The Young Child and the Environment

Issues Related to Health, Nutrition, Safety, and Physical Activity

Nancy E. Sayre
Clarion University

Jere Dee Gallagher
University of Pittsburgh

Allyn and Bacon

Boston ■ London ■ Toronto ■ Sydney ■ Tokyo ■ Singapore

Series Editor: *Traci Mueller*
Series Editorial Assistant: *Bridget Keane*
Marketing Managers: *Brad Parkins and Kathleen Morgan*
Production Editor: *Annette Pagliaro*
Composition Buyer: *Linda Cox*
Manufacturing Buyer: *Megan Cochran*
Cover Administrator: *Kristina Mose-Libon*
Electronic Composition: *Omegatype Typography, Inc.*

Library of Congress Cataloging-in-Publication Data

Sayre, Nancy E., 1943–
    The young child and the environment : issues related to health, nutrition, safety, and physical activity / Nancy E. Sayre, Jere Dee Gallagher.
        p.   cm.
    Includes bibliographical references and index.
    ISBN 0-205-30293-9
    1. Infants—Development.   2. Child development.   3. Early childhood education.   I. Gallagher, Jere Dee.   II. Title.

HQ774 .S28 2001
305.231—dc21

                                                                            00-064285

Printed in the United States of America

10   9   8   7   6   5   4   3   2   1   05   04   03   02   01   00

We would like to dedicate this book to all the children who have inspired us,
especially Kirk, Kelly, Kim, John Larkin, Barrett, and Chip,
and to W. G. who cooked and provided environmental insights.

CONTENTS

PREFACE

Almost daily we read in the newspapers, watch on television, or hear on the radio how Americans are becoming increasingly obese and developing cardiovascular risk factors that lead to either a decreased quality of life or premature death. Not only is this happening to adults, but it is also increasing at an alarming rate for children not having family histories of cardiovascular disease. Since children develop behavioral habits early in life, we as educators need to help children develop decision-making skills and acquire appropriate habits for healthy living. It is the purpose of this book to provide information that will assist educators and parents of young children in understanding the child and the impact of the environment on the child's future decisions. We want to empower the reader to become an advocate for young children. An additional purpose of this book is to discuss guidelines for making curriculum and learning environment decisions to help reverse the current health trends for young children in the United States. As Hubert H. Humphrey said, "Each child is an adventure into a better life—an opportunity to change the old pattern and make it new" (Cyber Nation, 2000).

We wrote this book for people who are interested in giving children a strong foundation by helping them to develop healthy behavioral habits early in life. Our first goal is to address Global Issues Concerning Infants, Toddlers, and Young Children. We cover the interaction of biological and environmental factors that influence the child. The National Health Standards and the components of Comprehensive School Health Education set the stage for the remainder of the book. The definitions of the term *developmentally appropriate* from the National Association for the Education of Young Children and the Council on Physical Education for Children are integrated and developmentally appropriate practices are discussed.

The second goal of the book is to provide a foundation of information on the Health and Safety Issues Concerning Infants, Toddlers, and Young Children. We provide background information on Nutrition and the Healthy Child, Principles of Environmental Hygiene and Infection Control, Safety in the Early Childhood Learning Environment, and Physical Fitness.

Developing an understanding of Movement Issues Concerning Infants, Toddlers, and Young Children is the third goal of the book. We discuss the various factors that influence movement skill development, and how to evaluate and plan developmentally appropriate movement programs for infants, toddlers, and young children.

The last goal of the book is to address Programmatic Development. We provide sample lesson plans for Developing Healthy Lifestyles (e.g., decision making, nutrition, safety, and movement skill development) and conclude by emphasizing the importance of developing Parents and Community Partnerships. We discuss the role of the family, the educator, and the social network in helping the child develop lifelong habits that may forestall chronic diseases in adulthood.

Key features of each chapter include a scenario, synopsis, and objectives that assist the reader in understanding and applying the main concepts. Throughout each chapter we tell true stories that illustrate how the respective theories are applied to early childhood settings. At the end of each chapter the reader is given a variety of suggestions about how to become an advocate for young children.

"There are only two lasting bequests we can hope to give our children. One is roots; the other, wings" (Cyber Nation, 2000). We hope we have given you wings in this book so that your children will fly!

Acknowledgments

We would like to thank Brandy Burzese for the line drawings that effectively enhance our concepts. In addition we would like to thank the following reviewers of the text whose comments contributed to the book's development: Patricia J. Otis, Kirkwood Community College; Barbara Pollack, SUNY Empire State College; and Alice Whiren, Michigan State University.

REFERENCES

Cyber Nation. (2000). Retrieved July 31, 2000 from the World Wide Web: http://www.cyber-nation.com/victory/quotations/authors/quotes_carter_hodding.html
Cyber Nation. (2000). Retrieved July 31, 2000 from the World Wide Web: http://www.cyber-nation.com/victory/quotations/authors/quotes_humphrey_huberth.html

PART ONE

Global Issues Concerning Infants, Toddlers, and Young Children

1

Health and Fitness Concerns of Infants, Toddlers, and Young Children

CHAPTER OBJECTIVES

Knowledge

■ The reader will understand the health indicators of a healthy lifestyle.

Skills

■ The reader will analyze the role ecological theory plays in a healthy lifestyle.

Dispositions

■ The reader will appreciate the role of the early childhood educator in helping children develop and maintain healthy lifestyles.

CHAPTER SYNOPSIS

Health Indicators
  Reversing Health Indicators
  Ecological Systems Theory

The Early Childhood Educator and Reversing Health Indicators
  Health Education and the Early Childhood Educator's Concerns

Scenario

Ms. Espacido was talking to the 4-year-old children in her program about what they felt were healthy behaviors. The children were eager to provide answers.

Mara said, "Eat good food."

Juan wanted everyone to know that, "Mom makes me healthy."

Ralph stood and stated in a firm voice, "Mom and dad make food, and we eat it."

Lindsay raised her voice over Ralph's and replied, "Love each other!"

Rollin excitedly added, "Play in the snow, play outside, oh, do exercises!"

Bani showed the stitches in her knee and meekly said, "Be safe when riding your bicycle."

Finally, Selina provided a lengthy answer in a quiet but firm voice. "Eat healthy, nutritious food, exercise, swing on the swing set, take vitamins, drink orange juice and water, and eat applesauce, carrots, and grapes."

Ms. Espacido was pleased that her children had such a well-developed concept of what it takes to have healthy lifestyles and develop into healthy adults.

The children in Ms. Espacido's child care classroom could write this book! Clearly, they have accurate, unclouded concepts of what behaviors are essential to be healthy. The children know that appropriate nutrition, safety, exercise, and a positive family environment are the foundations of a healthy life. The main goal of this book is to assist the educators of infants, toddlers, and young children in developing the knowledge, skills, attitudes, and behaviors necessary to provide a strong foundation in health practices so the children can develop into healthy adults.

Health Indicators

Unfortunately, the children in Ms. Espacido's classroom may be the exception, not the rule. Mara, Ralph, and Selina realize the important role a nutritious and balanced diet plays in their health. Research shows that the typical American diet leads to obesity, which is correlated with, or is the cause of, several major chronic diseases such as arteriosclerosis, stroke, coronary heart disease, and a form of diabetes. The majority of children between the ages of 2 and 5 years consume more cholesterol, total fat, and saturated fat than is recommended (Thompson & Dennison, 1994). This type of diet can lower the quality of the child's adult life and lead to future medical problems.

The increased sedentary life of children, due to factors such as increased television viewing, video and computer game playing, and the breakdown of the social network, has resulted in the rapid growth of childhood obesity. Unfortunately, there is growing evidence that the next generation of children is likely to be fatter and less fit than the current generation (Hill & Trowbridge, 1998). Rollin mentions to Ms. Espacido that you should "play in the snow"—acknowledging the need for exercise.

Juan and Ralph recognize the role that the family and others play in the development of a healthy lifestyle. They realize that adults provide the foods they need to be healthy. Bani knows that safety is important while Lindsay and Selina recognize that adults provide safe exercise areas and play opportunities. Additionally, Lindsay acknowledges that children need the love that family and caregivers provide in order to be healthy. Healthy lifestyles are enriching and enhance the life of the child, and the adult that child will become.

Reversing Health Indicators

It is the goal of this book to provide information that will assist educators of young children in making curriculum and learning environment decisions that will help to reverse the current health trends for young children in the United States. We initially set the stage by discussing the term *developmentally appropriate.* Infants, toddlers, and young children are different from older children and adults. The components of a healthy life, nutrition, environmental hygiene, safety, motor development, and fitness are discussed as well as the role of the family, the educator, and the social network in the development of a healthy child. Promoting the development of a healthy lifestyle during early childhood is an important step in creating lifelong habits that may help forestall chronic diseases in adulthood. Providing the child with an enriching, safe environment where the child can develop the appropriate decision-making skills and health habits is important to minimize the risk of illness and injury and to promote physical and emotional health throughout the lifespan.

Various agencies in the child's supporting social network have recognized the need to make a change in the current health trends of children in the United States.

Recommendations.   The American Academy of Pediatrics (1993) and the American School Health Association (1985) advocated that for children to learn they must be healthy. Only when children are healthy can schools fully meet their goals (Smith, 1996). The National Education Goals (NEGP, 1999) emphasize the importance of the comprehensive school health program. The comprehensive school health program includes health instruction, health services, a healthful environment, and a coordination of the program. Healthy lifestyles and behaviors in addition to the control of environmental factors can reduce the need for medical and hospital care and prevent many of the health problems of children not only throughout childhood but later in life as well.

Two recent developments have helped the nation focus on the importance of disease prevention by promoting healthy lifestyles. *Healthy People* (1990, 1998) and *Comprehensive Health Education* (American School Health Association, 1985) focused national attention on prevention by providing information and strategies on how to improve health. Healthy People is a series of documents produced by the government focused on setting national goals for health promotion.

Healthy People.   *Healthy People: The Surgeon General's Report on Health Promotion and Disease Prevention* (1979) was aimed at setting goals to prevent health problems. Broad goals were directed at reducing mortality among infants, toddlers, children, adolescents, and adults while increasing independence among older adults. Over 30% of the specific goals were directly related to improving the health of school-aged children by 1990. The second step in working toward the goal of healthy people was published in *Goals for Healthy People 2000* (1991). The objective of these recommendations was to increase attention to a variety of preventive health problems while focusing on three broad goals (*Healthy People 2000*, 1990, p. 6):

1. Increase the span of healthy life for Americans
2. Reduce health disparities among Americans
3. Achieve access to preventive services for all Americans

The specific goals were organized into 22 priority areas and grouped into three general categories that included health promotion, health protection, and preventive services.

Health Promotion.   Strategies for health promotion are related to an individual's lifestyle and are focused on decision-making strategies related to the quality of life. Health promotion takes into account physical activity and fitness; nutrition; tobacco, alcohol, and drug use; family planning; mental health and mental disorders; violent and abusive behavior; and educational and community-based programs. Since this book is looking at infants, toddlers, and young children we focus on nutrition, physical activity and fitness, and educational programs.

Health Protection.   Health protection strategies cover environmental and regulatory measures that provide protection for the individual. They include preventing accidental injuries, occupational safety and health, environmental health, food and drug safety, and oral health. We address safety, environmental hygiene, and infection control. The major health protection strategies in this book include suggestions for prevention of problems in these areas.

Preventive Services.   Preventive services focus on the social network that provides individual support. These services may include maternal and infant health, heart disease and stroke, diabetes and chronic disabling conditions, HIV infection and sexually transmitted diseases, immunizations and infectious diseases, and clinical preventive services. Throughout the lifespan a social network is critical. Teacher, parent, and family relationships are included in this book.

The *Healthy People 2000 Review* (1998) indicates that 15% of the objectives were reached or surpassed. These included a decline of 26% from 1987 of child and adolescent death rates. Thus the stage has been set to improve the health of America's children and to continue this positive beginning. The next step is outlined in *Healthy People 2010* (2000), the third set of decade-long goals, now attempting to refocus health policies and expenditures on developing a lifetime of good health. The new report sets goals not only to increase longevity but also to improve the **quality of life.** It is important to note that goals are set to eliminate racial and ethnic disparities in health.

Although these reports have not been directed at early childhood education, we feel that much of the information is directly related to the development of attitudes and behaviors that begin in early childhood. The focus of this book is to extrapolate the information from these reports to provide the early childhood educator with information aimed at developing healthy behavior for a lifetime.

Comprehensive Health Education.   According to the American School Health Association (1985) a Comprehensive School Health Program extrapolated the objectives listed in *Promoting Health/Preventing Disease: Objectives for the Nation* (U.S. Department of Health and Human Services, 1980) that directly apply to or have implications for health education. Eight categories should be included in a comprehensive school health program: health education; health services; safe and healthful school environment; school-community integration; physical education; food services; counseling; and school site health promotion for faculty and staff (Allensworth & Kolbe, 1987).

Health Education.   Typically, heath education has been a well-developed curriculum for school-aged children. The health curriculum provides the outline for teaching children the knowledge, skills, attitudes, and behaviors necessary to become health literate, maintain and improve health, prevent disease, and reduce health-related risk factors. At the early childhood level, health education addresses the physical, mental, emotional, and social dimensions of health. Thus, teachers use a sequential curriculum to help children develop the skills and attitudes that will foster healthy lifestyles. The chapters in this book assist the teacher in developing the skills to plan developmentally appropriate lessons and experiences in nutrition, safety, and physical activity for the young child.

Safe and Healthful School Environment.   Safe and healthful school environment is part of the comprehensive school health program. The teacher must ensure that the physical, aesthetic, and social-emotional environments of the school promote health and safety for the children and staff. The healthful school environment includes both the physical and psychological environments in which children and educators exist. The psychological environment includes the emotional and social environments of the classroom and the development of self-concept and self-esteem. The atmosphere of the child care early education setting should be one of acceptance and understanding. The teacher needs to be sensitive to the individual needs of each child and the individual backgrounds that may temper the learning environment and the interactions within the learning environment.

The physical environment covers safety hazards on the outdoor play area and in the building including chemical agents, electrical hazards, temperature, humidity, noise, lighting, and radiation. Chapters 4 and 5 provide information on creating a healthful learning environment for young children.

Physical Education or *Movement Education.*   Physical education or movement education is important in helping children develop a love of movement and physical activity. We feel that this is critical; children must continue to be physically active as they age. Quality movement or physical education programs, not sport development, are a critical part of a comprehensive child care early education program.

Young children develop the skills, attitudes, and dispositions necessary to be physically active for their entire lives. Chapter 2 provides an overview of the term *developmentally appropriate* while Chapter 6 discusses the importance and types of fitness. Chapter 7 covers information on how children develop motor skills and Chapter 8 applies that information to developing movement programs for young children. Chapter 9 provides examples of lesson plans that can be used with young children to develop good eating habits, develop proper personal hygiene, make safe choices, engage in movement, and develop physical fitness.

Nutrition Services.   It is important to provide children with nutritionally balanced meals and snacks that are appealing and varied in content. Chapter 3 covers important nutritional information for developing infants, toddlers, and young children.

Parent and Community Involvement.   Chapter 10 highlights the important partnerships between the parent, the child care early education setting, social agencies, and businesses working together to address the health needs of children and their families. Early childhood programs should actively recruit parent involvement and use community resources to provide for the health-related needs of children. A comprehensive health education program cannot take place without involving the entire social networking structure.

Recommendations to meet the goal of a healthy lifestyle can be made, but it is the individual who must carry out these recommendations. Children are unable to accomplish this so it becomes the responsibility of the family and the educational community to ensure that healthy lifestyle changes are made.

This process may be further complicated by the fact that each child is unique in terms of genetic characteristics and developmental level. Therefore, any curriculum and learning environment design decisions should take into account the uniqueness of the child as well as the family and the complete social network. This concept parallels the ecological systems theory of Urie Bronfenbrenner (1979). The ecological systems theory and the National Health Education Standards (1995) are used as the infrastructure of this book. Each chapter is organized around a standard as outlined and the mutual interaction between the child and the parent-social network that affect the child's development.

Ecological Systems Theory

Urie Bronfenbrenner's (1979) **ecological systems theory** places children with all their unique biological predispositions at the center of all environmental interactions. It is the interaction between the biological makeup of a child and the environmental influences that affects a child's development and behavior.

Children and their biological characteristics influence their surroundings or environment. In return, their substantive environment, family, peers, school, and neighborhood as well as socioeconomic environmental factors and cultural environmental factors influence children's development in several areas including social/emotional, cognitive/language, and physical/motor. This theory emphasizes the influence that parents and the entire social network, schools, peers, neighborhood, social services, church, mass media, extended family, and culture have on the child.

Bronfenbrenner outlines multiple ecologies or settings that affect the developing child. The theory uses concentric circles increasing in size to depict the various layers of interaction. The first layer is the microsystem. This circle includes the family, education program, medical services, and peers that have an immediate effect on the child. The second layer is the mesosystem that represents the interaction between the institutions within the microsystem. The exosystem layer is comprised of institutions such as legal services and welfare regulations that indirectly affect the child. The outermost circle is the macrosystem that takes into account the culture, laws, and customs of the society in which the child lives. This is an interactive process that involves the child and contributing factors in the environment: primary, socioeconomic, and cultural.

The ecological systems theory is extremely important when planning, implementing, and assessing programs for young children. While early childhood educators may be dedicated and committed to providing an educational environment that will enhance the health and lifespan of the children in their care, the ecological systems theory makes it painfully clear that this cannot be accomplished by the educator alone. Additionally, it is evident that not only the genetic makeup, but also the child's family plays a key role in the child's adoption of a healthy lifestyle. The bioenvironmental reciprocity model that is used throughout this book is a simplification of Bronfenbrenner's theory.

Bioenvironmental Reciprocity Model.   This model emphasizes the interaction of the biological and environmental factors that affect a child's development (see Figure 1.1).

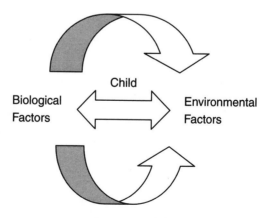

FIGURE 1.1   Bioenvironmental Reciprocity Model

Components of the Bioenvironmental Model.   The components of the bioenvironmental model are the child, the biological characteristics of the child that program the child's development, and the environmental factors that affect the child's development. This is an interactive process; each component influences the others.

The child's development begins at conception when the sperm, the reproduction cell or gamete of the male, fertilizes the ovum, the reproduction cell or gamete of the female. A zygote is the single cell that is formed from the fertilization process. The zygote contains the genetic code or chromosomes of both parents. Each child is a unique combination or mix of the parents' chromosomes. The 46 chromosomes present at the time of fertilization contain the genetic substance, deoxyribonucleic acid (DNA). Genes are short segments of DNA and are the blueprint for cells to reproduce themselves and to manufacture proteins that will maintain life (Santrock, 1999).

Abnormalities in genes and chromosomes can compromise the health of the child. Some health problems that occur due to major gene or chromosome defects are: Down syndrome, phenylketonuria (PKU), cystic fibrosis, and sickle-cell anemia.

Down syndrome is a form of physical and mental retardation caused by the presence of an extra chromosome. The health of the male sperm or the female

Environmental Biological

ovum may be involved in this condition. Care of a Down syndrome child might be difficult because of breathing and feeding problems due to the abnormal facial characteristics.

Phenylketonuria is a genetic metabolic disorder that if left untreated can cause mental retardation. It occurs primarily in Caucasians. The treatment for this disorder is a special diet to prevent an excess accumulation of the amino acid phenylalanine.

Cystic fibrosis is a glandular dysfunction that interferes with mucus production. The child has difficulty breathing and death may result. The child will need assistance in clearing mucus from the respiratory system.

Sickle-cell anemia affects the red blood cells and occurs most often in African Americans. In this condition, the red blood cell is hook-shaped rather than the normal disc shape. These cells die quickly, therefore the child fails to get the oxygen needed for survival.

The above are examples of problems in the genetic code of the child that cause developmental problems. These in turn can lead to problems with the child's prenatal and postnatal environments. Additionally, although the child might have a good genetic blueprint, changes can occur in the genetic code due to environmental factors such as prenatal exposure to drugs or alcohol.

Agents that cause damage to the fetus during the prenatal period are termed teratogens. Teratogens such as alcohol, drugs (illegal and legal), hypervitaminosis, radiation, and environmental pollutants can play havoc with the genetic blueprint of the developing child causing malformation, retardation, and illness. Poor nutrition and maternal illness can also cause problems for the developing fetus.

To have a healthy child it is important for the mother to avoid drugs and environmental pollutants and receive prenatal care and screenings. An infant born to a mother who received prenatal care is less likely to have a low birth weight or health problems later in life (U.S. Department of Health and Human Services, 1991). There are added benefits to prenatal care; research shows that women who receive prenatal care are more likely to seek preventive care for their infants following delivery (Bates, Fitzgerald, Dittus, & Wolinsky, 1994). Additionally, parents should take part in an educational program about nutrition, labor, delivery, and infant care.

When Ms. Espacido plans learning activities for Roberto, a child in her classroom, she must individualize the plan since Roberto has a heart murmur and is allergic to milk. Ms. Espacido must ensure that Roberto, while at the child care center, is receiving calcium from a source other than milk and dairy products. When selecting appropriate foods, she must consider his Hispanic background and food preferences. Her program has limited financial resources so she is further limited by lack of money to purchase essential food products for Roberto and the other children in her program who may also have conditions requiring adaptation. Another problem facing Ms. Espacido is that, although she has access to a nurse consultant regarding the precautions she needs to take for Roberto when designing physical activities, the nurse is only available once a month. The remainder of the time she must use her own judgment. To increase the complications, Roberto's mother, contrary to the nurse's recommendations, feels strongly that he should not be restricted from any physical activities at the child care center. As you can see, when planning and implementing programs for your children many factors influence the plan.

Educators must always recognize that it is the reciprocal interaction between the biological factors (heart murmur and family tendency toward dairy product allergy, for example) and environmental factors (ethnic background, social services, family) that affect the child's development and behaviors.

The Early Childhood Educator and Reversing Health Indicators

This book addresses the issue of providing a healthy child care early education environment, and providing health and physical education learning experiences while taking into account the reciprocity between genetic and environmental factors. To help assist the educator in planning and implementing instruction, the National Health Education Standards can be used. Each child needs to be health literate. This means an individual is a critical thinker and problem solver, a responsible, productive citizen, a self-directed learner, and an effective communicator. The goal of these standards is to provide an instructional program that enables children to become and remain healthy (AAHE, 1995, p. 1). The National Health Education Standards describe the health knowledge and skills required to be health literate (see Table 1.1).

Effective programs have moved from emphasizing knowledge to focusing on skills, behaviors, and attitudes. Communication skills and goal-setting activities are emphasized. The classroom environment supports various viewpoints and recognizes the multiplicity of values from the home, the teacher, the religious community, and the social group. The reciprocal process is recognized and used in planning, implementing, and assessing learning activities.

TABLE 1.1   The National Health Education Standards

Children will:

- Comprehend concepts related to health promotion and disease prevention
- Demonstrate the ability to access valid health information and health-promoting products and services
- Demonstrate the ability to practice health-enhancing behaviors and reduce health risks
- Analyze the influence of culture, media, technology, and other factors on health
- Demonstrate the ability to use interpersonal communication skills to enhance health
- Demonstrate the ability to use goal-setting and decision-making skills to enhance health
- Demonstrate the ability to advocate for personal, family, and community health

I'm getting healthy just carrying around the National Health Standards!

Health Education and the Early Childhood Educator's Concerns

Historically, health education focused on the reduction of communicable diseases that compromised people's health. Today, however, the outbreak of communicable diseases is decreasing and in many instances has been completely obliterated. Health education currently focuses on chronic disease as a major factor that compromises people's health. Initially these diseases were thought to be diseases of adults, diseases such as heart disease, diabetes, arthritis, and cancer. However with current research we now understand that lifestyles and behaviors that begin in early childhood influence these diseases.

In addition to a changing focus on disease prevention, the family unit has influenced health education. More and more two-working-parents and single-parent families exist. With parents spending less time at home, children's learning about health in the home has also decreased—thus increasing the responsibility of the child care early education center. Children spend less time observing the health habits of the parents and more time watching the health habits of their teachers and classmates.

School children come from an expanding multiethnic community. This variety of sociocultural and ethnically guided health behaviors influence the children's personal lifestyles and behavioral choices.

Television also has a major impact on children's health behavior and choices. They are constantly viewing commercials for unhealthy food and programs containing inaccurate health information. Additionally, children do not have a developed decision-making ability and, consequently, cannot always decipher fact from fiction.

The Role of the Early Childhood Educator.   Classroom teachers are influenced by their own personal interests in health and the responsibility they feel toward the health needs of their students. It is difficult to plan and conduct lessons in which teachers are unfamiliar or perhaps uncomfortable with the subject matter. The parents, community, district mandates, state regulations, and other social institutions also influence the commitment of the early childhood educator.

The Early Childhood Educator as Role Model.   Teachers influence children's health habits through modeling. The average child in an early childhood education setting observes the teacher's habits for over 8 hours a day, 5 days a week, for approximately 50 weeks a year. That means they observe the teacher for about 2,000 hours a year. This is a significant amount of time to demonstrate appropriate health habits.

Developmentally Appropriate Health Education: A Healthy Lifestyle.   Using a comprehensive health education program throughout the education of the child helps to protect the individual from the six categories of risk behaviors identified by the Centers for Disease Control and Prevention:

1. Behaviors that result in both unintentional and intentional injuries
2. Dietary patterns that contribute to disease
3. Insufficient physical activity
4. Tobacco use
5. Alcohol and other drug use
6. Sexual behaviors that result in HIV infection, other STDs, and unintended pregnancy

This book concentrates on preventing the first three behaviors during the early childhood years.

Health knowledge and life skills are developed throughout life. Health knowledge is the information needed to develop health literacy, maintain and improve health, prevent disease, and reduce health-related risk behaviors. Health knowledge is derived from the National Health Education Standards and includes the six categories of risk behaviors. The content areas for the health knowledge and life skills that are the focus of this book for young children are: growth and development; nutrition; environmental health; mental and emotional health; injury prevention and safety; communicable and chronic diseases; personal health; and family living. During the elementary and secondary school years, additional content areas include consumer and community health, and the use of alcohol, tobacco, and other drugs. This book focuses on the early developmental years, the educator, the family, and the social network surrounding the child, family, and educator.

Summary

The health of the child is dependent on the reciprocal interaction between genetic and environmental factors. This interaction has not been favorable to the child for developing a healthy lifestyle. Chronic diseases such as strokes, heart attacks, diabetes, and cancers have been directly linked to poor choices such as a diet comprised of fats and sugars and a sedentary lifestyle.

The National Health Education Standards describe the health knowledge and skills required to be health literate. It is very important for the early childhood educator to be familiar with the National Health Education Standards and to use them when planning learning activities, menus, and learning environments for infants, toddlers, and young children. This book is designed to assist the educator in this process.

CHANGE AND ADVOCACY

1. Design ways to help families achieve access to preventive services.

2. Write a state and/or federal legislator to request reduction in health disparities among children.

REFERENCES

Allensworth, D. D., & Kolbe, L. J. (1987). The comprehensive school health program: Exploring an expanded concept. *Journal of School Health, 57,* 409–412.

American Academy of Pediatrics: Committee on School Health. (1993). *School health: Policy and practice.* Elk Grove Village, IL.

American School Health Association. (1985). *Marketing kit.* Kent, OH.

American School Health Association. (1999). *National health education standards: Achieving literacy.* Kent, OH: American School Health Association.

Association for the Advancement of Health Education (AAHE). (1995). *National health education standards—Achieving health literacy.* Reston, VA: AAHE.

Bates, A., Fitzgerald, J., Dittus, R., & Wolinsky, F. (1994). Risk factors for underimmunization in poor urban infants. *The Journal of the American Medical Association,* 1105–1110.

Bronfenbrenner, U. (1979). *The ecology of human development: Experiments by nature and design.* Cambridge, MA: Harvard University Press.

Center for Disease Control. (1993). *Suicide surveillance summary report 1980–90.* Atlanta, GA: Centers for Disease Control.

Hill, J. O., & Trowbridge, F. L. (1998). Childhood obesity: Future directions and research priority. *Pediatrics, 101,* 570–574.

National Education Goals Panel. (1999). *The national education goals report: Building a nation of learners, 1999.* Washington, DC: U.S. Government Printing Office.

Santrock, J. W. (1999). *Life-Span Development.* Boston, MA: McGraw-Hill.

Smith, D. R. (1996). *Healthy children are prepared to learn. School health: Programs in action.* Austin, TX: Department of Health.

Thompson, F. E., & Dennison, B. A. (1994). Dietary sources of fats and cholesterol in U.S. children aged 2 through 5 years. *The American Journal of Public Health, 84*(5), 799.

U.S. Department of Health and Human Services. (1979). *Healthy people—The Surgeon General's report on health promotion and disease prevention.* Atlanta, GA: U.S. Department of Health and Human Services, Centers for Disease Control and Prevention, National Center for Chronic Disease Prevention and Health Promotion.

U.S. Department of Health and Human Services. (1980). *Promoting health/Preventing disease: Objectives for the nation.* Washington, DC: U.S. Department of Health and Human Services.

U.S. Department of Health and Human Services. (1990). *Healthy people 2000—National health promotion and disease prevention objectives* (Conference ed.). (p. 6). Washington, DC: U.S. Department of Health and Human Services.

U.S. Department of Health and Human Services, U.S. Government Office. (1991). *Healthy people 2000: National health promotion and disease prevention objectives.* Washington, DC: U.S. Department of Health and Human Services, U.S. Government Printing Office.

U.S. Department of Health and Human Services. (1998). *Healthy people 2000 progress review adolescents and young adults.* Washington, DC: U.S. Department of Health and Human Services.

U.S. Department of Health and Human Services. (2000). *Healthy people 2010* (Conference ed.). Washington, DC: U.S. Department of Health and Human Services.

Developmentally Appropriate Foundations for Infants, Toddlers, and Young Children

CHAPTER OBJECTIVES

Knowledge
- The reader will understand the factors that must be evaluated to demonstrate developmentally appropriate practice.

Skills
- The reader will analyze children's development to determine where they are on the developmental continuum.

Dispositions
- The reader will value children as unique individuals.

CHAPTER SYNOPSIS

Developmentally Appropriate Philosophy
  Development
  Developmentally Appropriate Guidelines
  Developmental Perspective

Individual Differences
  Maturation
  Learning
  Motivation
Cultural Influences

Scenario

The children are at the edge of the pool as the starter pulls the trigger. All the 5-year-old children dive into the pool to begin the race. Kelly swims to an early lead that she maintains throughout the race. After she touches the edge of the pool, yards ahead of her nearest competitor, she climbs out and immediately looks at the clock to see her time. Kelly realizes she has not improved her time from the last race, and her body language shows her disappointment. The father of one of her competitors notices her reaction and approaches to provide encouragement. Congratulating Kelly on her win, he tells her she should be pleased with the win. Kelly responds that she is upset because she did not improve her time from the last competition. The father counters with "Yes, but that doesn't matter, you beat all the other children and WON!" Kelly's parents, following developmentally appropriate practice, taught her to be concerned about improvement and NOT with winning. She therefore responded, "I didn't improve and that is what matters!"

Kelly's story provides an important lesson for parents, teachers, and children. Improvement is important, not winning and "beating" someone else. Today Kelly wins because she is the biggest and strongest in class, but tomorrow she could lose because another child might have gained the size advantage. Physical activity is necessary for a lifetime of health. The child care early educator must understand what is appropriate for the individual child in order to accomplish this. Today's parents are exposing young children to cognitive, physical, and motor development programs in record numbers. Fitness clubs have added elaborate facilities where a child as young as 6 years of age works out on child-sized lifecycles, free weights, and weight machines. Athletic competition during the childhood years has become increasingly popular. Individual and team sport competition can begin as early as the age of three, even earlier if one considers baby track competitions where babies crawl along a pathway to beat the other babies to the finish line so their parents can receive a prize. Additionally, organized movement programs for children in dance, gymnastics, and swimming begin at very young ages.

Many young children are enrolled in movement and sport programs based on the assumption that early experience facilitates the acceleration of the child's physical, emotional, and social development. Any organized movement experience that is properly conducted in an appropriate environment will nurture the child's attainment of skilled movement. However, parents and teachers of young children need to make informed decisions about what activity is appropriate, when the child should begin participating, and what the level of participation will be. The purpose of this chapter is to first understand a developmentally appropriate philosophy; second, how individuals differ in development; and finally, how culture influences these differences.

Developmentally Appropriate Philosophy

Children are not miniature adults. Not only do they have different body proportions in comparison to adults, but they also think very differently. A 2-year-old does not have the arm length to swim like an adult, and a 5-year-old, when asked to count as high as she can, climbs to the top of a chair, stands on tiptoes, puts her hands in the air, and starts counting. Teachers of young children must understand how children develop individually. What is considered developmentally appropriate for one child is not necessarily developmentally appropriate for another child of the same age. The National Association for the Education of Young Children (NAEYC) published a position statement on *developmentally appropriate* based on an understanding of how children develop in the context of their family and culture (Bredekamp & Copple, 1997). Child care early educators need to value the child for who she is and provide support for what she might become.

Development

To understand *developmentally appropriate,* the concept of development needs to be discussed. *Development* is a widely used term that in casual conversation is interchanged with *growth, maturation,* and *learning.* Motor development textbooks typically define development as a change in behavior (Gabbard, 2000; Gallahue & Ozmun, 1998; Haywood, 1993). This change can be progressive as seen in the infant developing a walking motion where she has a wide base of support, arms held high, and uses short steps. Development can also be regressive as noted by the elderly individual displaying a pattern similar to a young child. The infant continues to change and acquire the normal walking motion whereas the elderly individual might eventually regress to using a walker and subsequently cease walking altogether.

During childhood we hope that development is progressive and leads to organized movements that can be specialized to acquire functional tasks. In other words, a child develops from crawling to creeping to standing to walking, running, and jumping and eventually combines these skills to participate in game playing. At each level of development the child continually hones his skills to "go where he wants to go and do what he wants to do!"

Lifespan Development

The Motor Development Academy (1994) in the American Alliance for Health, Physical Education, Recreation, and Dance (AAHPERD) views development as including six components:

- Qualitative
- Sequential
- Cumulative
- Directional
- Multifactorial
- Individual

Qualitative.   Qualitative change suggests that not only does the child run faster and throw farther, but she also changes the way she runs and throws. As the ball is thrown, the child tries to grasp it with her fingers while locking her elbows. The child changes from merely flexing and extending at the elbow when throwing to taking a large step with the foot opposite the throwing arm. The movement pattern increases in mechanical efficiency by typically increasing the range of movement of the body segments involved, increasing the number of body segments used, creating a smoother and better-timed movement, allowing for better body positioning, and including more subroutines into the total movement. Chapter 7 covers increased mechanical efficiency in greater depth.

Sequential.   Sequential change indicates a progression from simple to complex. The child can catch a large ball prior to catching a small ball, or he can throw a ball prior to striking a ball. Throwing and striking use similar motions, but striking is more complex. When striking, the child must analyze the speed and spatial location of the ball and match his movement to that of the oncoming ball.

Cumulative.   Change is also cumulative. Previously learned skills are "building blocks" for skills that develop later. Prior to skipping (step-hop, step-hop) a child must demonstrate a good walking pattern and the ability to hop on one foot without losing balance. Attainment of prerequisite skills prior to instruction ensures success in learning the skill.

Directional.   Directional change means that development moves toward something, whether progressing toward a goal or regressing due to lack of practice, disease, or aging. The young child progresses from walking with short, wide steps to long, narrow strides, but with age and disease the older individual returns to walking with short wide steps.

Multifactorial.   Change can also be attributed to many factors; change is multifactorial. A child is able to walk when he has sufficient cognitive understanding, strength, balance, and motivation. Laura was 3 years old and in child care. One day the teacher excitedly called Laura's parents to invite them to come to the center. When Laura's parents arrived and viewed her behavior behind a one-way mirror there were tears in their eyes. Laura was talking to the other children. Prior to that day, although she spoke at home, she did not speak at school. Previously, when she interacted with the other children, they understood her through body language. Her parents had taken her to a variety of psychologists to determine why she would not talk around others. She had the motor coordination and the skill, just not the motivation. From that day forward, she has not stopped talking. Today, Laura is a successful attorney. Intrinsic motivation is an important component of skill development.

Individual. Finally, change is individual. Generally, all individuals progress through the same sequence, however they do so at their own rate. One child might walk at nine months of age while another child in the same family walks at fourteen months. Comparing the age of onset of a skill among children is inappropriate. A home video of two children at 2 years of age cannot differentiate who walked first. Early attainment of the skill *does not* indicate superior skill. Todd did not learn to swim until 10 years of age, but was awarded a swimming scholarship to attend college.

Since development is qualitative, sequential, cumulative, directional, multifactorial, and individual, development is age related *not* age determined.

> One problem in studying development is that we come to think of age as being development, that age becomes an agent of change, perhaps even *the* agent of change. It is easy to look at a graph of improved performance across age and think that age determines or influences change. We must remember that time itself is not causal and that age merely marks the passage of time or a period of time. Agents of change, such as biological processes or social interactions, function during the passage of time to determine or influence change. This means that we must consider what is happening during a given period of time rather than view age as the agent of change. To reiterate, age is merely time, and our problem is to identify and understand the changes in movement development across time. (Keogh & Sugden, 1985, p. 20)

Comparing individual children within an age group is inappropriate due to their different developmental levels. Setting individual expectations based on the individual's physical, cognitive, and emotional maturational levels provides guidelines to assist the child in learning.

Developmentally Appropriate Guidelines

After acquiring an understanding of the concept of development, the child care early educator must then apply that concept to construct developmentally appropriate guidelines. These guidelines can assist the child care early educator in providing young children with the experiences that allow them to develop to their fullest potential. In addition, developmentally appropriate guidelines assist the early child care educator in making developmentally appropriate decisions about curriculum and content, how to present content, and how to evaluate the curriculum and teaching methods (Bredekamp & Copple, 1997).

NAEYC developed guidelines that provide information on creating a caring community of learners, enhancing development and learning, constructing appropriate curriculum, assessing learning and development, and establishing reciprocal relationships with families. The Council of Physical Education for Children (COPEC, 1994) developed guidelines for movement programs for children 3 to 5 years of age and a separate document for school-aged children.

The guidelines presented in this book are an integration of NAEYC's and COPEC's guidelines. The first set of guidelines directing movement programs works on the principle that infants are different from toddlers, toddlers are different from young children, young children are different from older children, and that a child is not a miniature adult. Infants and toddlers cannot be expected to sit, watch, and listen. Young children learn by interacting with their environment. All children need to actively participate, not sit, watch, and listen. Too often we expect toddlers to patiently wait while lengthy explanations are given. It would be better to design the learning environment to facilitate discovery learning and to provide the child with opportunities to make appropriate decisions.

Children do not learn through interaction with the environment alone, but also through following the guidance of teachers. Instruction is child centered, not subject or teacher centered. The teacher structures the environment to promote learning. Various areas of the room are designed to actively engage children, and to aid in the development of a variety of skills such as fine and gross motor skills and dramatic play.

Children also learn and develop in an integrated fashion. Providing stimulation through multiple senses enhances their learning. Since movement is the primary source of learning for young children, a combination of play and movement experiences is beneficial. Play allows the child to practice and understand complex concepts without stress and on his own terms. Ask a child under 5 years of age to show you how high he can jump. You can even say, "I want to see a vertical jump." Now watch how the child jumps. The child might jump high with his feet, but his trunk barely moves. On the other hand, hold up a candy bar and see how high he can jump to reach the candy. To reach the candy bar the child will display a form that looks more like the mature vertical jump pattern of a highly paid professional basketball player.

A teacher of 3-year-olds interacts with children differently than a third grade teacher working with 8-year-olds. The educational environment of 3-year-olds provides the young child with exposure to a variety of tasks, and movement is critical to learning. The environment is structured to ensure specific behaviors. A structured environment provided young Aris with the skills to perform his traditional Greek dance. Soula, Aris's mother, loved to dance. When he was in the womb, she danced quite frequently, and as she did, she felt he was also dancing. After his birth, she continued to dance and structured the environment so that Aris was exposed to music and dance. At community Greek dances, Aris's father would dance holding Aris on his shoulders. From experiencing the music and moving to the beat, Aris eventually learned the Greek line dances. At 2 years of age, Aris was applauded for his dancing ability at a Greek Family Festival. Aris was capable of four steps on the beat that included a kick on the fourth beat!

In contrast to young children, older children are expected to persist in self-directed behaviors. This is glaringly obvious in the seating arrangements of an early education classroom and an elementary classroom. The 3-year-old children's classroom does not have desks, and the children move about freely whereas a first-grade classroom contains individual desks arranged in rows. The expectation for first graders is that they remain seated and do not move around. If fact, we have been in first-grade classrooms where children are deprived of recess if they move or talk.

A second set of developmentally appropriate guidelines relates to the importance of being physically active for a lifetime. Children need to participate in physical activity and become physically educated. Participation in physical activity begins early and must continue throughout life. Aris started dancing in the womb, danced well at 2 years of age, and will certainly follow in his mother's footsteps and continue to dance at 50 years of age and older.

Being physically active is important for health and wellness but too often parents and educators confuse being physically active with playing sports. Physical education programs and sport programs have different objectives and are not interchangeable (COPEC, 1999). This is a very important point. All children need to participate in physical activity and become physically educated. Not everyone wants or needs to participate in athletics.

I'm into the three "Ps", PLAY, PLAY, PLAY!

Each movement program needs to be designed specifically for the individual; developmental needs of the child must be the primary concern. A child with cerebral palsy cannot be expected to perform a throwing motion similar to a child without cerebral palsy. Borrowing from the youth sport literature, children want to participate in physical activity for a variety of reasons—to have fun, socialize, learn skills, and to be physically fit. They do not choose to participate merely to win. Winning is generally a motive of parents.

Educators also need to understand that what children are learning today will not necessarily be important in tomorrow's world (COPEC, 1999). Times are changing rapidly. To prepare children for the future, emphasis must be placed on the value of intrinsic motivation, decision making, exploration, and risk taking. This will enable children to discover new and different challenges.

Valuing the uniqueness of children and applying that knowledge to developmentally appropriate guidelines and a developmental perspective is important in allowing children to develop to their fullest potential. Adopting a developmental perspective provides the child care early educator with a guide that will help to determine when children are ready to learn a specific skill.

Developmental Perspective

A developmental perspective suggests a continuum of behaviors. Subsequent behaviors are built on earlier learned behaviors. If Wagner has not mastered the earlier behaviors he will not succeed when attempting to learn a more complex skill. The key point is that if a child cannot perform a skill, he is not wrong, he merely has not practiced and learned the prerequisite skill. The initial level of catching a ball, for example, consists of arms extended with palms facing in or up. The child might also display a fear reaction. Five-year-old Rose should not be faulted for displaying a fear reaction when she catches, as this is her level of development. Rose needs to catch using a light, large ball so that it won't hurt when she misses the ball and gets hit in the face. If a child can only demonstrate this beginning level of catching, even at 5 years of age, that is simply her individual level of development.

Numerous factors can explain a child's level of development: prior experience, physical maturational level, cognitive development, motivation, and environmental conditions. When teaching third graders, we find many children who cannot skip. We do not consider their performance wrong. They either do not have some of the **multiple factors** needed to perform the skill (i.e., strength and balance), or they lack the required **cumulative experience.** An understanding of developmental perspective leads to planning developmentally appropriate physical activity for children.

Espenschade and Eckert (1967) provide another example of a developmental continuum for jumping. The first skill that leads to hopping on one foot would be stepping down from a height with support. The physical factors that change as the child moves up the continuum are strength and balance (see Figure 2.1).

An understanding of development and developmentally appropriate practices assists the early childhood educator in understanding similarities among children.

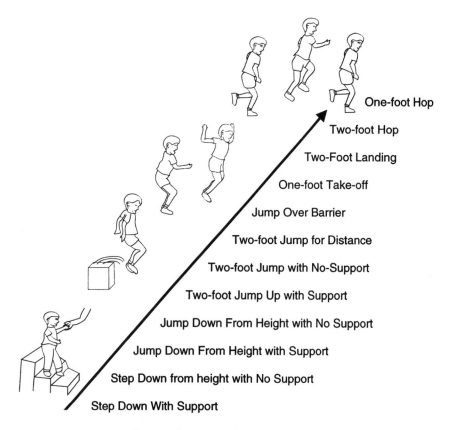

One-foot Hop

Two-foot Hop

Two-Foot Landing

One-foot Take-off

Jump Over Barrier

Two-foot Jump for Distance

Two-foot Jump with No-Support

Two-foot Jump Up with Support

Jump Down From Height with No Support

Jump Down From Height with Support

Step Down from height with No Support

Step Down With Support

FIGURE 2.1   Intertask Developmental Sequence for Jumping
(Espenschade & Eckert, 1967)

This information is useful in designing learning environments and curriculum activities. Additionally, this information must be interpreted in light of individual differences.

Individual Differences

To understand where a child is on the developmental continuum we can look at a readiness model. Traditional readiness models include three main factors: maturation (physical, cognitive, emotional), learning, and motivation (Magill, 1988).

Maturation

Maturation includes biological, cognitive, and emotional components. *Growth, maturation,* and *development* are terms that have been used interchangeably. Growth is the quantitative increase in physical size that includes an increase in cell number, cell size, and intracellular matter while maturation is defined as the qualitative, functional changes that occur with age (Malina & Bouchard, 1991). Maturation controls growth. When the individual is physically mature, growth has ceased. Children's movement is limited by growth factors that include height, weight, limb length, body shape, and maturation-related factors that include proportional changes. David, Jane, Ted, and Nancy are cousins. The traditional family picture taken of the cousins at all family gatherings was a stair-step formation. David, the eldest and tallest, was at the head of the line, Ted and Jane, who are the same age, were in the middle, and Nancy, the youngest and shortest, was at the end of the line. As the cousins grew and matured, the stair-step formation changed drastically. Nancy, as an adult, is now the tallest of the cousins. At a recent family gathering Nancy asked that the stair-step formation be used for a family picture, but David replied, "We don't do that anymore!"

Even young children understand developmental differences. Cousins 5-year-old Sidney and 4-year-old Alexandra were at their grandmother Meme's house. As they were getting ready for bed, Alexandra started to fold her clothes. Meme commented to Sidney about how Alexandra was folding her clothes and helping to keep things neat. Without thinking, Sidney responded, "Everyone is different, Meme!"

Biological Maturation.   Biological makeup begins with heredity and plays a continuing role in the development of the child. The interaction of the primary environment and the hereditary blueprint has a strong impact on health. Body type, temperament, and inherited diseases such as diabetes, cancer, and heart disease may contribute to the health of the developing child.

In this section we cover neural maturation, physical growth, and physiological functioning. Neural maturation is very important and sets the stage for interaction with the environment. Rapid changes in physical growth and physiological functioning can be related to an increase in performance outcomes.

Neural Development.   Neuron development and elaboration is dependent on the early spontaneous movements and the later directed or learned motor behaviors. Movement increases neuron elaboration and is vital to the cognitive, social, and emotional development of children. Neurons are produced between 10 and 26 weeks after conception. These cells then migrate from their production site near the center of the brain to their appropriate location. Once this is completed—around the seventh month of prenatal development—the next stage, cell elaboration, begins (Santrock, 1999). The stage of elaboration continues until the child is around 10 years old. The period of heaviest elaboration is from birth to around the fifth year.

During cell elaboration the axons and dendrites of the neuron grow and form millions of connections with other neurons. These trillions of pathways, connecting in a web-like mass, establish connections between neurons to make communications more complete. If pathways are not established or used, over time these connections diminish—making it difficult to establish new connections as the child grows older. Physical activity through movement, spontaneous or learned, helps to increase dendrite growth as well as to increase myelination. Myelination, the development of fatty insulating material, assists the axon in conducting the signal.

Neurological development continues for a prolonged period following birth. The average brain weight for a full-term male is about 370 grams (about one-fourth of adult size) and by the third year of life the average brain weight has tripled to about 1,080 grams (about 90% of its adult size). By 6 years of age, 95% of the neural system is developed. The brain weight between 6 and 14 years of age is approximately 1,350 grams and parallels adult size. However, even after the adult brain weight has been reached, there are continued maturational changes (Chugani, 1994).

Neurons first appear during the second prenatal month. At this time the neurons are also growing in size—which occurs from about the sixth prenatal month through the first year. At birth the brain contains almost all of the nerve cells it will ever have. The most rapid growth spurt will occur from about the third trimester of gestation until 4 years of age. New research suggests that during this time the brain has an opportunity for optimal development. After this rapid growth spurt the brain's ability to reorganize is limited. This is a time of neuronal plasticity. If the brain receives insult or injury—which causes functional deficits—reshaping can occur. Between 8 and 10 years of age there is a decrease in the recovery and reshaping function of the brain.

A link has been established between movement, experience, and neurological development. Experiences appear to strengthen the connections within the brain such that if connections are not made or are weak, they are pruned away. If the connections are made and used, they are strengthened and become part of the brain.

With the rapid expansion of connections through use and the pruning due to disuse, there appear to be windows of opportunity for brain development. The main circuits required for responses such as breathing, regulation of heartbeat, and reflexes are set and windows of opportunity do not exist; however, the environment shapes and refines the connections for conscious control. The variety of sensory experiences progressively refines these connections, making environmental stimulation extremely important.

Researchers are discovering the importance of early stimulation. Children lacking in stimulating environments have brains that are 20 to 30% smaller than normal. The years of development prior to age 5 are extremely important, and a child has the ability to overcome some devastating problems during this time. Children below the age of 3 years who have lost a complete hemisphere of the brain have matured into highly functioning adults. During this time of development, the brain is very plastic and new connections are made. Experience is critical in the wiring of a child's brain. However, the ability of the child to rebound from serious problems declines as the child gets older.

A series of studies on children between the ages of 4 months and 8 years who live in disadvantaged environments found that intensive early education using blocks, beads, and games had positive long-term effects on IQ and academic achievement (Ramey & Ramey, 1994). An important finding was that the earlier children enrolled in the programs, the longer the results lasted. Children enrolled after the age of 5 demonstrated few benefits.

Gabbard (2000) summarized research on brain development suggesting windows of opportunity for various functions. Windows of opportunity occur while the child is growing physically—frequently during the rapid growth spurt for the specific system. Gross motor development has a sensitive period prenatally to about age 5 whereas fine motor development takes place shortly after birth until approximately 9 years of age. Visual development demonstrates a window of opportunity from birth to age 2. The vocabulary-building opportune period extends from birth to about 4 years while that for second language learning extends from 1 year to about 10 years of age. The window of opportunity for music is from about 3 years of age until 10. The math logic window of opportunity ranges from 1 year to about 4 years.

Physical Growth.   Physical growth includes changes in height and weight. The child grows very rapidly during the first year of life. During this time the infant typically increases in length by 10 inches (from 20 inches for boys and 19.75 inches for girls to 30 and 29.25 inches respectively) and in weight by 14 to 15 pounds; in many cases children increase their birth height by nearly 50% and triple their weight to 22.5 pounds for boys and 21 pounds for girls. The second year of life shows continued growth but at a slower rate, growing an average of 4.75 inches. Until the adolescent growth spurt the child increases in height and weight at a slow and steady pace, although some will experience a small growth spurt in middle childhood.

Not only does stature and weight change throughout childhood but the absolute and relative sizes of body parts also change. A newborn's head accounts for 25% of the body size in relation to body length while the legs make up about three-eighths of the stature. On the other hand, the head is one-eighth and the legs half of the total height for an adult. To help understand what a child is dealing with, think of how hard it would be to balance if you had two heads, one on top of the other!

Not only are there proportional differences in relation to total height, but there are width differences also. The width of the head of a newborn is similar to the shoulders and hips whereas the width of an adult's head is only one-third the width of the shoulders. During infancy and early childhood, the legs grow faster than the trunk and undergo a growth spurt during early adolescence. Think of early adolescents: They appear to be all legs! During the adolescent growth spurt the legs and the trunk become proportional to each other. Think of the infant with her hand raised: The hand barely reaches the top of the head. Yet for the adolescent and adult, the elbow is above the head. A younger child is not physically ready to swim due to the length of her arms; she is unable to generate the required force.

The rate at which individual children physically grow differs. Children can be categorized as early, average, or late maturing. Early maturing children tend to be bigger and stronger than their late maturing counterparts. This size advantage can predispose a child to early success in movement merely due to a size

Body proportions change with age.

advantage. Late maturing children on the other hand might not experience success in movement. The child might be skilled demonstrating a mature pattern, but due to size mismatching, not perform well when playing with others. In the opening scenario, Kelly might have the advantage in swimming because she is bigger and stronger, not because she demonstrates advanced skill. Emphasizing skill development—not outcome—is critically important for young children.

Physiological Factors. Physiological factors are related to movement performance constraints. Generally the ability of the child to sustain moderate to intense physical activity over time (aerobic endurance) increases with physical growth, but when the child's level is considered relative to his body size, these measures are comparable to adults. This means children should not be restricted from participating in aerobic activities that require moderate to intense physical activity, however, distance and time must be scaled to their individual body size. For example, the length of time that a child is physically active should be less than that for an adult.

The ability to produce short bursts of muscular force (anaerobic activity), even when factored relative to body size, is not similar for adults and children. Muscular strength increases with age due to increases in muscle mass and improvements in skill performance. The strength and power increases associated with the aging process directly influence the ability of the child to perform many movements successfully. For example, without the level of strength needed to lift the body weight, a 4-year-old child's attempts to jump up will not be successful. Also pairing children to compete against each other can predispose the smaller child to failure. The larger child will win merely because he is stronger than the smaller child, not because of superior skill.

The physiological parameters of cardiovascular endurance, muscular strength, and temperature regulation can affect motor performance. A child's state of biological maturation may require an alteration of activities. When playing catch with a child, for example, the educator needs to use a soft, light, and large ball while standing fairly close by. Due to immature development of the eye, the child is somewhat nearsighted; thus she is unable to organize space at a distance. Another example is pitching a ball for a child to strike. The child moves closer to the pitcher to be able to track the ball whereas the pitcher moves away in order to avoid being hit!

As the child grows and matures it is necessary to match equipment to the child. By asking young children to learn on adult-sized equipment or adult-sized fields, they are put at a disadvantage. We tested the success of children using child-sized golf clubs (Wood, Gallagher, & Martino, 1990). When John Larkin used a child-sized golf club, he demonstrated a skilled swing pattern. When he used either a woman's club or a cut down man's club, however, his skill deteriorated.

Cognitive Maturation.   In addition to the physical maturational level of the child, the cognitive and emotional maturational levels also need to be considered. Children who are under 2 years of age are in Piaget's sensorimotor level of cognitive development. During this phase, movement is critical to thinking, and the child basically learns through movement by interacting with the environment. The second stage of development, preoperational thought, is from 2 to approximately 8 years of age. During this stage, the child begins to use symbols to represent objects in the environment and verbal communication emerges. Pretend play appears at this time and enhances motor development. The concrete operations stage generally spans ages 7 through 11. Problem-solving skills are enhanced and children start to use memory strategies (attention, rehearsal, and cuing) to improve learning and retention. The final stage of cognitive development is formal operations, which begins at approximately 11 or 12 years of age. Abstract thought is the major emphasis during this stage.

Knowledge development and play go hand in hand. Piaget believed that play assisted the child in the construction of knowledge. He outlined three major types of knowledge: physical knowledge, logical-mathematical knowledge, and social knowledge.

As Kara plays with the keys she is developing physical knowledge, knowledge about the physical properties of the objects she manipulates. A second type of knowledge is logical-mathematical. Logical-mathematical knowledge provides the child with a comprehension of relationships between objects, people, and ideas. The last time Sara cared for Sam she read him the book *Good Night Moon;* when Sara arrived to care for Sam a week later he ran for the book *Good Night Moon.* Sam formed a relationship between an object, the book, and Sara, a person. At the same time Sam was developing logical-mathematical knowledge, he was also developing cognizance about social knowledge. He has constructed his own knowledge through stimulation and a self-selected activity. The child is constantly adding information to his knowledge patterns and/or changing the format of existing knowledge patterns through assimilation and accommodation.

The child constructs knowledge through play and the interactive process of assimilation and accommodation. During assimilation the child uses knowledge and skills without adaptation. Accommodation involves changing current ways or patterns of thinking to take into account the new information. In T-ball Jesse practices hitting a ball off the tee. The ball is always at the same place in space so that each time Jesse hits the ball he is assimilating the information into replicating the same pattern or schema. During an actual game, however, Jesse, who could hit the ball off the tee 100% during practice, strikes out. The coach and his parents pronounce that he is nervous. No, Jesse needed to practice accommodation to change his hitting pattern or schema to adapt the pattern to account for the various positions in space that the ball may occupy. Instead of practicing hitting the ball in the same position he needs to practice striking the ball in different positions in space.

Emotional Maturation.   Affective development focuses on the social and emotional development of the child. For movement programs we need to be concerned with the development of self-concept and a positive attitude toward physical activity. Self-esteem and self-concept have been used interchangeably. Gruber (1985) in a review of 84 different studies concluded that involvement in directed play or physical education enhanced self-esteem. Around 8 years of age children begin to verbalize their feelings of self-worth and make judgments about their self-esteem. By 12 years of age they are able to differentiate academic and athletic competence, peer social acceptance, physical appearance, and their own conduct.

In summary, the readiness and success of most movement-related skills is heavily dependent on the biological, cognitive, and social/emotional maturation of the individual. Due to physical constraints of the child, many activities should be limited in time and distance, with any equipment matching the child's body size. Skills should be presented to the child in a manner that capitalizes on the cognitive development and enhances memory strategies to aid retention. Finally, the self-concept of the individual needs to be developed. The child needs to feel competent in order to continue the activity.

Learning

The term *learning* has also been used interchangeably with *development.* We define learning as a relatively permanent change in behavior as a result of experience. Chip (10 months old) lives in the south and learned to say "hey" when a phone was held to his ear. However, Eliza, a child in the north, learned to say "hi" under similar circumstances. Marcella, who lived in Brazil for her first two years, answered the telephone using "alo"; at 3 years old she now says "hi" to her American grandparents and "alo" to her grandparents from Brazil. Infants without phones in the home will say "hi" when someone enters the room but do not know what to do with a telephone. Chip, Eliza, and Marcella learned how to interact with others due to experience and the environment in which they were raised; they did not learn merely due to the passage of time.

Learning motor skills during the early childhood years is important for several reasons relating to the windows of opportunity discussed earlier. Childhood seems to be the most efficient time to learn fundamental motor skills; basic motor skills such as running, jumping, kicking, catching, and throwing are precursors to sport-specific skills (Haubenstricker & Seefeldt, 1986). Additionally, skills and activity habits acquired in early life often persist into the adult years (Beach & Jaynes, 1954; Kohl & Hobbs, 1998, Rarick, 1964); and motorically skilled children are more relaxed and willing than unskilled children to attempt new motor challenges (Rarick, 1964, McGraw, 1935). Williams (1986) adds that environmental experience in the form of play or physical activity may be important for the young child in that it provides her with the opportunity to sort out important sensory information relevant to task performance. This provides the child with an opportunity to learn how to use information from within the body to produce appropriate movements while suppressing inappropriate ones. Pedro ran into his grandmother's house, knocking over a lamp. On the return visit, he made a wide arc around the lamp—thus avoiding a collision.

Children acquire motor skills at very young ages. However, for optimum learning to occur, an appropriate progression of activities must be designed. To determine this, the skills the child can already perform must be analyzed. Matching the child's level of performance to a developmental progression of the skill assists the teacher in guaranteeing success during learning.

The environmental conditions, task demands, and prerequisite skills the child can perform (cumulative experience) influence future learning. The teacher of young children needs to evaluate the task demands and match those to the cumulative experience of the child to determine the *sequence* of learning.

Finally, manipulation of the environmental conditions can either increase or decrease task success. For example, to teach throwing, the teacher first needs to evaluate the child's physical, cognitive, and emotional maturational levels. Physically—does the child have the appropriate strength, balance, and fine motor control to step, swing the arm, and release the ball in sequence? Many young children go through the appropriate movement sequence but do not release the ball. Is the child cognitively capable of understanding and following the appropriate cues of look, step, and throw? Is the child emotionally capable of working within a small group and not hitting other children with the ball? Does the child listen to the teacher?

While we have given the readiness sequence for throwing as an example, this same assessment and planning should go into the teaching of any movement concept or fundamental motor skill. The assessment, planning, and implementation stages of teaching a skill should not be seen as a formal or structured lesson, but rather a way to facilitate learning in a child who is developmentally ready and intrinsically motivated to learn a skill. We must remember that the best way to help a child learn a skill is to provide a learning environment that helps to develop the skill. Children should be provided with balls of varied shapes and sizes and the space to throw without hurting anyone within the learning environment.

Motivation

A child can have the prerequisite skills and demonstrate the appropriate social behaviors but still not participate in physical activity. Motivation of both the child and parent are important in participating in physical activity.

Child's Motivation.   The child's motivation to participate in physical activity must be considered. We typically think that children have short attention spans—and for many activities this is true. However, when playing ball with your 3-year-old nephew, who stops first? We are sure it is you! On the other hand, you ask a child to do a chore and you have to persist in getting him to complete the task. What is the cause of the child persisting at one task and not the other? First, playing ball is fun whereas the chore probably is not.

A feeling of competence is also important in motivation. As mentioned in affective development, it is important that children develop a feeling of self-confidence in the activity. Children need to be successful and thus feel competent. It does not take too many experiences of failure for a child to discontinue participation in an activity. It is always disappointing to hear a child say "I can't."

Parents' Motivation.   The motivation of the parent or caregiver to expose a child to early participation in structured physical activity is essential. Is the parent interested in having the child develop prerequisite skills for lifetime participation in physical activity? Or does the parent want to develop an Olympic competitor or a professional athlete? Typically, a parent who places a child in one specialized movement activity or sport may be attempting to foster a high level of success. A parent might think that to achieve the national recognition of Tiger Woods her child needs to start playing golf at 3 years of age. Although the commercials indicate that Tiger played golf as a young child, the majority of elite competitors do not begin sport competition early. In fact, many athletes who do specialize in a sport as young children will also burn out of sport and movement programs altogether. Parents need to understand the likelihood of a child becoming an elite competitor is small. Sage (1980) indicated that the chances of a high school football player playing professional football is 15 in 100,000, and the likelihood of a high school basketball player achieving pro ranks is 3 in 700,000. The probability of reaching the elite level of athletics decreases exponentially for even younger participants. Frequently, parents fail to realize that genetic endowment, in conjunction with movement skill and intrinsic motivation, play strong roles in determining the success of the athlete at the elite level. Such information may permit parents to have realistic expectations and avoid placing excessive pressure on their child for unattainable success.

Parental pressure on children to participate in movement programs and youth sports can lead to the child discontinuing participation. Children who feel it is not their own decision to participate in movement and sport programs are less likely to be satisfied with their experience and more likely to discontinue involvement (McGuire & Cook, 1983). It is no longer play; it has not been designed by the child and is not spontaneous. Those children who participate to please their parents have higher levels of stress (Scanlin & Lethwaite, 1984). Young children are especially sensitive to comments and reactions of adults and sometimes in ways that adults do not realize. Rebecca's father was the community soccer coach. Throughout the season, she heard about the good soccer players, but her name was never mentioned. As a result, when she played soccer she did cartwheels rather than attending to the game.

Parents should understand that participation in physical activity is important in the child's development. Research clearly indicates the benefits of physical activity for adults and children alike. We want children to begin to participate in physical activity early in life and continue for a lifetime. Young children are initially excited about physical activity but with growth, development, maturation, and learning, many turn into couch potatoes. Running everywhere they go, young children are highly motivated to be physically active. When teaching physical education to first graders, we recall the excitement of children. It was clear physical education was their favorite class, and they loved to come to the gym. However, this same enthusiasm no longer exists in middle school children. By the time children reach high school, many students hate gym. They do not want to sweat and would prefer to sit rather than be physically active.

Two of the factors that are central to maintaining a love of movement are development of self-esteem and success. Self-esteem and success interact. With success, self-esteem is enhanced; with enhanced self-esteem, the child practices more and becomes more successful. Many children are unsuccessful and consequently their motivation to continue participating diminishes. Teachers must plan lessons so that children are successful in developing the required skills.

Cultural Influences

Not only do we need to know if an activity is developmentally appropriate to the age norms and to individual differences, but we also need to know if it is culturally congruent (Bredekamp & Copple, 1997). Cultural differences relate to a specific group of individuals—which differ from individual differences. The child care early education educator needs to understand and value the cultural rules of the home in order to facilitate learning. Teachers can cause conflict in children if they do not understand the cultural environment of the child. We want to develop expectations for children that are consistent with the home, not confuse them by giving conflicting information.

Kirk was raised in a family that liked to play soccer, cross-country ski, and swim. The family participated in these sports as a family activity. Kirk had been in the water since infancy and had been on many ski outings with his mother, father, and sister. However, the area where the family lived placed a great deal of emphasis on the sports of football and baseball. Kirk was not aware of this sports culture conflict until he started kindergarten. During his first gym class the class played baseball. Needless to say, Kirk did not do well with this sport. The gym teacher called the mother and told her that Kirk was motorically delayed and needed to take a remedial gym class. Clearly the family culture and the regional culture were in conflict. Teachers of young children must remember that cultural differences do exist and must be sensitive to this aspect of learning when assessing, planning, and implementing motor activities.

School populations in the United States are increasingly diverse ethnically, racially, linguistically, and economically (Jackson, 1993/4). With these changes, increasing importance is focused on multicultural understanding. Education in all areas must meet the needs of a diverse society by encouraging understanding and appreciation of others. Children and adults alike need to understand and value diverse cultures. Sparks (1994) suggests that for teachers to effectively integrate multicultural education within their discipline, they need to have the knowledge and skills to promote social justice and equality for everyone and foster these attitudes among their students. Culturally responsive content appreciates the influences of culture, language, race, gender, and other characteristics that indicate differences (Huber, Higer & Parschal, 1992).

Jackson (1993/94) identified seven strategies to build a culturally responsive approach to teaching: build trust, become culturally literate, build different methodological approaches, use effective questioning techniques that promote critical thinking processes, provide effective feedback, and establish positive home-school relations. These strategies are covered separately in other parts of the text. It is important to remember that each child is a unique individual and it is essential to do everything possible to set the environment for all children to develop to their fullest potential.

Summary

Success in movement can provide a positive sense of accomplishment in the child, and subsequently build the child's desire to continue activities that promote healthy living through participating in physical activity. In order to ensure that the child achieves success in movement, the parent and teacher must consider the following factors:

1. Participation in physical activity is important for a lifetime. The purpose of participating during childhood is to develop behaviors that exist in adulthood. Movement is important in developing connections.
2. A stimulating environment is important in the early development of the child. The stimulating environment helps in developing connections in the brain that can last a lifetime.

3. The maturational level of the child can restrict or enhance performance. With age, children increase in size, and aerobic and anaerobic fitness levels. Therefore expectations, fields, equipment, play time, and rules need to be modified in all movement activity in which the child participates.

4. The learning environment is critical to promoting a positive attitude toward movement. Children need to work at the appropriate developmental level of the skill. A child who has not learned an efficient kicking pattern will not be successful in games that require kicking skills.

5. Motivation of the parent and child is important. Parents must understand that children participate in movement to have fun, to learn, and to socialize with their friends.

6. Educators, parents, and children need to value and appreciate diverse cultures.

In conclusion, for organized movement activities to thoroughly nurture the growing child, parents and teachers must be cognizant of the large combinations of factors that influence the child's performance. The focus of movement programs is to develop participation in physical activity for a lifetime, not the development of elite athletes. During the childhood years, fun and skill development should be the primary goal of the activity. Exercising by moving has been shown to positively influence the quality of life. During the childhood years care must be taken that adequate skill development and a desire to move is developed in the child.

CHANGE AND ADVOCACY

1. Evaluate toys to determine their developmental appropriateness for specific age groups of children. If they do not match, write a letter to the manufacturer to explain why the toy is inappropriate for the age(s) listed on the box.

2. Analyze an early childhood program to determine developmentally appropriate practices. Provide the child care center with ways to enhance their developmentally appropriate practices.

REFERENCES

Beach, F., & Jaynes, J. (1954). Effects of early experience upon the behavior of animals. *Psychological Bulletin, 51*(3), 239–263.

Bredekamp, S., & Copple, C. (1997). *Developmentally appropriate practice in early childhood programs* (Rev. ed.) Washington, DC: National Association for the Education of Young Children.

COPEC (Council on Physical Education for Children). (1994). *Developmentally appropriate practice in movement programs for young children, Ages 3–5.* Reston, VA: American Alliance for Health, Physical Education, Recreation, and Dance.

COPEC (Council on Physical Education for Children). (1999). *Developmentally Appropriate Physical Education Practices For Children.* Reston, VA: American Alliance for Health, Physical Education, Recreation, and Dance.

Chugani, H. (1994). Development of regional brain glucose metabolism in relation to behavior and plasticity. In G. Dawson, & K. Fischer (Eds.), *Human behavior and the developing brain* (pp. 153–175). New York: Guilford.

Espenschade, A., & Eckert, H. (1967). *Motor development.* Columbus, OH: Merrill.

Gabbard, C. (2000). *Lifelong motor development.* (3rd ed.). Boston: Allyn and Bacon.

Gallahue, D., & Ozmun, J. (1998). *Understanding motor development: Infants, children, adolescents, adults.* New York: WCB McGraw-Hill.

Gruber, J. (1985). Physical activity and self-esteem development in children: A meta-analysis. *The Academy Papers, 19,* 30–48.

Haubenstricker, J., & Seefeldt, V. (1986). Acquisition of motor skills during childhood. In V. Seefeldt (Ed.), *Physical activity and well-being* (pp. 41–102). Reston, VA: American Alliance for Health, Physical Education, Recreation, and Dance.

Haywood, K. M. (1993). *Life span motor development* (2nd ed.). Champaign, IL: Human Kinetics.

Huber, T., Higer, S., & Parschal, J. (1992). Case studies in culturally responsible pedagogy. *Mid-Western Educational Researcher, 5* (2), 9–14.

Jackson, F. R. (1993/94). Seven strategies to support a culturally responsive pedagogy. *Journal of Reading, 37,* 298–303.

Keogh, J., & Sugden, D. (1985). *Movement skill development.* New York: Macmillan.

Kohl, K., & Hobbs, K. (1998). Development of physical activity behaviors among children and adolescents. *Pediatrics, 101,* 549–554.

Motor Development Academy. (1994). *Looking at physical education from a developmental perspective: A guide to teaching.* Reston, VA: American Alliance for Health, Physical Education, Recreation, and Dance.

Magill, R. (1998). Critical periods as optimal readiness for learning sport skills. In F. Smoll, R. Magill, & M. Ash. (Eds). *Children in sport* (pp. 53–65). Champaign, IL: Human Kinetics.

Malina, R. M., & Bouuchard, C. (1991). *Growth, maturation, and physical activity.* Champaign, IL: Human Kinetics Books.

McGraw, M. B. (1935). *Growth: A study of Johnny and Jimmy.* New York: Appelton-Century. (Reprinted in 1975 by Arno Press)

McGuire, R. T., & Cook, D. L. (1983). The influence of others and the decision to participate in youth sports. *Journal of Sport Behavior, 6,* 9–16.

Monighan-Nourot, P. (1997). Playing with play in four dimensions. In Isenberg, J., & Jalongo, M. (Eds.), *Major trends and issues in early childhood education: Challenges, controversies, and insights* (pp. 123–148). New York: Teachers' College Press.

Rarick, G. (1964). Research evidence on the values of physical education. *Theory Into Practice, 3,* 108–111.

Ramey, C., & Ramey, S. (1994). Which children benefit the most from early intervention? *Pediatrics, 94,* 1064–1066.

Sage, G. H. (1980). Social development. In V. Seefeldt (Ed.), *Physical activity and well-being* (pp. 343–372). Reston, VA: American Alliance for Health, Physical Education, Recreation, and Dance.

Santrock, J. W. (1999). *Life-span development.* Boston: McGraw-Hill.

Scanlin, T. K., & Lewthwaite, R. (1984). Social psychological aspects of competition for male youth sport participants: I. Predictors of competitive stress. *Journal of Sport Psychology, 6,* 208–226.

Sparks, W. G. (1994). Culturally responsive pedagogy: A framework for addressing multicultural issues. *Journal of Physical Education, Recreation, and Dance, 65* (9), 33–61.

Williams, H. (1986). The development of sensory-motor function in young children. In V. Seefeldt (Ed.), *Physical activity and well-being* (pp. 104–122). Reston, VA: American Alliance for Health, Physical Education, Recreation, and Dance.

Wood, C. A., Gallagher, J. D., Martino, P. V. (1990). Large equipment, small children: Implications for club fitting based upon age and standing height for junior golfers. In A. J. Cochran (Ed.), *Science and golf: proceedings of the First World Scientific Congress of Golf* (pp. 87–92). London: E.&F.N. Spon.

PART TWO

Health and Safety Issues Concerning Infants, Toddlers, and Young Children

3 Nutrition and the Healthy Child

CHAPTER OBJECTIVES

Knowledge

- The reader will identify the components of the Food Guide Pyramid and explain the elements of a balanced diet for infants, toddlers, and children.

Skills

- The reader will design a balanced diet for infants, toddlers, and young children using the Food Guide Pyramid and recommended servings guidelines.

Dispositions

- The reader will appreciate the role a balanced, healthy diet plays in the development of infants, toddlers, and young children of varying ethnicities.

CHAPTER SYNOPSIS

Nutritional Preferences and Guidelines
    Guidelines for Nutritional Planning
Shopping for a Healthy Lifestyle
    The Food Guide Pyramid

Nutrition for a Lifetime
    Prenatal Development
    Early Childhood Development
    Nutritional Programs to Aid Development

Scenario

In a child care setting, a group of children and a teacher were sitting around a table discovering and designing with clay. As fingers and wooden tools were manipulating the clay, the children were discussing various activities. The teacher, Miss Franco, was having a conversation with Julius, the child seated next to her. The teacher said, "My Daddy gave me a box of chocolates, and I ate every one! Julius, did your Daddy ever give you chocolate?" Julius gave the teacher a very thoughtful reply, "Yes, but I can't eat chocolate all the time."

The conversation between Julius and his teacher was very insightful regarding his knowledge level. Food is enticing. We all love to eat and talk about food. Eating involves all of the senses. The sound of the crunchy apple; the sight of the vivid colors of oranges, red beets, and avocados; the smell of fresh-baked bread; the slippery touch of wet pasta; and the taste of sweet, salty, and bitter foods. Julius realized that chocolate may be delicious, but it is not a food that is good to eat all the time. It certainly is not a food that helps in obtaining optimal health.

Smith (1979) felt that optimal nutrition would maintain a person in the best health possible considering his particular genetic endowment. If an individual is not healthy it could be due to nutritional deficiencies. By eating the right foods, the health of an individual can be maintained or improved and the development of diseases can be hindered. Smith (1979) connected nutrition and well-being to indicate five levels of health ranging from total optimal health to terminal illness. Optimal nutrition contributes to maintaining a higher level of health while poor nutrition leads an individual to slipping into an unhealthy state.

On Level 1 of a healthy lifestyle the child grows to adulthood free of illness and has indicators of a healthy lifestyle such as freedom from rashes, headaches, depression, constipation, and insomnia. He is a flexible person who is happy and has few problems as he progresses through cognitive, physical, social, and emotional development. To maintain a child on Level 1 the child must have optimum nutrition that provides the right amount of required nutrients such as grains, fruits, vegetables, meat, and fish, and small amounts of fats. In this chapter we discuss the types and amounts of nutrients that a child must have to stay on Smith's Level 1, and we provide the early childhood educator with ideas on what she can do to help the child's family maintain this optimum level. We do not want the child to slide into an unhealthy state outside of Smith's Level 1.

Level 2 marks the beginning of a backward slide. While there are no major problems, we begin to see slight problems in the child's health such as colds and the flu. He might not be as flexible as a child on Level 1 but will, nonetheless, progress well through the developmental milestones. The child who is on Level 2 and beginning to make a backward slide healthwise may not be receiving the right types and/or amounts of nutrients.

A child on Level 3 probably had problems very early in his development. His mother may have had a stressful pregnancy, or he may have been born prematurely. Problems such as diarrhea, vomiting, or eczema appear shortly after birth. The child may have a temperament that causes him to avoid contact with the caregiver. This may present bonding problems between caregivers and the child.

Children on Level 4 require almost constant medical attention for a variety of illnesses and personality and cognitive problems. Finally, the child who is classified as Level 5 will be terminally ill and bedridden, and will display developmental delays or deficiencies.

Optimum amounts of nutrients are required throughout pregnancy and postnatal development to enable the child to operate throughout life at Level 1. The early childhood educator must work with the family to ensure that the child receives the proper amount of required nutrients each day. This means that two-way communication must take place between the family and the child care early educator about the types and amounts of foods that the child eats both in the home and in the child care early education setting. Educators of young children must have a working knowledge of the nutrients necessary to maintain children's health at the optimum Level 1 (Smith, 1979) and how to prepare healthy food in ways that are interesting and enticing to children.

Clearly, Julius, who is 3 years old, has a grasp of the role food plays in helping him remain a healthy individual. While many people would like to eat chocolate all the time, everyone should realize that this is not healthy eating nor is it a part of a healthy lifestyle. The remainder of the chapter covers nutritional guidelines, planning and shopping for food, and the role nutrition plays in a healthy lifestyle.

Nutritional Preferences and Guidelines

When infants are born they begin to communicate their taste preferences through increased sucking and tense or relaxed facial muscles. The preferred taste in newborns is sweet—which is vital since early growth is dependent on sweet-tasting mother's milk. Like adults, infants tend to react to sour and bitter tastes by movement of their facial muscles. By 4 months of age infants begin to prefer salty-tasting foods—which prepares them to accept solid foods (Beauchamp, Cowart, Mennella, & Marsh, 1994).

The genetically prescribed taste preferences are tempered in the developing child through cultural and environmental influences. Children living in the United States as well as other countries will develop a strong preference to the foods they are exposed to through their environmental and familial interactions. As a result some children eat a diet rich in grains, legumes, vegetables, and fruits while the diet of other children consists of meat, potatoes, and gravy or highly processed fast foods. Educators of young children must be aware of the genetic, environmental, cultural, and metabolic influences that affect the food choices children make and assist them in making the right choices for a healthy lifestyle.

Guidelines for Nutritional Planning

Educators are involved in the selection of foods for daily snacks, breakfasts, lunches, and—in some cases—dinner. The burden falls on these individuals to make sure children in early childhood programs receive healthy and nutritional foods in the appropriate amounts for the developmental age of the children. They must also be sure that these foods are tasty and appealing while meeting the cultural and ethnic preferences of the children involved in the program. It should be noted that some programs provide a nutritional consultant or contract food services from agencies that employ a nutritionist, but this practice is the exception rather than the rule. The early childhood educator acts as the nutritionist in the majority of programs.

Ethnic and Cultural Food Considerations.   When planning menus caregivers need to take into consideration the familial, cultural, and religious backgrounds of the children in their programs. Each cultural group has basic foods that are staples in their diets. African Americans tend to eat a diet that is rich in dark, leafy greens, beans, and starches. Hispanic Americans tend to follow a vegetarian diet containing beans and corn. Native Americans consume a diet of starches, fruits, and dairy products. Asian Americans tend to eat a diet of starches, vegetables, and fruits. European Americans' diet will reflect their particular cultural and ethnic heritage. Italian Americans may prefer pasta dishes with white and red sauces. Irish Americans will eat a boiled dinner consisting of corned beef with potatoes, cabbage, and carrots. German Americans enjoy sausages with potatoes and whole grain breads. The Jewish American diet, depending on the country of origin, may contain either a variety of high-fat and high-sodium foods due to following of the Kosher preparation of foods or may contain a diet of grains and vegetables (Leeds, 1998).

Families tend to especially follow their cultural and ethnic background food preferences during special holidays. Children who are accustomed to familial or ethnic foods feel more comfortable in a care situation if they are given these foods with which they are familiar.

When meal-planning, attention should also be given to religious holidays. Many religious holidays have food customs and traditions and families may expect the teachers of the child care early education program to respect and follow these customs. Many Catholic families prefer their children eat fish on Fridays while other families want their older children to participate in fasting. To involve the cultural and religious preferences of the family, extra effort is required but the rewards are extensive. The children are more comfortable in the child care early education setting and their self-esteem is enhanced. Of equal importance is that other children in the early childhood setting become aware of ethnic foods and that cultural understanding increases.

Ethnic food preferences are not only associated with certain types of foods but also with the spices used to prepare the food. Foods representative of different cultures use certain amounts of spices and flavorings such as curry, soy sauce, ginger, and garlic. Children's acceptance of a spice depends on how familiar they are with the spice. Varying the menus in programs provides children with different textures, colors, and tastes. Both children and staff alike benefit from this exchange of flavors and smells.

Socioeconomic and Ethical Considerations.   Socioeconomic considerations also need to be a part of menu planning. There are some nutritional foods that children are not exposed to because the cost of the food item is excessive for the food budget of the program. While this could be a rationale to exclude certain foods from programs for infants, toddlers, and young children, teachers should, nevertheless, make the effort to expose children to unusual and nutritious food items. When shopping for food, teachers or nutritionists should consider purchasing those mangoes!

Another item related to food selection and ethnic or socioeconomic status is the use of foods in art projects. This a controversial issue because some individuals feel that it is offensive to use food items in art projects since some children, in their home settings, do not have enough food for daily subsistence. Teachers of young children should be aware of this sensitive issue and make a personal judgment when planning creative projects.

Recommended Dietary Allowances. A healthy diet for infants, toddlers, and young children should provide the sufficient amount of nutrients appropriate for the age and developmental level of each child. The concept of optimum nutrition is based on the relationship between quantities required and quantities supplied (Smith, 1979). The Food and Nutrition Board of the National Academy of Sciences established the Recommended Dietary Allowances. The RDAs provide average daily intakes for protein, vitamins, and minerals—based on age, weight, and height—that are necessary to maintain good nutrition and health. The age groups categorized in the RDAs pertinent to this text are:

- Birth through 5 months
- Six months through 12 months
- One through 3 years
- Four through 6 years
- Seven through 10 years

The RDAs for many nutrients increase with age, but some, such as calcium, decrease with age. Appendix A shows the RDAs for the above age groups. When planning diets for young children it is necessary to know not only the recommended dietary allowances but also the nutritional content of foods that you will be using to meet the recommended dietary allowances. Food labels assist parents and caregivers in this process.

Food and Nutrition Labeling. The 1990 Nutritional Labeling and Education Act made labels more user friendly by providing the buyer with the name of the product, its net weight, and the manufacturer's name and address. The label lists the ingredients in order of their prominence in the food, and provides the nutrition content per adult-sized serving as well as an evaluation of the nutrition content of each serving. Manufacturers must also include on the label scientifically reliable information regarding any health claims (see Figure 3.1 on page 46).

Calories. The food label will give the amount of calories per serving. *Calorie* is a term used by nutritionists to describe the amount of heat produced by metabolizing a food item that a child's body can then use as energy for play, to build body tissues, and to maintain the body temperature at 98.6 degrees Fahrenheit. An apple has 81 calories. This means that when the body metabolizes the apple it produces 81 calories of heat the body can use for energy. One gram of protein has 4 calories; 1 gram of fat has 9 calories; and 1 gram of carbohydrate has 4 calories (Rinzler, 1997). When planning healthy snacks and meals for children or adults,

Nutritional Facts

Serving Size 1/2 cup (125g)

Servings Per Container about 6

Amount Per Serving

Calories 60	Calories from Fat 15
	% Daily Value*
Total Fat 2 g	3%
Saturated Fat 0g	0%
Cholesterol 0 mg	0%
Sodium 590 mg	25%
Total Carbohydrate 9 g	3%
Dietary Fiber 3 g	12%
Sugar 7 g	
Protein 2g	
Vitamin A 13%	**Vitamin C** 0%
Calcium 6%	**Iron** 10%

*Percent Daily Values are based on a 2,000 calorie diet

FIGURE 3.1   Food Label

keep in mind that 1 gram of protein plus 1 gram of carbohydrate still has fewer calories than 1 gram of fat. Therefore, eating ice cream as a snack should be minimized while bread or turkey snacks should be encouraged.

The recommended energy, or caloric, intake is based on a person's age and weight (Birch, 1991). Table 3.1 lists the amount of calories needed for each pound based on a child's age and estimated growth rate. It should be noted that while averages can be given, the actual caloric need of each child will vary depending on the child's individual level of activity and growth rate.

TABLE 3.1   Recommended Energy or Calorie Intake By Age

1–3-Year-Old Children	46 calories/pound of body weight
4–6-Year-Old Children	41 calories/pound of body weight
7–10-Year-Old Children	32 calories/pound of body weight
Adults	13 calories/pound of body weight

In addition to the amount of calories that a food provides per serving, the labels give the protein, carbohydrate, and fat content per adult-sized serving. Nutritional planners should remember this when planning menus for young children. Adaptations must be made to provide the appropriate nutrition content for infants, toddlers, and young children.

Proteins.   Proteins are commonly referred to as the building blocks of the body. They are required for building and maintaining all body tissues and synthesizing many compounds vital to the body's functioning (Leeds, 1998). Proteins are made up of amino acids that are broken down by the body and then reassembled as specific compounds the body needs to build nails, skin, muscle tissue, and bone (Rinzler, 1997). The body uses 20 different amino acids, but only 9 of these amino acids are essential. Table 3.2 lists the amino acids.

Complete proteins contain all nine of the essential amino acids in balanced amounts, and are typically found in animal foods such as meat, fish, poultry, eggs, and dairy products. Incomplete proteins either do not contain all the amino acids, or they may be present in limited amounts. The nutritional value of legumes, nuts, seeds, and grains is not as high as foods containing complete proteins. The only exception to this is the soybean; it contains all nine of the amino acids. Common cultural combinations such as beans and rice or corn tortillas and beans will provide all nine of the amino acids. These are meals planned using the concept of complementary proteins. Each of the above foods is an incomplete protein, but when they are paired they complement each other and together become a complete protein.

Carbohydrates.   If proteins are the building block of the body, carbohydrates are considered the fuel of the body. Carbohydrates come in three types: simple carbohydrates, complex carbohydrates, and dietary fiber. All carbohydrates are composed of sugar. Simple carbohydrates (monosaccharides) are made up of 1 unit of

TABLE 3.2   Amino Acids

Essential Amino Acids	Nonessential Amino Acids
Histidine	Alanine
Isoleucine	Arginine
Leucine	Asparagine
Lysine	Aspartic acid
Methionine	Cysteine
Phenylalanine	Glutamic acid
Threonine	Glutamine
Tryptophan	Glycine
Valine	Proline
	Serine
	Tyrosine

sugar. Fructose, glucose, and galactose are examples of simple sugars. Disaccharides are carbohydrates that have 2 units of sugar linked together. Examples of disaccharides are sucrose, lactose, and maltose. Polysaccharides are many sugars linked and are referred to as complex carbohydrates. Starch, cellulose, pectin, and gums are examples of complex sugars. Dietary fiber is similar to a complex carbohydrate—a polysaccharide—with the one exception that the bonds that hold the sugars together cannot be broken down by the digestive enzymes. The fiber passes through the digestive system without undergoing a great deal of change. Dietary fiber cannot be considered a source of energy but is very important in the diet. Fiber promotes regular bowel movements and may reduce the risk of hemorrhoids, colon cancer, and perhaps diverticular disease (Stamler & Dolecek, 1997).

Carbohydrates also protect the muscles in the body. If carbohydrates are not available, the body will begin to use protein tissue as energy. This is why severe reducing diets or poor nutrition can be detrimental to the developing child—and may even result in death.

Fats.   Fats or lipids are another nutrient listed in the content of foods. Lipids increase the palatability and aroma of foods. Once a teacher was eating several frosted wafer cookies and commented, "Why are these cookies so good?" A student fired back, "FAT!"

Fats or lipids have functions besides adding taste to foods. They provide stored energy to the body, serve as body insulation, produce nerve cell myelin, carry fat-soluble vitamins, and supply the body with fatty acids. European countries have recognized the importance of fats in the diet of infants and toddlers. All infant formulas in Europe are required to contain pro-omega fats from fish—to enhance neural development. Low-fat diets should not be used for infants and toddlers. This population should drink whole milk to get the fats necessary for development.

The main function of lipids is to provide fuel for the body's immediate energy needs. Fats are a more concentrated form of energy than are proteins or carbohydrates because fats, with nine calories per gram, have more than twice the amount of calories of proteins or carbohydrates.

Excess dietary energy from proteins, carbohydrates, or fats is stored as one of the three types of fat: triglycerides, phospholipids, and sterols. Adipose tissue, the fat-storing cells on hips, abdomen, thighs, and breasts, helps to give the human body its shape and is composed of triglycerides. The more active an individual is, the smaller the amount of adipose tissue present. This same tissue also helps to insulate the body. Fatty material forms the myelin that covers the axon of nerve cells—permitting faster communication in voluntary and involuntary behaviors. The first 5 years of a child's life are very important in myelination and nerve cell growth, which are the foundation for all cognitive and motor development. Therefore, it is essential that a child receives proper nutrition during this time period to ensure optimum physical, motor, and cognitive growth.

Triglycerides supply the body with two essential fatty acids—linoleic acid and linolenic acid. These fatty acids may be present in the forms of saturated, monounsaturated, and polyunsaturated fats. A saturated fat stays solid at room temperature and gets harder when chilled. Monounsaturated fats are liquid at room temperature and will get thicker when chilled. Polyunsaturated fat is liquid at room temperature and will remain a liquid when chilled.

Another form of lipid—phospholipids—carries hormones and fat-soluble vitamins A, D, E, and K throughout the body via the blood. An important phospholipid in the body is lecithin. Lecithin, a major component of cell membranes, is found naturally in egg yolks and is often added to processed foods to help mix fats and water. The third form of lipids is the sterol group. The major sterol in the body is cholesterol, the base that the body uses to build hormones and vitamins.

A diet high in fat has been associated with an increased risk of obesity, diabetes, heart disease, and various forms of cancer. Saturated fats increase the amount of cholesterol thereby increasing the risk of heart disease and stroke. Diets must provide the right balance of fat to provide the nutrients necessary to promote growth and a healthy body but not enough to cause obesity. Therefore, the American Health Association and American Cancer Society recommend that fats should not account for more than 30% of total daily calories (Leeds, 1998). Parents and caregivers must be educated consumers to ensure the health of themselves and the children under their care. Low-fat diets may be maintained by avoiding fats such as flavorings, meat, and some dairy products. Caution should be followed when putting children on low-fat diets because balance must be maintained for normal development to occur. In this situation, a nutritionist's advice should be followed.

Vitamins and Minerals.   Vitamins and minerals are also listed on food labels. Vitamins encourage good health through the prevention of disease and the promotion of healing. Minerals assist the body in building tissue and regulating various body functions. Vitamins are named by the letters of the alphabet in the chronological order of their discovery. A number (B-1, B-2, B-3, B-6, and B-12) further distinguishes vitamins within a group, such as the B-complex vitamins, from one another.

The human body needs at least 13 vitamins:

- Vitamin A
- Vitamin D
- Vitamin E
- Vitamin K
- Vitamin C
- B-Complex Vitamins
    - Vitamin B-1 (thiamine)
    - Vitamin B-2 (riboflavin)
- Niacin
- Vitamin B-6
- Folate
- Vitamin B-12
- Biotin
- Pantothenic acid

The news media has heralded the ability of certain vitamins—called the antioxidant vitamins—in preventing the effects of certain chronic diseases such as cancer, heart disease, and premature aging. It is felt by some researchers that vitamin E, vitamin C, and beta-carotene (vitamin A) are partners in combating disease and will clean the body of toxins that could cause disease and conditions associated with aging.

Deficiency of certain vitamins in children will cause a variety of health problems as shown in Table 3.3.

Vitamin Deficiencies.   Parents and caregivers should provide a balanced diet with a variety of grains, fruits, vegetables, and animal or dairy protein to meet the vitamin as well as the mineral needs of the growing child.

Minerals.   Minerals are natural substances that are not plant or animal though they are present in plants and animals. Plants get minerals from the soil while animals get minerals from eating the plants. Minerals have names that reflect the place where they are found or a unique characteristic such as their color (Rinzler, 1997).

The minerals essential for human beings are:

- Calcium
- Chloride
- Phosphorus
- Potassium
- Magnesium
- Sulfur
- Sodium

TABLE 3.3   Vitamin Deficiencies

Vitamin	Deficiency Symptoms	Food Sources
Vitamin A	Night blindness, xerophthalmia (hard cornea)	Liver, milk, butter, orange vegetables, apricots, leafy greens, sweet potatoes, mangoes, peaches
Vitamin C	Scurvy, fatigue, bleeding gums	Citrus fruit, red and green pepper, strawberries
Vitamin D	Rickets (poor bone format), osteomalacia (bone softening)	Milk
Vitamin E	Hemolytic anemia	Vegetable oils, peanuts and peanut butter, tuna fish, wheat germ, leafy greens
Vitamin K	Poor blood clotting	Broccoli, cabbage, brussels sprouts, asparagus, liver

Other elements that are also essential for human beings in trace amounts are:

- Copper
- Chromium
- Fluoride
- Iodine
- Iron
- Manganese
- Molybdenum
- Selenium
- Zinc

The two minerals that are most likely to be lacking in the American diet are iron and calcium (Leeds, 1998).

Iron. The most common nutrient problem among children in the United States is iron deficiency, which is particularly prevalent among infants, toddlers, and children up to 4 years of age. Iron is the major component of hemoglobin and myoglobin, two proteins that store and transport oxygen in the bloodstream. If a child has inadequate levels of iron she can have reduced energy production as well as decreased attention span and learning ability (Leeds, 1998). The best sources of iron are organ meat (liver, heart, kidney), red meat, egg yolks, wheat germ, and oysters. Certain plants (e.g., whole grains, wheat germ, raisins, nuts, seeds, and potato skins) contain iron, but the human body has a hard time using the iron from these sources.

Calcium. The most prevalent mineral in the human body is calcium. About three pounds of an adult's body weight is calcium and most of it is packed into bones and teeth. It is also present in the fluid around the cells of the body. Calcium strengthens bones, helps regulate the flow of water through the cell walls, assists in communication between cells, and keeps muscles moving. It has also been shown that calcium helps to lower the risk of colon cancer and lowers blood pressure. The best sources of calcium are milk and dairy products, fish such as sardines and salmon, tofu, and leafy greens.

Mineral Electrolytes. The main mineral electrolytes of the human body include sodium, potassium, and chloride. Electrolytes help to maintain the body's fluid balance. The major source of sodium and chloride is sodium chloride, also known as table salt. Excessive amounts of sodium in the diet may cause edema, or fluid retention, and in more extreme cases hypertension or high blood pressure. The cultural and socioeconomic use of certain foods such as soy sauce, bacon, ham, fast foods, canned vegetables, and snack foods contribute to high intakes of sodium. Avocados, baked potatoes, watermelon, and bananas are the major sources of potassium.

Fluoride.   An essential nutrient, fluoride, is a controversial issue with many researchers. The human body stores fluoride in the bones and teeth. Research shows that intake of fluoride by children during tooth development helps to make teeth resistant to decay. Researchers also suspect that fluoride helps to strengthen bones. Sources of fluoride are fluoridated drinking water, seafood, and seaweed. Some water supplies are naturally fluoridated, but many other communities add fluoride to the municipal water supplies. In areas where fluoride is not in water supplies, children may be directed by physicians or dentists to take fluoride supplements to prevent tooth decay. Dentists may also apply fluoride directly to the teeth; it is also contained in the majority of toothpastes. Mottles, dark spots on the teeth, may appear when the child is given too much fluoride. Excessive fluoride (fluorosis), can also result in brittle bones.

Vitamin and Mineral Supplements.   Children in various geographical areas of the United States may take fluoride supplements as well as other vitamin and mineral supplements. The American Dietetic Association, the American Academy of Pediatrics, and the American Medical Association agree that routine use of vitamin or mineral supplements for normal, healthy children is not recommended (Leeds, 1998). The one exception to this is giving fluoride to children when fluoride is not in the water supply.

Children should be able to obtain all the nutrients necessary for a well-balanced diet but in cases where the child might not be able to obtain all the nutrients, sometimes it is advisable to provide children with vitamin and mineral supplementation. Children who may be at nutritional risk, and who may benefit from the use of routine vitamin and mineral supplementation, may be from low socioeconomic situations, have poor appetites, or be on restrictive diets (e.g., vegetarian diets). If supplementation is used, the amount of each vitamin and mineral should never exceed 100% of the daily recommended RDA. It should also be remembered that the RDAs are determined for adults, and what is appropriate for an adult is not appropriate for an infant, toddler, or child. Supplements should be approved by a pediatrician and should be appropriate to the age level of the child.

Chemical Additives.   Finally, chemicals may be used in foods as coloring agents, flavoring agents, or preservatives. If the food contains FDA color additives, flavors, flavor enhancers, caseinate (a milk derivative in nondairy foods), or preservatives they must be declared on the food label. These chemicals in foods may cause toxic, carcinogenic, or allergenic reactions.

Since children may be allergic to these items, they need to be listed on labels to avoid allergic reactions. Color dye additives and flavor enhancers make food more appealing. Food producers have added a variety of substances to foods to tempt the consumer. Anyone who has worked with children knows that if the food is not appealing to the child, regardless of how nutritious the food is, the child will not eat it. The variety of colorful dyes added to cereals is a glaring example. Dyes may be carcinogenic (cancer causing) and should be avoided (National Research Council, 1996).

Nitrite has traditionally been used to preserve cured meats such as hot dogs, bacon, and luncheon meats. There have been repeated studies linking childhood cancers and the consumption of these meats (Bunin, Kuijten, Buckley, Rorke, & Meadows, 1993; Preston-Matin, Pogoda, Mueller, Holly, Lijinsky, & Davis, 1996). In the last two decades the food industry has greatly reduced nitrite levels in these foods, and this action has led the National Research Council (NRC, 1996) to conclude that these foods do not pose a risk of cancer to adults. Because of the continued controversy in this area, early childhood professionals must decide whether to use these inexpensive, tasty, and popular preserved meat products.

Water.   Water is the most important substance for good health. The body uses it as a solvent and a nutrient. Human beings can live for several weeks without food, but if the human body does not receive water, death will occur in a matter of days. The adult body is approximately 50 to 60% water by weight. The actual amount varies according to the percentage of muscle mass. On a percentage basis the average male has more water than a female, and young children have more water than adults. Adult males have a higher water content than females since they have a higher proportion of muscle mass.

Water, as a solvent, carries dissolved nutrients through the bloodstream to the cells of the body and waste products out of the body. It also helps regulate body temperature and acts as a lubricant for movement of the joints, eyelids, and gastrointestinal tract.

The main sources of water are drinking water and some other beverages. Drinks containing caffeine and alcohol, however, act as diuretics and increase urination. These beverages should not be used to provide the daily requirement of water. Other sources of water are foods high in water content such as fruits and vegetables.

Since drinking water is the major source of water it is important that children are encouraged to drink water frequently throughout the day. Children should have easy and child-accessible sources of water. More and more desks in public school settings have water bottles placed on them so that children may drink from them throughout the day. Clearly someone is getting the message that water is important to the developing child. Homes should have unbreakable drinking containers for children. Child care early education settings should provide indoor and outdoor drinking fountains at child-level or unbreakable drinking containers.

All water supplies should be laboratory tested to ensure that the water is safe for drinking. Municipal water supplies are tested at the water treatment plant following the requirements of the Safe Drinking Water Act. However, water should also be tested at the point of use for lead content. Lead is one of the most dangerous contaminates in water. Excessive consumption of water contaminated with lead can lead to diminished height and intelligence levels in children. The plumbing pipes and water coolers in older buildings may have lead solder in copper pipe joints. Water leaches the lead from the solder and contaminates the drinking water. The United States Environmental Protection Agency has set maximum contaminate levels for more than 76 drinking water contaminates such as bacteria and chemicals. The odor and taste of the water is also regulated (Code of Federal Regulations, 1999).

When children are ill, particularly from fever, diarrhea, or vomiting, it is essential that they are frequently given water to prevent dehydration. Excessive loss of water due to inadequate water intake will cause an imbalance between the water content inside and outside the cells as well as the loss of electrolytes. It is vital to the health and survival of the cells and systems of the body that this balance be maintained.

Recommended Dietary Allowances and Label Analysis Summary.   It is clear that the RDAs and food labels should be consulted when planning nutritious snacks and meals for young children, but many educators of young children have a wide variety of other duties and may not have the time to use this table. The Food Guide Pyramid (Figure 3.2) is a quick and easy-to-use reference that educators will find beneficial in such instances. By following this guide educators will ensure that the children are meeting their RDA requirements.

The United States Department of Agriculture (USDA) created the first food pyramid in 1992. The impetus for the creation of the food pyramid was a reaction to criticism that the Four Food Groups Plan (vegetables and fruits, breads and cereals, milk and milk products, meat and meat alternatives) introduced in 1957 placed too much emphasis on high-fat, high-cholesterol foods from animals (Rinzler, 1997). The Four Food Groups Plan provided a foundation to teach nutrient ade-

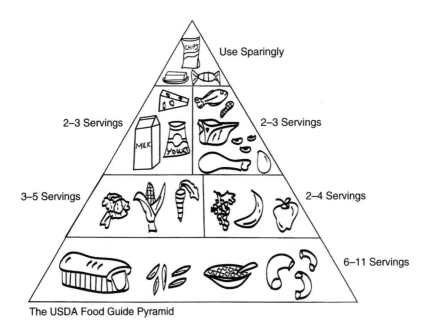

The USDA Food Guide Pyramid

FIGURE 3.2   Food Guide Pyramid

quacy and to guard against nutrient deficiencies (Achterberg, McDonnell, & Bagby 1994). The 1992 Food Guide Pyramid is the official food guide for the United States, and it is the only one recognized by federal agencies and departments. It is designed to address nutrient excess as well as nutrient deficiency (Achterberg et al., 1994). The Food Guide Pyramid identifies six distinct food groups:

- Grains (bread, cereal, rice, and pasta)
- Vegetables
- Fruits
- Dairy (milk, yogurt, and cheese)
- Protein (meat, poultry, fish, eggs, dry beans, and nuts)
- Additional foods (fats, oils, and sweets)

Mr. Swartz found that the Food Guide Pyramid was a beneficial checklist to use when planning menus for the children in his classroom of 4- and 5-year-olds. He also found the pyramid to be a beneficial symbolic representation to help the children develop an awareness of proper nutrition and the concepts necessary to plan their own menus. He showed the children the Food Guide Pyramid and asked them to describe their favorite foods. Interestingly, the children focused on bread, fruit, and chicken in their discussion. This interest in nutrition was also evident when the children were asked to draw their own Food Guide Pyramid. Mr. Swartz, through this activity, helped the children develop an understanding of a healthy diet, and what strategies could be used when planning menus.

Food Pyramid Guidelines.   The Food Guide Pyramid illustrates the three principles that guide individuals, such as Mr. Swartz, in planning menus:

Variety
Balance
Moderation

Variety.   No single food can provide all the nutrients that children need. The greater the variety of food that a child eats, the higher the chances are of receiving all the essential nutrients, vitamins, and minerals that she needs.

Balance.   A balanced diet will have different serving amounts of the foods in the Food Pyramid. A pyramid was used to depict the healthy choices individuals can make because it can be divided into blocks of different sizes. A pyramid cannot be built with identical blocks, nor can a healthy body be built from equal portions of foods from the Four Food Groups. Some foods—such as bread, cereal, rice and pasta—require more daily servings than foods from the milk, yogurt, and cheese group or from other food groups. Balance or proportionality is needed.

Children need a balanced diet for optimum growth. Eating a variety of foods in moderation will provide a balanced diet. Many children in the United States do not eat a balanced diet. The United States Department of Agriculture conducted a survey to analyze the food intakes of 3,307 children and teenagers. The results of the survey were compared with the minimum recommendations for the five food groups according to the Food Guide Pyramid. The survey revealed that the diets of children in the United States greatly exceed Food Pyramid recommendations for fat and added sugars. Additionally, children do not meet Pyramid recommendations for the other food groups, especially the fruit, grain, and dairy products groups (Munoz, Krebs-Smith, Ballard-Barbash, & Cleveland, 1997).

Moderation.   When planning diets for young children some consideration is needed, especially when considering the foods located in the peak of the pyramid. While these foods (fats, oils, and sweets) provide some value in the form of energy they must be eaten in moderation because they are of limited value to health, and they certainly are not required in large amounts. Many times, certain foods in the peak of the pyramid are termed "empty calorie foods." It is not that these foods are void of calories; how nice if they were! Rather these foods provide calories, but they are considered empty in nutritional value. At some level Julius knew this when he stated, "I can't eat chocolate all the time."

In Mr. Swartz's class a lengthy discussion took place about sweets. The children listened to Mr. Swartz explain that the tip of the pyramid consists of fats and sweets. When he was done explaining this concept the majority of the children expressed that sweets and potato chips along with fruits were their favorite foods. Mr. Swartz knew that the children were expressing their own and also their parents' knowledge of the Food Guide Pyramid. An American Medical Association (AMA) survey of 700 parents, with children ages 6 to 11 years, found that 4 out of 5 parents were familiar with the Food Guide Pyramid, but fewer than 2 out of 5 use it to plan their children's meals. In addition, about 70% of parents in the survey were not concerned about their children's consumption of foods at the tip of the pyramid (Dairy Council MidEast, 1999).

Recommended Servings.   Recommended servings suggestions provide recommendations for a different number of daily adult servings depending on the different amount of calories consumed each day. Adults should receive:

> 6–11 servings of breads, cereals, rice, or pasta
> 2–4 servings from the fruit group
> 3–5 servings of the vegetable group
> 2–3 servings from the milk, yogurt, and cheese group
> 2–3 servings from the meat, poultry, fish, eggs, dry beans, and nuts

Sparingly use foods, such as oils and sweets, from the tip of the pyramid. The variance in the number of servings is dependent on the suggested caloric intake and activity level of each adult. The above guidelines are for adults; this means that variances must be made for children.

Our friend Julius, who is 4 years old and weighs 46 pounds, should receive on an average 1,886 calories a day. If he is a very active child he may need more calories, or if he is inactive he may need fewer. Julius will need more servings from the Food Guide Pyramid than an adult but fewer total calories. He should have 9 servings from the bread, cereal, rice, and pasta group; 3 servings from the fruit group; 4 servings from the vegetable group; 2 to 3 servings from the milk group; and 2 to 3 servings—or about 6 ounces—from the meat group each day (Rinzler, 1997). The next question is, "What is a serving?"

In a society that encourages Americans to order "biggie" meals, it is important to understand the size of a food serving. Table 3.4 provides the USDA-defined serving sizes for the six food groups. These serving sizes are for adults and again it is important to remember that they must be adjusted for children.

Serving sizes for the food substances such as butter, olive oil, and sucrose that are fats, oils, and sweets have not been set. These foods should be used only in moderation, and they should not be eaten in place of any other foods in the Food Guide Pyramid. Unfortunately, many of these foods are served and eaten in large quantities in the American Diet.

As mentioned, the problem with the above portion size chart is that they have been established for adults, not children. Children have lower nutritional requirements (RDAs) than adults. They may need to eat more frequently, but at

TABLE 3.4 Serving Sizes for the Food Groups in the Food Guide Pyramid

Food Group	Serving Size
Grains	1 slice bread ½ cup cooked cereal, rice, or pasta 1 ounce ready-to-eat cereal 5–6 small crackers
Vegetables	1 cup raw leafy vegetables ½ cup other vegetables, cooked or chopped raw ¾ cup vegetable juice
Fruits	1 medium apple, banana, or orange ½ cup chopped, cooked, or canned fruit ½ cup fruit juice
Dairy	1 cup milk or yogurt 1½ ounces natural cheese 2 ounces processed cheese
Meat, Poultry, Dry Beans, Eggs, Nuts, or Seeds	2–3 ounces cooked lean meat, poultry ½ cup cooked dry beans 1 egg 2 tablespoons peanut butter ⅓ cup nuts or seeds
Fats, Oils, Sweets	None specified

Source: International Food Information Council, 1995.

I want an upside down Food Guide Pyramid!

the same time the portion sizes are smaller. Some nutritional experts recommend serving slightly less than 1 tablespoon of a food item for each year of life (Leeds, 1998). This means that when planning a breakfast for Julius, who is 4 years old, the following guidelines should be loosely followed:

4 tablespoons or ¼ cup cereal
¼ to ½ cup milk
¼ to ½ cup orange juice

Children should not be given portions larger than the recommended amount. Adults should avoid encouraging children to "clean their plates," or using food as a bribe or reward. All of these behaviors encourage overeating—which may lead to a lifetime of health problems.

Children can benefit from parents and caregivers following these basic planning guidelines and serving sizes when planning nutritional meals and snacks. Children like to eat frequently; schedules and portions should be adjusted accordingly. Children may eat six or more times each day. Staff members in child care early education centers should avoid having set times when all children eat morning and afternoon snacks. The times for snacks should be adjusted to the individual child's eating patterns. Open snack time periods should be established to allow for individual flexibility.

Mediterranean Food Pyramid.   It should also be noted that a second food pyramid could be used to guide food choices but it is not the official pyramid approved by the U.S. Federal Government. The Mediterranean Food Pyramid (see Figure 3.3) was developed in 1993 by the World Health Organization, Harvard School of Public Health, and Oldways Preservation and Exchange Trust to describe the diet of countries bordering on the Mediterranean Sea, such as Greece and Italy (Rinzler, 1997).

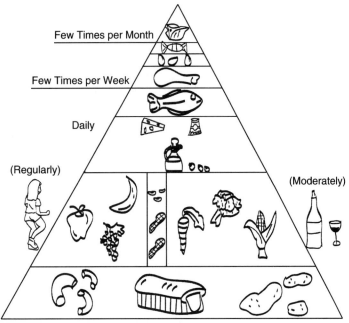

Few Times per Month

Few Times per Week

Daily

(Regularly)

(Moderately)

The Mediterranean Diet Pyramid

FIGURE 3.3   Mediterranean Food Pyramid

This food pyramid does not provide recommended amounts of daily servings. Instead, it gives more of an overview of healthy eating habits. Each day, individuals should eat grains, fruits, legumes, nuts, vegetables, olive oil, cheese, yogurt, and fish. Sweets, eggs, and poultry should be eaten a few times per week, and red meat should be eaten a few times per month (Rinzler, 1997). Studies indicate that individuals who follow the Mediterranean Food Pyramid will more likely have a lower risk of cancer, especially colon cancer and, consequently, a longer lifespan (Rinzler,1997). This pyramid provides a very good overview of healthy eating habits and could be used as a reference or guide when working with menu planning.

Diet Variances.   The two aforementioned food pyramids are the most common diet guides for children who consume a wide variety of animal and plant foods. There are, however, alternative diets. Some of these diets, such as vegetarian diets, are acceptable for children provided that satisfactory substitutions are made. Other diets, such as macrobiotic and megavitamin diets, can be harmful to a child because a balanced diet may be difficult to maintain. This is especially true for a developing child. The macrobiotic diet gradually calls for the elimination of animal products, fruits, and vegetables until grains are the only food left. The megavitamin diet is used to counteract diseases, metabolic disorders, and brain malfunctions. Specific vitamins have been found to be advantageous for metabolic imbalances but not beneficial in the correction of other problems. There is concern that such diets can do damage to systems of the body. Caregivers may be asked to provide children with supplements during the hours of care. The management of such diets by caregivers should be avoided without expert medical advice and written medical and parental authorization.

Vegetarian Diets.   Interest in vegetarian diets has increased in the United States for health, philosophical, cultural, and religious reasons. It is quite likely that individuals working with young children will have to face the challenge of planning balanced and interesting vegetarian diets for young children in their care. Be sure to ask the parents prior to the child's entrance into the program if there are any diet concerns. Once this has been determined, it would be to the caregiver's advantage to consult with the parents and/or nutritional experts on the best way to establish a balanced diet for vegetarian children in the program.

Vegetarians may be classified as vegans, people who eat only plant foods (fruits, vegetables, grains, legumes, nuts, and seeds). They may also be further classified as lactovegetarians. These individuals eat all the foods in the vegan diet plus milk and milk products. Ovolactovegetarians are people who include eggs, milk, milk products, and vegan foods in their diets. Pescovegetarians eat fish, eggs, milk, milk products, and vegan foods. A pollovegetarian will eat everything except red meat (Leeds, 1998).

A vegetarian diet is high in foods that provide bulk, thus young children, particularly toddlers, may feel full before they have obtained the calories they need for growth and development. Additionally, food planners must take more care to provide balance so that the child receives the appropriate amounts of protein, carbohydrates, and fats. Individuals who strictly follow the vegan diet must pay attention to eating foods that provide them with adequate amounts of protein, vitamin B-12, vitamin D, riboflavin, calcium, iron, and zinc (Leeds, 1998). Vegetarian children should receive diets in which plant proteins have mutually complementary amino acids (such as dried beans with rice or wheat flour tortilla with cheese).

Shopping for a Healthy Lifestyle

The 1990 Nutritional Labeling and Education Act helps to provide the shopper with an awareness of the calories, fat, protein, carbohydrates, vitamins, and minerals in each serving of a processed food. Shopping by reading labels is a time-consuming process because each label should be read and analyzed to see if the items will enhance or hinder the health of children. In addition, the educator who is purchasing food by bulk for an education program may not be provided nutritional information on the packaging. Ensuring that children have a healthy lifestyle through diet is an important duty of parents and caregivers. At least 4 of the 10 leading causes of death in the United States—heart disease, cancer, stroke, and diabetes—are directly related to the way people eat. Most children between 2 and 5 years consume more than the United States Department of Agriculture's recommended allowances of fat and cholesterol (Thompson & Dennison, 1994). The major source of fat and saturated fatty acids in the children's diet is whole milk and the major source of cholesterol is eggs (Thompson & Dennison, 1994). This does not mean that eggs or whole milk should be eliminated from the diets of young children. The National Cholesterol Education Program Guidelines (1991) recommend whole milk for children 1 to 2 years of age and a gradual shift to 2% milk between 2 and 3 years of age. Eggs, according to the Food Guide Pyramid, should be eaten in moderation.

The Food Guide Pyramid

Copy the empty food pyramid in Figure 3.4 and use it as a guide in planning daily meals and snacks that will provide optimum nutrients for energy and tissue building. Educators should plan on providing two-thirds of the servings a child will need for daily nutrition if the child is being cared for from 7:00 a.m. to 5:00 p.m.

Plan a Meal Pyramid Guide. An example of using the Plan a Meal Pyramid Guide for Julius is shown in Figure 3.5. If you remember, Julius needs 9 servings of grains, 3 servings of fruits, 4 servings of vegetables, 2 to 3 servings of milk products, and 2 to 3 servings of meat, dry beans, and nuts.

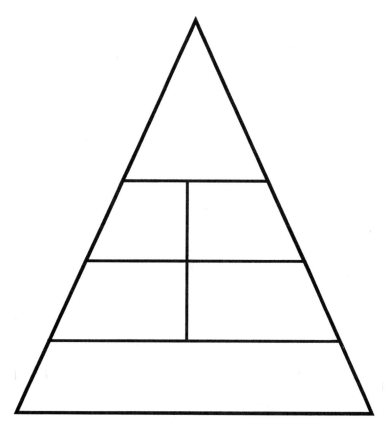

FIGURE 3.4   Plan a Meal Pyramid Guide

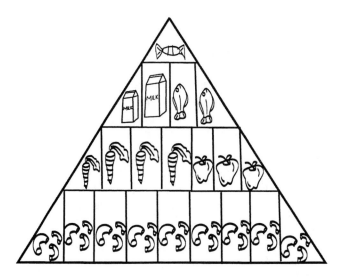

FIGURE 3.5   Julius's Food Guide

The following menu (Figure 3.6) provides two-thirds of Julius's dietary needs while he is at his child care program.

The same menu could be used with minor adjustments for Julius's friend, Dudley, whose family is ovolactovegetarian. The stock base for the vegetable soup

Breakfast
Cereal, 1/4 to 1/2 cup (1 grain)
2% milk, 1/2 cup (1 dairy)
Banana (1 fruit)
Whole wheat bread, 1 slice (1 grain)

Snack
Carrots and celery, 1/2 cup (1 vegetable)
Yogurt dip, 1/4 cup (1 dairy)
Whole wheat crackers, 4 (1 grain)
Water

Lunch
Vegetable soup, 1 cup (1 vegetable)
Turkey on whole wheat pita bread (1 meat, 1 grain)
Orange juice, 1/2 cup (1 fruit)

Snack
Peanut butter on whole wheat crackers (1 nut, 1 grain)
Water

FIGURE 3.6   Sample Menu

must be made from vegetables—not beef—and hummus could replace the turkey in the pita sandwich.

The above menu could be served family style to young children. This is a requirement in some programs such as Head Start. If this is the case it is important that the adult who is supervising the meal pay attention to the number and size of servings each child is taking.

Nutrition for a Lifetime

Prenatal Development

Eating right for a healthy lifestyle begins during pregnancy. Pregnant women are eating for two, but the developing child has higher needs for protein, vitamins, and minerals than for calories. During pregnancy a woman's energy requirements increase by about 300 calories per day during the second and third trimesters (Leeds, 1998). When planning meals and snacks during this time, the shopping list should include vegetables, fruits, nonfat or low-fat yogurt, milk, legumes, and lean meats. Caffeine, cigarettes, alcohol, and illegal drugs should be avoided. Alcohol can cause irreversible damage to the developing fetus. Fetal alcohol syndrome (FAS) causes a recognized group of mental, physical, and behavioral symptoms seen in children born to women who drink during pregnancy. Children born to women who use drugs often have birth defects and physiological addictions. These drugs may inhibit prenatal development which results in retarded cognitive and social development. The smoke from cigarettes restricts the supply of blood to the fetus, restricting the supply of oxygen and nutrients needed for normal development. Caffeine causes dehydration which may also have an effect on the developing fetus.

Early Childhood Development

After a child is born, the first nutrition a child receives is through breast milk or formula. Breast-feeding has emotional, physiological, and practical advantages for both mother and child. A mother whose infant is fed only breast milk needs an additional 500 calories above her pre-pregnancy intake to maintain her weight (Leeds, 1998). Besides the additional calories, lactating women need additional protein and slightly higher intakes of vitamin C, vitamin E, magnesium, zinc, and selenium (Leeds, 1998). To avoid dehydration, alcohol and caffeine should not be consumed. Child care centers having infants who are being breast-fed should do everything to encourage the process. A quiet, comfortable place away from center traffic should be arranged for the mother to sit when she is feeding her infant or when using a breast pump. The staff should do everything to support the mother and should not provide the child with any supplement, water, and/or formula, without the parents' permission. Some parents may choose to use formula. Human milk is the standard by which formulas are measured.

However, manufactures cannot duplicate the anti-infection and antiallergenic attributes of breast milk.

It is important that formula not be prepared from contaminated water supplies. A recent concern is the nitrate and nitrite contamination of water supplies due to run-off of chemical fertilizers. Nitrites and nitrates should not exceed the Environmental Protection Agency's (EPA) limit of 10 milligrams of nitrate or nitrite per liter of drinking water. Breast-feeding women who drink contaminated water supplies may pass the chemical to the infant through their breast milk. These chemicals interfere with the transportation of oxygen and could negatively affect the developing infant.

Both breast milk and formula provide the fluid needs of the infant unless the child develops a fever, is vomiting, or has diarrhea. If any of these conditions persist a physician should be contacted to avoid dehydration and consequent electrolyte imbalance. Infants should not be given sugar water.

Solid foods should not be introduced until the infant is between 4 and 6 months old. Prior to this time the infant may not be physiologically ready to swallow solid foods and introducing solids too soon may increase the risks of allergies. Until 4 to 6 months of age breast milk and formula provides all the nutritional needs of the infant. Leeds (1998) recommends the schedule shown in Table 3.5.

Foods should only be introduced one at a time, and the waiting period before introducing a new food should be at least 72 hours. Parents and caregivers should not add butter, salt, or sugar to food. Parents might decide to provide homemade baby food for their child that they have made and frozen in ice cube trays. Frozen homemade food should be thawed in the refrigerator overnight or over low temperatures on the stove.

Foods that might cause choking such as nuts, popcorn, seeds, hard candy, grapes, raw vegetables, hot dogs, large pieces of meat or cheese, raisins, corn, and peanut butter should also be avoided. The above foods should not be given to any child under 3 years of age.

It is important that developing fetuses and children receive the nutrients for optimum growth. This does not always occur for children in the lower socioeconomic level of American society.

TABLE 3.5   Schedule for Introduction of Foods to Infants

Age	Type of Food
0–4 months	Only breast milk or infant formula
4–6 months	Infant cereal (rice) diluted with breast milk, formula, or water
5–7 months	Strained, diluted fruit juices
7–8 months	Strained vegetables, fruits, meats, egg yolks
9–10 months	Toast and crackers, cubed soft fruits, mashed vegetables
10–12 months	Strained fruit juices from a cup
12 months	Whole milk, cooked egg whites

Nutritional Programs to Aid Development

To combat the poor nutritional start that some children may receive, it is important to have intervention programs to provide effective prenatal and postnatal care. The Supplemental Feeding Program for Women, Infants, and Children (WIC) is an effective program sponsored by the federal government to provide adequate nutrition, nutrition education, and prenatal health services to low-income families. Each state can set the income criterion within the federal guidelines of 100% to 185% of the poverty level. Five groups are served by WIC:

- Pregnant mothers
- Breast-feeding mothers up to 1 year after delivery
- Mothers who do not breast-feed up to 6 months after delivery
- Infants
- Children up to the age of 5 years

WIC participants receive vouchers for specific food items, fruit juices high in vitamin C; cereals high in iron; milk; cheese; dried beans; and peanut butter. Bottle-fed babies will receive formula fortified with iron. The program also mandates nutritional education. Research clearly shows that the WIC program reduces low birth weight, small head circumference, the rate of infant mortality, and medical costs. Clearly good nutrition has improved the lives of some children.

Child care programs can receive federal nutrition funding. To qualify, the center must serve meals and snacks that meet the established federal guidelines reflected in the RDA requirements and the Food Guide Pyramid. Public schools can participate in two federally funded nutrition programs, the School Breakfast Program and the School Lunch Program. These programs must also furnish meals that provide at least one-third of the RDAs. The U.S. Department of Agriculture (USDA) monitors these programs.

Once children are through infancy, the challenge is not only to provide nutritional meals and snacks but also to assist the child in the development of good eating habits. It is important that children are given the opportunity to plan meals and snacks and to shop for food. It is through these activities that children develop concepts of good nutrition and a healthy lifestyle. Children should be encouraged to learn about nutrition by making choices between nutritional foods and nonnutritional foods. During this time it is also important to follow the Food Guide Pyramid when planning meals and selecting snacks. Child care early education workers and parents should avoid snacks that focus on the top of the pyramid—fats, oils, and sweets. Snacks have historically meant cookies, potato chips, and similar foods. While these treats certainly taste delicious they should only be eaten in moderation. Potato chips are high in calories, fat content (43%), and sodium—with very little nutritional value. To encourage children to develop a healthy lifestyle, snack foods high in sodium should also be avoided.

It should also be noted that educators are often faced with the difficult dilemma of monitoring snacks and meals sent from home. More and more children are coming to their child care or public school setting with prepackaged lunches. Parents need to be familiar with the nutrition requirement outlined in this chapter so that they will avoid these prepackaged meals that are based upon adult Recommended Dietary Allowances. When given to children these meals are high in calories (470), fat (280), and the fat calories total 60% of the adult's daily needs. In addition, these food items are high in sodium. We have seen the prepackaged lunches accompanied by prepackaged drinks composed of sugars, water, and dyes. These items do not provide a healthy diet for children and should be discouraged through parental nutritional education programs.

Summary

Recent evidence suggests that dietary patterns set in childhood may predict occurrence in adulthood of obesity, cardiovascular disease, and cancers. Many leading causes of death in the United States are directly related to the way people eat (John Hopkins Intel: Health Information, 1999).

Excesses of these foods set children up for a lifetime of disease. Foods need to be compared to the Food Guide Pyramid and must be analyzed for content to determine if they are too high in fat, added sugars, and salt (sodium). Foods should be analyzed to determine if they provide the developing child with all the necessary nutrients based on age and individual level of development. Cultural and ethnic sensitivities should also be considered. Eating the proper foods is a major part of a healthy lifestyle.

CHANGE AND ADVOCACY

1. Write a series of newsletters for parents explaining the importance of nutrition in the lives of their children.

2. Offer a workshop for parents on how to plan healthy lunches for their children.

3. Develop a puppet show for the children about decision-making strategies when selecting snacks.

REFERENCES

Achterberg, C., McDonnell, E., & Bagby, R. (1994). How to put the food guide pyramid into practice. *Journal of the American Dietetic Association, 94*(9), 1030–1036.

Beauchamp, G. K., Cowart, B. J., Mennella, J. A., & Marsh, R. R. (1994). Infant salt taste: Developmental, methodological, and contextual factors. *Developmental Psychology, 27,* 353–365.

Birch, L. L. (1991). The variability of young children's energy intake. *New England Journal of Medicine, 324,* 232.

Bunin, G. R., Kuijten, R. R., Buckley, J. B., Rorke, L. B., & Meadows, A. T. (1993). Relationship between maternal diet and subsequent primitive neuroectodermal brain tumors in young children. *New England Journal of Medicine, 329,* 536–541.

Code of Federal Regulations. (1999). *Title 40 (141.0.App.A).* Washington, DC: U.S. Government Printing Office.

Dairy Council Mid East. (1999). Survey reveals many parents know, but don't use nutritional guidelines. *FYI A Nutritional Education Newsletter, 1* (2), 1.

Johns Hopkins InteliHealth. (1999). *The importance of nutrition.* Baltimore, MD. Retrieved January 22, 1999 from the World Wide Web: http://www.intelihealth.com.

Leeds, M. (1998). *Nutrition for healthy living.* Boston, MA: McGraw-Hill.

Munoz, K., Krebs-Smith, S., Ballard-Barbash, R., & Cleveland, L. (1997). Food intakes of U.S. children and adolescents compared with recommendations. *Pediatrics, 100*(3), 323–327.

National Research Council. (1996). *Carcinogens and anticarcinogens in the human diet* (pp. 127–180). Washington, DC: National Academy Press.

Preston-Martin, S. J., Pogoda, J. M., Mueller, B. A., Holly, E. A., Lijinsky, W., & Davis, R. L. (1996). Maternal consumption of cured meats and vitamins in relation to pediatric brain tumors. *Cancer Epidemiology, 5,* 599–605.

Rinzler, C. A. (1997). *Nutrition for dummies.* Foster City, CA: IDG Books.

Smith, L. (1979). *Feed your kids right.* NY: Dell Publishing Co.

Stamler, J., & Dolecek, A. (1997). Relation of food and nutrient intakes to body mass in the special intervention and usual care groups in the multiple risk factor intervention trial. *American Journal of Clinical Nutrition, 65,* 366S.

Thompson, F., & Dennison, B. (1994). Dietary sources of fat and cholesterol in U.S. children aged 2 through 5 years. *The American Journal of Public Health, 85,* 799.

4 Principles of Environmental Hygiene and Infection Control

CHAPTER OBJECTIVES

Knowledge

- The reader will identify the four types of environmental hazards and their various components.

Skills

- The reader will analyze health promotion practices and policies.

Dispositions

- The reader will value the role health prevention practices and policies have on the health of the young child.

CHAPTER SYNOPSIS

Environmental Hazards
  Biological Hazards
  Physical Hazards
  Chemical Hazards
  Ergonomic Hazards
Focus on Health Promotion
  Preventive Practices and Services
  Steps to Prevention

Current Problems Facing Today's Children
  Reduction in Health-Care Differences
  Child Abuse
  Rural Environment
  Homeless
  Disabilities

Scenario

Three-year-old Roberto is a thumb-sucker. Roberto wraps his favorite blanket around his arm and strokes his face while he sucks his thumb. Now that he is going to a child care center his mother and father have tried various strategies to stop his thumb-sucking, but little progress has been made. The exasperated parents finally told him that his thumb was dirty and covered with germs that would make him very sick! Roberto looked at his parents, dropped his blanket, ran to the bathroom, and washed his hands vigorously. He returned to his blanket, picked it up, and continued sucking his thumb contentedly now that the germs were gone.

Roberto used problem solving and showed that—on his developmental level—he has a strong grasp of one of the key concepts of how to prevent childhood illness and promote a healthy lifestyle. Roberto knew that in order to control potential infection he needed to wash his hands. It is important to **anticipate, recognize, evaluate,** and **control** the biological, chemical, physical, and ergonomic hazards in the child care early education environment to reduce health hazards that may endanger life and inhibit the development of the child to his fullest potential in body size, positive lifespan health, and full economic productivity. All areas are important in the development of a child.

In the past, developmental potential has narrowly focused on body size. To help a child reach his fullest potential, educators of young children need to focus on the anticipation, recognition, evaluation, and control of environmental factors that will both increase the lifespan and improve its quality. This chapter initially provides background information on environmental hazards, and how their effects can be eliminated or minimized. After discussing biological, physical, chemical, and ergonomic hazards, suggestions are provided for avoiding problems that arise from these hazards in the child care early education setting. This chapter also stresses the importance of a health appraisal and concludes by discussing the challenges facing the child, parent, child care worker, and educator in the 21st century.

Environmental Hazards

Environmental factors that can cause illness or reduction in a child's potential can be classified into four hazard areas (Plog, Niland, Quinlan, 1996):

- Biological hazards
- Physical hazards
- Chemical hazards
- Ergonomic hazards

Each area alone or in combination with other areas can cause harm to the developing child. Parents and educators can recognize these hazards and take steps to evaluate and eliminate the hazards and their effects. This section covers each hazard and provides suggestions to the early child care education center staff.

Biological Hazards

Biological hazards occur through exposure to living organisms that have adverse effects on individuals. Approximately 200 biological agents, such as infectious microorganisms, biological allergens, and toxins are known to cause infections and allergic, toxic, and carcinogenic responses in people (Plog et. al., 1996).

Biological hazards can be categorized into three groups (Plog et. al., 1996):

- Microorganisms and their toxins (viruses, bacteria, fungi, and their products)
- Arthropods (crustaceans, arachnids, insects)
- Allergens (plant and vertebrate animals)

Each day children and educators are exposed to these microorganisms, arthropods, and allergens. On some level Roberto understood this when he washed his hands before continuing to suck his thumb.

Microorganisms. Microorganisms are viruses, bacteria, and fungi. They can enter the body through inhalation, absorption through the skin, ingestion, and injection and can result in infection or allergy. The effect of the microorganism may be a general infection, or the infection may be localized to specific tissues or organs. Furthermore, the consequences will also depend on the virulence or strength of the microorganism, the route of the infection, and the immune system and health of the child. State Public Health Departments will provide early childhood professionals and parents with information on communicable diseases and the prevention of these diseases.

Child care early education professionals should have a general understanding and knowledge of the biological hazards caused by microorganisms. Programs should maintain a reference library on this subject and have a nurse and/or physician who will act as a consultant to the program. Some infections resulting from microorganisms that may be present in early learning environments are listed in Table 4.1.

Additional comment should be given to Hepatitis B and HIV/AIDS, listed in Table 4.1. Both of these diseases are extremely dangerous and deadly. These viral diseases are transported through blood-borne contamination. The American Academy of Pediatrics and the Centers for Disease Control and Prevention recommend that all children receive the Hepatitis B vaccine. Adults who, in the daily performance of their job, come in contact with blood or body fluids should also be vaccinated. HIV is transmitted through sexual intercourse, breast-feeding, and exposure to blood containing the virus. Children with Hepatitis B and HIV/AIDS cannot be excluded from child care early education programs. Administrators and teachers must make every effort to maintain confidentiality and eliminate potential transmission to other children and staff in the program.

It is important that programs for young children adopt a policy of universal precautions to reduce the risk and transmission of Hepatitis B, HIV/AIDS, and other communicable diseases. The design of such a policy should emphasize the importance of always establishing an infection-control barrier between persons. Universal precautions are discussed in detail later in the chapter.

Another disease that is becoming more of a serious concern in schools and child care early education settings is tuberculosis, a bacterial disease. A simple skin

TABLE 4.1   Biological Microorganisms Diseases

Disease	Cause	Signs/Symptoms	Treatment
Chicken pox	Virus	Fever, fluid-filled vesicles	Globulin (VZIG) medication, anti-itching medications, vaccine
Colds	Virus	Runny nose, sore throat	Monitor symptoms
Conjunctivitis	Bacteria	Whites of eye pink, discharge	Antibiotic
Coxsackie virus (Hand, foot, and mouth syndrome)	Virus	Fever, sore throat, stomach pain, diarrhea	Monitor symptoms
Fifth disease	Virus	Headache, chills, sore throat, rash symptoms	Monitor
Hepatitis A	Virus	Tiredness, nausea, jaundice, appetite loss	Monitor symptoms
Hepatitis B	Virus	Fever, appetite loss, jaundice	No treatment, vaccination, prevention
HIV/AIDS	Virus	Developmental delays, repeated infections	Varies according to symptoms
Impetigo	Bacteria	Oozy rash	Wash and cover rash
Meningitis	Bacteria	Fever, chills, rash	Hospitalization
Ringworm	Fungi	Rash of skin, nails	Anti-fungal ointment
Roseola	Virus	Fever, rash	Monitor symptoms
Salmonella	Bacteria	Diarrhea, fever	Monitor symptoms
Shigella	Bacteria	Diarrhea, dehydration	Antibiotic
Strep throat	Bacteria	Fever, swollen glands, headache	Antibiotic
Tuberculosis	Bacteria	Coughing, fever, weight loss, infected sputum	Medications

test can be used to determine if children or teachers have been exposed to the disease. All individuals working with young children should have this test to determine if they have tuberculosis or are carriers of the disease.

Arthropods. The second category of biological hazards is the arthropod group. Arthropods include insects, spiders, and crustaceans. Two of the most common types of arthropods that we have to deal with in early childhood settings are head lice and scabies.

Head Lice. A common nuisance for the child care early education setting is infestation of head lice. Head lice are parasites the size of a small ant or sesame seed that survive on the blood of their host. It is common to find them on the scalp, the nape of the neck, and behind the ears. Lice are transmitted from child to child by hopping or by riding on an object such as a hat, comb, or brush. Head lice are very common and do not occur because the child is dirty; body lice are associated with poor hygiene. Head lice should be treated quickly because if left untreated a rash and infection can occur. During a particular stubborn outbreak in a public school, the school nurse met the buses each morning and checked the children's hair as they exited the bus. Those contaminated with lice were sent home.

The treatment of head lice involves the use of an over-the-counter shampoo containing the pesticides pyrethrum and piperonyl butoxide. Adults administering the shampoo should follow the directions on the container. Additionally, all clothing and bedding should be washed in hot water and placed in a hot drier. Rugs, car seats, and furniture should be vacuumed. When the vacuuming is completed the bag should be taken out of the vacuum, placed in a plastic bag, sealed, and destroyed. Children should not be permitted to return to the educational setting until the nits (lice eggs) are no longer present. Special lice combs can help to eliminate nits. Children's heads should be rechecked for approximately three weeks after treatment to guard against reinfestation from a new hatching.

The parents of all children in the program should be advised of the contamination and what precautions they should take. Head lice are very tenacious and, unless every step is taken, reinfestation will occur. Children have been removed from homes and placed in foster care because their families did not control the head lice. The children were missing too much school and were a health hazard to themselves and to the educational community. Social Services and their lawyer intervened by removing the children, treating them, and ensuring their return to school. The parents were given an intervention dealing with the importance of good hygiene. The children were returned to the parents and the hygiene of everyone in the family was improved.

Scabies. Another common skin infection caused by a mite, a miniature arachnid (spider family), is scabies. The female mite burrows under the skin and lays eggs. Symptoms of scabies include an itchy rash and short wavy lines on the skin. They are spread through direct contact. Diagnosis includes scraping of the skin and examination under a microscope by a physician. Treatment includes creams or lotions, with the child returning to the educational setting within 24 hours from the start of treatment. As with lice, all clothing and bedding should be washed and dried in a hot drier. Difficult to wash items can be stored in plastic bags for 4 to 7 days before using again. All furniture and carpeting should be vacuumed, and the bag handled in the same way as for lice contamination. All parents of children in the center should be informed and advised about this situation.

Additional Arthropods.   Bees, wasps, fire ants, and spiders present a safety problem for children. Bites from insects such as bees, wasps, and spiders can cause allergic reactions when the toxic formic acid mixture is delivered through injection into the child's skin. Some reactions to the bites of these and other insects can be especially dangerous to sensitive individuals and may even lead to death. Every precaution should be taken to eliminate insects from the environment of young children. Window screens should be used to avoid the presence of insects in the indoor learning environment.

Every precaution should be taken to provide an environment that is healthy for both children and staff. Outdoor environments should be examined for the presence of bee, wasp, and ant nests. Standing water areas that may serve to breed insects should be drained. When playing outdoors children should not wear scented soaps or lotions. Since food attracts insects, children should not play around food. Clothing can be used to provide a barrier between the insects and the children. Sweetened drinks are especially attractive to yellow jackets. There have been reports of people swallowing yellow jackets from drinking out of a pop-top

soda can, getting internally stung, and dying from swelling that closed their airways. All sweet drinks served in an outdoor setting should be in a closed container. If there is a drink opening, it must be able to be closed after each use.

Additional infestations caused by arthropods that may be of concern in an early childhood setting are listed in Table 4.2. The cause, disease, and symptoms are included.

Plant and Animal Allergens.   Plant and animal allergens can cause problems in the early childhood setting. Management of the biological hazards of animals such as their urine, feces, saliva, dander, and hair helps to lessen children's exposure and thus reduce dermatitis (skin rash), allergies, systemic intoxication (the entire body becomes inflamed and feverish), and transfer of infectious agents. Plants can also be an environmental hazard (for a complete listing see Chapter 5).

In addition to problems with animals, children and early childhood professionals may be allergic to the plants, or the plants may be poisonous if touched or ingested. A student teacher had planned a learning activity about native Americans for her kindergartners. The children were to build a habitat. She brought in a variety of tree branches that included pine branches. As the children started to work on building the habitat, Frank started to have difficulty breathing and broke out in a rash. The teacher and student teacher observed the changes in the child and quickly rushed the child to the school nurse. Frank was treated for an allergic reaction to pine and was able to return to his classroom once the pine branches had been removed. Many children may be allergic to certain plants. Medical files may provide professionals with this information and appropriate precautions should then be taken.

A type of plant that child care professionals also need to be concerned about is fungi, a plant without flowers, leaves, or chlorophyll. Molds or mildew are a type of fungi and grow in very dark and moist places and can enter the body through the respiratory system or the skin—causing skin infections and infections of the respiratory system, lungs, and bronchi. An example of a skin infection caused by fungi is athlete's foot. To kill mold spores and reduce the chance of contamination, a bleach solution of one part bleach to four parts water should be

TABLE 4.2   Biological Arthropod Diseases

Arthropod	Disease	Signs/Symptoms	Treatment
Deer Ticks	Lyme Disease	Rash	Medication
Parasite	Giardia lamblia	Diarrhea, cramping, weight loss, bloating	Medication
Mites	Scabies	Rash, seeping crusts	Topical medication
Worms	Pinworms	Anus itching	Medication

left in contact with the mold surfaces for two to five minutes (Aronson, 2000). Humidity levels should be controlled at 30 to 50% to limit the growth of mold and mildew (EPA & CPC, 1995). All surfaces should be dry and standing water should be avoided.

Physical Hazards

Physical hazards are caused by environmental factors such as noise, temperature extremes, and radiation (Plog et al., 1996). It is important for the staff in child care early education communities to be aware of the immediate or cumulative effect these factors may have on the physical and mental well-being of the child and adult.

Noise.   Children are sensitive to sound and will react to high or unpleasant sounds. Each individual has her own threshold for noise tolerance, and sensitivity should be shown. A little girl in a child care center could not tolerate high-frequency sounds. Consequently, the teacher had to adapt all audio presentations for this child.

Noise or unwanted sound can have the following effects on human beings (Plog et. al., 1996):

- Psychological effects from startling the individual—causing disruption in rest or concentration
- Interference with speech communication
- Physiological effects causing hearing loss

Teachers and children should not have to speak loudly or shout to be heard. Noise levels should be controlled to eliminate this type of hazard. Everyone cringes when thinking of the sound chalk makes screeching across a chalkboard!

High noise levels are a problem for child care early education settings. These settings are filled with the sounds of children interacting with friends and teachers and may lack sound-absorbing materials. To assist in noise control, soft materials such as pillows, carpeting, drapes, or curtains can be used and dropped ceilings can be installed.

Temperature Extremes.   Similar to noise levels, temperature sensitivity is also individual. The same temperature can be too high for one individual and too low for another. We have all been in a home, business, or theater where the temperature is either too high or too low for us, but not for others. Thermal extremes can make people uncomfortable—reducing their ability to concentrate and affecting mental well-being. Extremes of temperature can also cause heat and cold stress. Heat stress can result in heatstroke while cold stress results in hypothermia.

Children do not respond to environmental temperatures in the same manner as adults. Changes in the child's thermoregulatory system are discussed in Chapter 6. The temperature of a child care early education setting should be kept between 65° and 75° F in the winter and between 68° and 82° F in the summer (Kendrick, Kaufman, & Messenger, 1995). It should also be noted that the placement of the thermometer is critical. Hot air rises so the younger the child, the lower the thermometer gauge should be placed. The air should be well ventilated and circulating.

Radiation.   A major concern of educators of young children is the effect of radiation that may cause damage to the cells of the body. A common type of radiation is, of course, sunlight. Children should not be exposed to sun for long periods of time. Exposure to sunlight and microwaves should be avoided, particularly for young, developing children. When children are exposed to sunlight, they should wear protective clothing and play in shaded areas. Staff members may put sunblock on the children depending on state regulations. Many state child care regulations will not permit staff to apply sunblock without written permission from the parents.

Chemical Hazards

Educators of young children must recognize the chemical hazards that may exist in the child care early education environment and take steps to control or eliminate their effect on the health of young children and staff of the program. Children are far more sensitive to environmental chemical hazards because of their developing systems. Their immune system, liver, and kidneys are immature and do not function at optimum levels, thereby putting the children at risk.

Chemical compounds in the form of liquids, gases, mists, dust, fumes, and vapors can cause health problems. Chemicals can irritate the upper respiratory system causing increased mucus flow and edema on the surface of the skin causing dermatitis. Some other chemicals—in the form of gases—can reduce the amount of oxygen in the atmosphere and interfere with the transportation of oxygen to the cells of the body.

All product labels should be read to understand the toxicity of the material. If the label does not give complete information the manufacturer should be contacted. By law, manufacturers must provide Material Safety Data Sheets (MSDS) for all of their products. These sheets detail storage, handling, health hazards, and first aid recommendations. They should be readily available for all staff members to consult (see Appendix B). All chemical materials should be stored in their original containers.

Chemicals of major concern to the child care professional are carbon monoxide, cleaning solutions, pesticides, lead, paints, varnishes, radon, asbestos, formaldehyde, and tobacco smoke. In addition, potential chemical hazards that might exist outdoors are discussed next.

Carbon Monoxide.   Carbon monoxide is a colorless, odorless gas as well as a chemical asphyxiate. This gas decreases oxygen transport to tissues and it takes 16 to 30 days for detoxification to occur. Therefore, repeated low-level exposures become cumulative. An indication of low concentrations of carbon monoxide exposure is headache, dizziness, nausea, and confusion (EPA & CPC, 1995). This gas can enter the learning environment through ventilation ducts open to highways or from poorly ventilated fuel-burning furnaces and water heaters. It is important to have professionals check the ventilation system, furnaces, and water heaters. If wood-burning or oil-burning stoves are used in the learning environment, they should be properly vented to the outdoors to avoid carbon monoxide poisoning.

All child care early education environments should have carbon monoxide detectors placed at strategic locations in rooms isolated by doors. The detectors should be placed high in the room, out of the reach of the children. The batteries must be changed every six months.

Cleaning Solutions and Pesticides.   Extreme caution should be used when using organic solvents that are in cleaning solutions and pesticides. Organic solvents are solutions that contain hydrogen and carbon. Some common organic solvents are mineral spirits (similar to gasoline), ethyl acetate in fingernail polish and other varnishes, and acetone. This is a very small list of the common solvents used on a daily basis. These chemical substances should not be used around children and/or food supplies. Remember all cleaning solutions and pesticides should be kept in their original containers, and labeled storage instructions should be carefully followed. The Material Safety Data Sheet should be on file for all cleaning solutions and/or pesticides used.

Insect, rodent infestation, and molds are better controlled through good housekeeping practices with the use of barriers to prevent the entrance of these insects or rodents into the environment. If infestation is extreme, certified pest control exterminators should be contacted and research should be done on the effects of the chemical used by the exterminators. The Environmental Protection Agency (EPA) can be helpful in this process.

An additional pesticide concern to child care early education providers is pesticides on food. Modern farming methods use pesticides. Therefore, fruits and vegetables will be covered with pesticides and should be washed before eating. A way to avoid foods contaminated with pesticides is to purchase organic foods.

Lead.   One of the environmental chemical dangers to children is lead poisoning that can be from inorganic or organic lead. Inorganic lead is associated with compounds such as lead nitrate or lead chloride while organic lead is combined with carbon. Inorganic lead can cause physical abnormalities characterized by anemia, headache, anorexia, weakness, and weight loss (Plog et. al., 1996). Chronic exposure to high levels of lead can eventually lead to bone marrow changes (Plog et. al., 1996). Fetuses, infants, and children are more vulnerable to lead because it is easily absorbed into the system of the developing child. Children are exposed to inorganic lead poisoning by eating or sucking lead-painted surfaces or playing in soil contaminated with lead. Soil can be contaminated by paint dust or exhaust from automobiles that use leaded gasoline. Floors and window ledges should be washed with a solution of powdered automatic dishwasher detergent and warm water. Dishwasher detergent is recommended because of its high content of phosphate (EPA & CPSC, 1995).

Children can accumulate organic lead via two pathways. First, they may eat plants or animals grown in an area of high lead concentrations. Second, organic lead can be absorbed directly through the skin or the mucous membranes of the respiratory tract and tends to be concentrated in the fatty tissue of the brain because of its high solubility (Plog et. al., 1996). Fortunately, exposure to organic lead by respiration has been greatly reduced by banning tetraethyl lead additives to gasoline. The main means of accumulation is now ingestion.

Since 1960 most paints sold do not contain lead, but surfaces painted prior to the 1960s do probably contain lead. All paint surfaces should be checked and deteriorating paint surfaces removed. Children should never be present during the lead removal process, and safety procedures should be followed to reduce contamination in areas used by children. The Department of Public Health provides guidelines for lead removal. Do not remove lead paint without professional assistance.

In addition to painted surfaces, water supplies should be tested for lead levels. Water supplies may be contaminated with toxic levels of lead even though the water has been tested by state officials. In older homes and buildings the plumbing materials included lead pipes and solder. Today lead-free pipes and solder are used.

Paints and Varnishes.   Paints and varnishes used in the educational environment should be water based and labeled nontoxic to avoid contamination through inhalation—resulting in possible damage to the central nervous system. All art materials used by children should also be water based and nontoxic.

Radon.   Radon is a radioactive, carcinogenic gas that is inhaled into the lungs with the potential of leading to lung cancer. The most common source of indoor radon is uranium in soil or rock on which the structure is built. The gas enters buildings through dirt floors, cracks in concrete walls and floors, and through floor drains.

Child care early education settings, especially if they are located in a basement or below ground level, should be tested for radon levels. Inexpensive, do-it-yourself test kits can be obtained through the mail, at hardware stores, and at other retail stores. Do not purchase a kit unless it has passed the Environmental Protection Agency (EPA) guidelines.

Asbestos.   Asbestos is a fibrous material used in the manufacturing of insulation materials and tiles and is also used as a fire retardant. It enters the body as microscopic, needle-like fibers, and collects in the alveoli or air sacks of the lungs. The result is fibrous growth narrowing the ducts of the air sacks and limiting their effectiveness (Plog et al., 1996). The Asbestos Hazard Emergency Response Act of 1986 brought national attention to this material and to Public Law 99-579 (1986) and made additional money available for financially needy schools to help pay for abatement costs. This program was funded from 1985 until 1993. Owners of buildings must notify occupants of the presence, the location, and the quantity of asbestos-containing material and presumed asbestos-containing materials (29 Code of Federal Regulations, Part 1101). The American Academy of Pediatrics (1987) recommends that children not be exposed to asbestos.

Formaldehyde.   Formaldehyde was formerly used in construction materials, especially plywood and chipboard. It is also a by-product of combustion. Formaldehyde readily dissolves in fluids in the nose, throat, and lungs causing irritation and symptoms such as watery eyes, burning sensations in the eyes and throat, nausea, and difficulty breathing. After repeated exposure, formaldehyde can enter the bloodstream and cause central nervous system damage.

All building materials used today are formaldehyde free. Emissions from building materials that contain formaldehyde decline with time. When involved in the construction of a learning environment and purchasing new furniture, check to make sure that the building materials are free of formaldehyde. If furniture or other pieces of equipment in the learning environment contain formaldehyde, coating wood products with polyurethane finishes may reduce formaldehyde emissions (EPA & CPSC, 1995). To further reduce formaldehyde exposure, wood that has been pressure-treated should never be burned indoors.

Environmental Tobacco Smoke.   Environmental tobacco smoke (ETS) is a mixture of smoke that comes from cigarettes, pipes, or cigars. The compounds in the smoke are known to cause cancer in humans. The EPA estimates that passive smoke annually causes between 150,000 and 300,000 lower respiratory tract infections in infants and children under 18 months of age (EPA & CPSC, 1995). Middle ear infections can also be the result of exposure to passive smoke. The best way to handle this problem is to have a **NO SMOKING** policy in learning environments for young children.

Additional Chemical Hazards.   Additionally, children should not be exposed to any form of air pollution caused by chemical gases, vapors, or fumes such as adhesives and chemical air fresheners. At all times learning environments must have proper ventilation, natural or mechanical, to provide a healthy environment for young children. All exhaust fans and clothes dryers should be vented to the outdoors. Children should not be exposed to chemical hazards in the outdoor environment. Educational settings should never be located near chemical-producing businesses.

Outdoor Chemical Hazards.   Outdoor pollutants include ozone, carbon monoxide, oxides of sulfur, oxides of nitrogen, unburned hydrocarbons, and particulates. Oxides of sulfur and nitrogen and ozone are primary irritants that can cause reddening of the eyes, increased mucus flow, and breathing distress. They are especially dangerous to younger children with more immature lungs than adults and to people with asthma or other respiratory ailments. Children with flu or cold symptoms are even more susceptible to these outdoor pollutants.

Play areas should not be located near dusty parking lots or dirt roads because of the particulates. Once they have entered the lungs they never leave. Children who are closer to the ground receive larger doses of particulates due to their short stature and higher respiration rate. Also, play areas should not be treated with herbicides or insecticides. Children should not be exposed to harmful chemicals for the sake of a green and weed-free lawn.

Ergonomic Hazards

Ergonomics is the application of human biological science in conjunction with engineering science to achieve optimum adjustment between the physical task, equipment, and the human body (Plog et al., 1996). Individuals who purchase equipment for children should make sure that the following items are designed for children rather than adults:

- Chairs
- Tables
- Toilets
- Sinks
- Drinking fountains
- Stairs
- Handrails
- Movement and sport equipment

Additionally, adjustment should be made within and between age groups to meet the individual physical needs of each child. Educators should be particularly concerned about injury to the children or to themselves resulting from physical stress. Injury frequently occurs when lifting. The lift should be with the legs, not the back. Adults should practice "lift with the legs" and encourage children to do so also. Another area for concern is the diaper-changing area, particularly when changing toddlers. The changing table should be low enough or equipped with stairs so staff members are not lifting children every day on an hourly basis.

Repetitive motion should be avoided especially in young children. Such behaviors will result in injury to joints and growth plates of the bones. Children should not, for example, be asked to jump in place repetitively on a hard surface.

Focus on Health Promotion

The American Medical Association (1992) designed Project Target 2000 as a national program to promote disease prevention in children. The program has three major goals (Edelstein, 1995):

- Achieve access to preventive services for all Americans
- Increase the span of healthy life of Americans
- Reduce health-care differences among Americans

The concept behind Target 2000 and this chapter is to call attention to behaviors that will help children reach their fullest potential. The next section focuses on prevention.

Preventive Practices and Services

The first thing that educators of young children or parents can do to prevent future illness is to develop steps to prevention. The health policy should be directed toward the children, staff, and family. Both physical and mental health policies should be set. The policies should be the foundation for all future health practices that serve, protect, and promote the health of the children, their family, and the staff.

Kendrick, et al. (1995) suggested answering the following questions when developing health policies:

- What should be done?
- Why should it be done?
- Who is responsible?
- What is the process?

An example of this process would be the development of emergency procedures (see Appendix C). The opening statement of the emergency procedure must discuss what should be done and why it should be done if a child is injured. The next step is to include an authority list (who should be contacted about the injury). Finally, list the steps that should be taken after the child has been given care and is out of danger.

Health Policy.   Health policies outline procedures to eliminate biological, physical, chemical, and ergonomic hazards in the environment. We initially examine guidelines for health appraisal, immunizations, and dental care and subsequently discuss specific steps for prevention of illness.

Health Appraisal.   A major part of any prevention plan should be a health appraisal for each child, staff, and volunteer participating in the child care early education program. This appraisal should be updated on a yearly basis, earlier if needed and appropriate to the individual's age.

The age-appropriate health assessment should follow the **American Academy of Pediatrics Guidelines for Health Supervision.** The health assessment should contain the following information:

- Review of child's health history
- Results of a physical examination
- Assessment of the child's growth and development patterns
- Physician recommendations and assessments (disability, medication, and special diets)
- Immunization record (including TB test)
- Emergency diagnosis and treatment recommendations

All staff workers, food preparation personnel, volunteers, and children should have a health appraisal on file.

Immunizations. Immunizations are an important preventive policy to improve the health of young children. Immunizations provide the child with protection against diseases such as polio, diphtheria, pertussis, tetanus, mumps, measles, and Haemophilus influenza type B (Hib disease). The American Academy of Pediatrics (AAP), the Advisory Committee on Immunization Practices (ACIP), and the American Academy of Family Physicians (AAFP) has established an immunization schedule for healthy children.

Beginning at birth, children should receive scheduled vaccinations providing protection against:

- Hepatitis B
- Diphtheria
- Tetanus
- Pertussis
- Polio
- Measles
- Mumps
- Rubella
- Haemophilus influenza type B (Hib)

Immunizations are designed to assist the body in building the natural defenses that enable it to react to disease and build up antibodies. The medical community delivers some of the vaccines such as MMR (measles, mumps, rubella) and DPT (diphtheria, pertussis, tetanus) in the same inoculation so as to limit trauma to the child. The American Academy of Pediatrics and the family physician should be consulted for the proper immunization and up-to-date timetable.

Parents and teachers should be aware that there is a controversy over immunizations. There could be adverse reactions to the immunizations. The majority of parents and the medical community feel that the protection benefits outweigh the risks. Additionally, educators should be sensitive to cultural and religious perspectives regarding immunizations. Some religions and cultures are opposed to vaccination. While children are required to meet immunization schedules before entering child care and/or public school, exemption due to religious and/or personal belief can be obtained. Additionally, exemption from immunization for medical reasons can also be obtained.

Dental Care. Dental care is a major part of personal hygiene and a healthy lifestyle. Daily care of teeth and gums should be a major part of a child care early education program's health policy and should begin around 15 to 18 months. Dental caries are the result of bacteria forming a plaque on teeth. The bacteria forms an acid that degrades the enamel of the teeth (Edelstein, 1995). Children should be encouraged to see a dentist for regular checkups, beginning at age three, on a yearly or semi-yearly schedule. Young children should practice daily cleaning of their teeth with their own toothbrush labeled with their name. Toothbrushes should be stored upright in the open air so that the bristles do not touch.

The use of fluoride toothpaste should be based on the age of the child and whether the community water supply is fluoridated. Since swallowing fluoride toothpaste could result in mottled teeth (Kendrick, et al., 1995), the use of fluoride toothpaste should be avoided before the age of three.

Nutrition is an important part of dental care. High sugar foods should be avoided as well as sugary drinks. Infants and toddlers should not be given sugar water to drink. Propping a bottle to feed an infant or a toddler is not recommended because the formula, juice, or sugared water will stay pooled in the mouth, creating an environment conducive to the growth of bacteria and will result in tooth decay.

After establishing a health policy, the child care early education specialist needs to follow steps to prevent illness. This is extremely important when developing an environment for healthy children.

Steps to Prevention

Cleanliness.   A clean environment, free of pollutants, trash, and animal waste is the first step in infection control. This section covers cleanliness related to hands, diaper-changing, toileting, hygiene recommendations for play materials, and the environment. A universal precautions policy should be adopted when handling any body products such as fecal material, vomit, or blood. The main point of this policy is to provide a barrier between individuals through the use of disposable gloves, disinfectant solutions, and hand washing.

I'm using universal precautions!
I'm washing my hands very cautiously.

Hand Washing.   Hand washing is the first line of defense in the prevention of infectious diseases and universal precautions. Roberto enacted one of the most important infection-control procedures—hand washing—to control biological hazards and resulting infections. Caregivers and teachers of young children should wash their hands when they enter the child care early education environment and prior to and following these activities:

- Food preparation
- Feeding children
- Personal eating
- Toileting and diaper-changing
- Handling mouthed toys, body fluids (mucus, blood, vomitus), soil and sand (outdoors and indoors)
- Handling, feeding, or cleaning pets

Roberto would add to this list that hands should be washed before sucking your thumb! Caregivers and teachers should be diligent about thoroughly washing their hands with running water, rubbing all surfaces including the front, back, fingers, and nail beds of the hands. The hands should be rinsed well and dried thoroughly with a paper towel before using the towel to turn off the water. Cloth towels should never be used in a child care early education setting. The practice of using cloth towels will increase infection in the program. If cloth towels are used, each child should have his own towel, and it should be clearly labeled with his name. The cloth towels should hang so that they do not touch each other. Many state child care regulations prevent the use of cloth towels. Posters of the proper hand-washing procedures should be placed above all sinks in the education setting (see Figure 4.1).

Disposable gloves should be used when cleaning body fluids or changing diapers, but they should never replace hand washing. Once they have been used the gloves should be disposed of properly in a covered container. Disposable gloves should never be used a second time.

Diaper-Changing and Toilet Facilities.   Diaper-changing and toilet facilities are a major biological risk in child care facilities and other types of education settings

FIGURE 4.1   Hand Washing

for young children. All diaper-changing and toileting areas should only be used for these functions and they should be located as far as possible from food preparation areas. The diaper-changing surface should be covered with a disposable paper which is discarded, and the table disinfected after every use. The area should have running water for hand-washing.

There is always a dilemma concerning whether cloth or paper diapers should be used. This is particularly true of child care settings or other types of group settings for infants and toddlers. The American Public Health Association/American Academy of Pediatrics Standards (1992) state:

- Diapers should be able to contain urine and stool
- Diapers must have an inner absorbent lining attached to a waterproof cover
- Outer and inner linings must be changed as a unit
- Outer and inner linings should not be reused unless cleaned and disinfected

Presently, only disposable paper diapers with absorbent gelling material fully meet these criteria (Kendrick, et. al., 1995). Reusable cloth diapers with or without a separate, unattached plastic pant do not meet this requirement. Therefore, paper diapers are recommended for use in group settings. Disposable diapers should be placed in a lined, covered container, and the container should be emptied daily. Children should not be permitted to play in the container.

Gaining control of bodily elimination is a major step for toddlers and should be handled with the greatest degree of care and sensitivity. Toilet-training is the child's first major step toward autonomy and self-respect. Toilets and sinks should be cleaned daily with a sanitizing solution. A training chair should be made of a smooth, nonporous material and should be emptied and sanitized after each use. Many medical experts recommend that training chairs not be used in groups because of hygiene problems (Kendrick, et. al., 1995). If the facility has adult-sized toilets, washable plastic toilet seat adapters can be used.

Play Materials and Equipment.   All play materials and equipment should be disinfected frequently. This is particularly true of mouthed toys and all surfaces such as tables where children eat and diaper-changing tables. These areas should be cleaned with a bleach solution before and after use. A fresh disinfectant, bleach solution should be mixed daily because it looses potency as a consequence of chemical decomposition. Use the following formula:

- 1 tablespoon of bleach to 1 quart of water, or
- ¼ cup of bleach to 1 gallon of water

The solution should be sprayed on table surfaces and left on the surface for two minutes before wiping the surface dry. (Kendrick, et. al., 1995) recommends a stronger bleach solution, ¾ cup bleach to 1 gallon water to disinfect toys. This should be done weekly and immediately after the toys have been mouthed. The toys should soak in the bleach solution for approximately five minutes and be washed in a dishwasher on the sanitation temperature setting. Commercial alternatives to bleach can be purchased if they are Environmental Protection Agency (EPA) chemical germicides registered as hospital disinfectants (Kendrick et. al., 1995).

Water play is an important part of the early childhood curriculum, but for health and safety reasons precautions should be taken. Water tables should be cleaned with the bleach disinfectant before filling with clean and disinfected water. All water toys should also be cleaned with the bleach solution. The water tables should be emptied daily to reduce contamination and to prevent accidents. If water play is extended to pools or wading pools, teachers should make sure the pool water meets all state sanitation codes. Wading pools should contain ¾ teaspoon bleach to every 50 gallons of water (PA Code 55). The wading pool should be emptied daily and be cleaned with a disinfectant.

Sand play is another important aspect of the early childhood curriculum. All sand boxes/tables located outside should be covered to avoid biological hazard contamination from animal fecal material. Yearly, the sand should be turned over to a depth of 18 inches, and replaced every two years (Kendrick, et. al., 1995).

Environmental Hygiene.   Environmental hygiene should be practiced. Trash should be kept in containers lined with plastic bags and removed from the facility daily. Additionally, trash that has been contaminated with human or animal secretions or excrement should be contained in a plastic-lined container that has a cover. By keeping secretions contained, the risk of contamination and infection will be decreased.

Bedding used by children should be washed weekly or immediately after contamination with urine, feces, or vomitus. Laundry should be washed in water and dried at a temperature above 140° F or an approved disinfectant must be used in the rinse cycle (Kendrick, et. al., 1995). Clothes used for playing dress-up should be washed weekly following the same procedures. Cots, mats, or cribs should be washed at least monthly with a sanitizing solution.

To further prevent biological hazards and resulting infections, health procedures should be followed in food preparation areas:

- Work surfaces should be cleaned to avoid food contamination
- Food handling should be limited by using utensils
- Refrigerated foods should be covered and stored at 45° F or lower
- Frozen foods should be wrapped and stored at 0° F or lower
- Hot foods should be covered and must be kept at 140° F or higher
- Personal hygiene should be used at all times
- Hair should be covered with a hair net or cap
- Raw meat and eggs should be handled with care
- Expiration dates on food should be followed

Individuals with a communicable disease should not be involved in food preparation.

Air and Water Sanitation

The Water Supply.   The water supply should be safe for drinking. All child care and education facilities should provide a potable water supply in both the outdoor and indoor environments that meets federal safe drinking water standards (40 Code of Federal Regulations, Part 146). Children should be provided with disposable drinking cups or use drinking fountains. The latter should be made of materials impervious to water and should have a guard over the nozzle to prevent children from contacting the nozzle with the mouth or nose.

Air Quality.   Air quality is an important factor to consider in infection control. Infectious diseases can pass from one child to another through airborne contamination. When children are indoors they should be provided with adequate space to decrease airborne contamination. The National Association for the Education of Young Children (NAEYC, 1998) recommends a **minimum** of 35 square feet of useable indoor floor space per child and a **minimum** of 75 square feet of outdoor play space. The indoor space should be provided with natural or mechanical ventilation. If windows are used for ventilation they must be screened. If air conditioners are used for ventilation they should be cleaned and serviced regularly. Additionally, heating systems should be cleaned regularly to reduce airborne contaminates.

Animals in the Classroom.

Animals or classroom pets play an important educational role. While it is valuable to have animals in the child care early education setting it should be stressed that they should not compound health problems. To prevent this from occurring the following guidelines should be followed:

- All animals should be kept in spaces that provide for adequate movement and exercise
- The area should be clean and well ventilated
- The animal should be well fed on a diet designed for its species
- An animal should not be kept if any child is allergic to that animal
- Animals should be checked by a veterinarian and should have all the prescribed vaccinations
- Adults and children should wash their hands after feeding, cleaning, and handling the animals
- Litter boxes and/or materials containing urine and fecal material should be kept away from the children
- Children should learn the proper, humane way to handle animals (Figure 4.2)

Special care should be used when children are handling amphibious animals. Children and staff members should wash their hands after handling any pet but especially turtles, frogs, and salamanders. These animals have been linked to salmonella, a bacterial infection that can cause illness.

Trash should be removed from the facility daily, and all foods should be stored in closed containers to eliminate infestation and contamination from rodents or

---

Pet Adoption Pledge

1. I promise to give food and water to my pet daily.

2. I promise to keep my pet's cage clean and out of drafts at all times.

3. I will always treat my pet with kindness.

FIGURE 4.2   Pet Adoption Pledge

insects such as ants and cockroaches. These practices should help to avoid the use of chemical pesticides, a chemical hazard. Contaminated foods should be discarded. To further reduce unwanted insects and arachnids, screens should be used on all exterior doors and windows.

Current Problems Facing Today's Children

Many children in the United States are not receiving appropriate health care and prevention services. In addition, there are societal stresses that impact health. This section addresses reduction in health care differences, followed by a discussion of child abuse, children living in rural environments, children who are homeless, and children with disabilities.

Reduction in Health-Care Differences

Differences in the quantity and the quality of health care unfortunately exist in the United States. It important to improve the quality of children's lives by reducing differences that exist in health and health care among children of varying backgrounds.

More than 14 million children in the United States live in poverty; this equates to approximately one in five children. Additionally, the rate of child poverty has grown over the past several decades (Children's Defense Fund, 1998). Children living in poverty have more health problems. Some feel that the best way to reduce poverty is to ensure employment at fair and equitable wages. Others feel that tax relief, literacy training, or subsidized child care is the answer. Whatever the answer, poverty needs to be eliminated to improve the lives of children. Children need appropriate care and freedom from all forms of deprivation.

Immunizations and dental care are part of a routine to maintain a healthy child. Children must have adequate health care to prevent future illness and to treat current medical problems. More than 11 million American children lack health insurance; the percentage of children who do not have health insurance coverage has risen to the highest level ever recorded by the United States Census Bureau (Children's Defense Fund, 1998). Parents simply are unable to pay the high coast of health insurance, but coverage is vital to the child's well-being. Children's Health Insurance Program (CHIP) is helping uninsured children by providing funds to expand Medicaid and to provide state grants for funding for uninsured children. Insurance coverage for children is necessary to prevent illness and to provide for a healthy life. The professional staff can provide information to the parent or guardian on how to obtain health insurance.

Child Abuse

Child abuse is a problem that is increasing in the United States. It is estimated that 500,000 children are physically abused every year (Santrock, 1999). Teachers and doctors are required by law to report any suspected incidents of abuse. Forms of abuse or maltreatment are:

- Physical
- Sexual
- Emotional
- Neglect

Children can be subjected to physical or sexual abuse, nutritional, supervision, and education neglect, emotional abuse, and drug and alcohol abuse. Why individuals abuse children is multifaceted. Abusive behavior is linked to poor coping skills. Violence has become almost the norm. Media violence must be reduced. Children and adults alike model what they see on television. Children crash their cars, punch their dolls, and sometimes fight other children as though they were the tough characters on TV.

No matter what form the abuse takes, the repercussions to the child and the long-term effects are devastating. The long-term developmental consequences of child abuse include poor emotional regulation, attachment problems, problems in peer relations, and other psychological problems (Cicchetti & Toth, 1998). Maltreated children are at risk for a lifetime of problems and disorders.

All suspected cases of abuse must be reported to the appropriate state authorities. Early childhood professionals should familiarize themselves with their state laws concerning abuse. Some states hold medical personnel, social workers, and teachers legally responsible for reporting suspected child abuse situations. (See Chapter 5 for additional information on abuse.)

Rural Environment

Children living in rural areas are often at a disadvantage concerning health care and recreation opportunities. Distances complicated by lack of transportation often prevent children in rural areas from receiving timely preventive medical attention. They do not receive physical examinations, dental examinations, or immunizations simply because their parents lack transportation to take the child to the medical facility. Programs such as Head Start recognize these problems and provide transportation to medical centers for young children enrolled in their program. Additionally, children from rural areas do not have parks where they can participate in recreational and physical activity. This emphasizes the need for early movement stimulation and an adequate physical regime in the education environment for young children.

Homeless

Homeless children face problems similar to rural children but their greatest problem is that they do not have a safe environment in which to live. Homeless families with children are the fastest growing segment of homeless Americans (Children's Defense Budget, 1990). Other families are having problems because they use all their income on housing and have little expendable income left for other living expenses. Additionally, social service agencies may not be able to find homeless children to provide intervention services. It will take community awareness on this issue to provide equal care for the homeless child. The availability of low-income housing must increase to assist families in providing a safe environment for children.

Disabilities

Children with disabilities have unique health problems related to their disability. The education community needs to recognize this and must provide services and environments that permit the child with a disability to reach his fullest potential.

Summary

The health of a child can be compromised by biological, physical, chemical, and ergonomic hazards. Appropriate hygiene practices must be used to control biological hazards and related microorganisms. Hand-washing and the use of disinfectants are very important aspects involved in controlling microorganisms. A variety of infectious diseases resulting from microorganisms can cause long-term and short-term illness to children. Arthropod, plant, and animal allergens can cause allergies, dermatitis, and systemic intoxication. Environmental hygiene should be used to limit the effect of these biological hazards.

Physical hazards are caused by such environmental factors as noise, temperature extremes, and radiation. Chemical hazards can be absorbed through the skin, digested, or inhaled. A variety of actions can be used to reduce or eliminate the damage caused by chemical hazards.

Finally, educators should be aware of ergonomic hazards and make every effort, when purchasing or constructing materials, to eliminate damage to the health of the child.

Health appraisals are an important part of preventive health practices. Immunizations are part of the health appraisal and prescribed schedules should be followed. All children should have an equal right to a healthy lifestyle. Barriers such as lack of safe housing and insurance should be eliminated. All children regardless of their socioeconomic background have the right to be healthy.

CHANGE AND ADVOCACY

1. Examine state child care regulations and advocate to eliminate biological, physical, and chemical hazards.

2. Work with county planners to improve the problems associated with children living in rural areas and homeless children.

3. Discuss with local Head Start and child care directors ways to improve the medical and dental care of children.

REFERENCES

American Academy of Pediatrics, & American Public Health Association. (1992). *Caring for our children-National health and safety performance standards; Guidelines for out-of-home child care programs.* Washingon, DC: American Academy of Pediatrics.

American Academy of Pediatrics. (1987). Asbestos exposure. *Pediatrics, 79*(2), 301–305.

American Medical Association. (1992). *Healthy youth 2000.* Grove Village, IL: AMA.

Aronson, S. (2000). Environmental health in child care settings. *Child Care Exchange, 131,* 35.

Children's Defense Budget. (1990). *S.O.S. America!* Washington, DC: Children's Defense Budget.

Children's Defense Fund. (1998). *The state of America's children.* Washington, DC: NAEYC.

Cicchetti, D., & Toth, S. L. (1998). Perspectives on research and practice in developmental psychopathology. In W. Damon (Ed.), *Handbook of child psychology 4,* 479–584. NY: Wiley.

Code of Federal Regulations, Title 40. (1986). Washington, DC: Office of Federal Register National Archives and Records Service General Services Administration.

Code of Federal Regulations, Title 29. (1998). Washington, DC: Office of Federal Register National Archives and Records Service General Services Administration.

Commonwealth of Pennsylvania. (1998). *Pennsylvania Code, Title 55, Chapter 3270.* Harrisburg, PA: Office of Children, Youth, and Families.

Edelstein, S. F. (1995). *The healthy young child.* Minneapolis/St.Paul, MN: West Publishing Co.

Kendrick, Kaufmann, & Messenger. (1995). *Healthy young children: A manual for programs.* Washington, DC: NAEYC.

Leeds, M. J. (1998). *Nutrition for healthy living.* Boston, MA: McGraw-Hill.

National Association for the Education of Young Children. (1998). *Accreditation criteria and procedures.* Washington, DC: NAEYC.

Parizkova, J. (1996). *Nutrition, physical activity, and health in early life.* NY: CRC Press.

Plog, B. A., Niland, J., & Quinlan, P. J. (1996). *Fundamentals of industrial hygiene.* Itasca, IL: National Safety Council.

Robertson, C. (1998). *Safety, nutrition and health in early education.* Albany, NY: Delmar.

Santrock, J. W. (1999). *Life-span development.* Boston, MA: McGraw-Hill.

United States Environmental Protection Agency (EPA), & United States Consumer Production Commission (CPC). (1995). Washington, DC: Office of Radiation and Indoor Air. *EPA Document # 402-K-93-007.*

5 Safety in the Early Childhood Learning Environment

CHAPTER OBJECTIVES

Knowledge

- The reader will describe the components of psychological and physical safety.

Skills

- The reader will analyze equipment and materials to ensure physical and psychological safety for the children.

Attitudes

- The reader will value the role psychological safety and physical safety play in the lives of young children and their families.

CHAPTER SYNOPSIS

Psychological Safety
Bioenvironmental Reciprocity Model
Emotional Intelligence
Oppositions to High Emotional Intelligence

Physical Safety
Poisoning
Falls
Burns
Suffocation

Drowning
Cuts
Electrocution

Injury Prevention
Supervision
Equipment Inspection
Additional Hazards

Emergency Procedures

Scenario

Danny and Kyle were students in Mrs. Brown's 4-year-old class. One day they were role-playing their version of a scene from a popular crime show. Danny, who is the son of the local chief of police, was the policeman. Kyle, who had a mother dying from a chronic illness, was the robber. The 4-year-old boys designed the plot and set the stage. Danny followed Kyle the criminal about the room in a low-key pursuit until he closed in on Kyle and delivered the fatal shot. Kyle role-played a very slow and dramatic death. When Kyle completed his dying and was lying prone on the floor, Danny walked over to Kyle and stood over him. Danny removed his policeman hat, placed it on his chest over his heart, and bowed his head. Mrs. Brown watched the entire scene take place and was pleased that Danny and Kyle felt safe, both psychologically and physically, to act out this role in her classroom. She realized that this was a major accomplishment.

Danny and Kyle's role-playing was significant on many levels. The boys were able to problem solve and to plan a dramatic play that went on for an extended period of time. Additionally, Danny was able to emulate his father and his father's role in society, and Kyle was able to begin to understand, on his own developmental level, his mother's illness through role playing a death situation. Danny and Kyle needed to feel safe in their environment to be able to role-play and to resolve issues that are important for each child's cognitive, social, and emotional development. Unfortunately, this scene is not a reality in the daily environment of many children.

Children today are exposed to an alarming amount of violence in their homes, schools, and streets. They are bombarded with inappropriate material through television, movies, popular music, computer games, and on-line interactions. Mass media poses real psychological and physiological dangers to the development of children. Pressure must be placed on society, political leaders, industry executives, and child and family advocates to improve the lives of children so they can function safely in today's society. Children need to be able to form strong, stable attachments with caring adults, but they must experience an environment that ensures their safety from psychological and physical dangers. This environment must not only provide safety from violence and inappropriate materials, but also from accidents that can cause injury or death.

The objective of this chapter is to understand the relationship between psychological and physical safety in the learning environment and the development of a healthy child. It is vital that infants, toddlers, and young children feel secure and safe in their environments for maximum motor/physical, cognitive/language, and social/emotional development. That safe feeling must occur at both the psychological and physical levels.

Psychological Safety

All environments, including learning environments, must provide psychological safety for young children to develop into healthy children and adults. Children must feel secure in order for positive mental processes to develop and for positive feelings and behaviors to dominate their lives.

Bioenvironmental Reciprocity Model

As was stated in Chapter 1, the child is a product of the interaction of her biological and environmental components, and it is the reciprocity of these components that determine the physical, mental, and behavioral actions of the developing child. The interrelationship of the mental processes and the anatomy and physiology of the child is important. This interrelationship begins in the prenatal period and can be affected by numerous environmental and biological factors. Beginning at the prenatal period, the child develops a blueprint of expectations for herself and others that develops into responsiveness or indifference, success or failure (Karr-Morse & Wiley, 1997). Developmental research has shown that the developmental window of opportunity for emotional development is 0 to 2 years of age (Afifi & Bergman, 2000). Children must feel positive about themselves to develop into emotionally happy and stable adults. Mental health is certainly a strong component of a healthy adult. Based on research, Pool (1997) feels that emotional well-being is the strongest predictor of achievement both in school and on the job. Additionally, noted criminologist Dorothy Lewis found that adult criminal violence results from the interaction of two or more internal factors or vulnerabilities such as cognitive delays, neuropsychiatric disorders, and early negative family circumstances (Karr-Morse et. al., 1997). It is the gentle balance between the genetic code and the environment, both prenatal and postnatal, which affects later behaviors. When this balance suffers any loss of equilibrium at critical times in development, the result may be devastating. Educators and policy-makers need to come to the realization that greater emphasis should be placed on the care of young children and the interaction between the family and the child care early education facility. This is especially true during the first years of life, including the prenatal period, to ensure positive physical, emotional, and cognitive development. If this is not done, we may continue to see children developing poor mental health coping strategies and using sad, angry, or anxious emotions as outcomes. We want children to have happy and stable emotions to use when analyzing their behaviors. We want them to have high emotional intelligence.

Emotional Intelligence

Goleman (as cited in Pool, 1997), felt that there are five dimensions to emotional intelligence that should be incorporated into the child's environment. These dimensions are:

- Self-awareness
- Handling emotions
- Motivation
- Empathy
- Social skills

Self-awareness.   To have emotional intelligence a child should be aware of his strengths and weaknesses and have a positive self-concept about these strengths and weaknesses. Each child must see himself as a part of society and understand his role in that society.

Handling Emotions.   Children must learn to handle their emotions in a variety of situations. Two-year-olds are notorious for having "temper tantrums." Anyone who has worked with this age group is quite familiar with the lack of control that may be seen in some 2-year-olds. While developmentally this is understandable for this particular age, we are not as accepting of this behavior in older children. As children age there is the expectation that they gain control of their emotions. Children who do not control their emotions are perceived as being impulsive. Pool (1997) states that there are consequences to being impulsive. Impulsive boys are three to six times more likely to be violent by the end of adolescence, and impulsive girls are three times more likely to become pregnant during adolescence.

Motivation.   Helping children to set goals, to persevere, and to achieve their goals will increase children's motivation. Educators of young children should make a conscious effort to use these three steps to increase motivation—thus increasing children's emotional intelligence.

Empathy.   Empathy is the ability to understand the feelings of other individuals. We convey our emotions through the tone of our voices or by our facial expressions. Very young children are capable of reading emotions, and should be encouraged to react positively to the emotions. Bullies are considered to lack empathy.

Peter, at 2 years of age, was enrolled in a child care program where he repeatedly hit and pushed other children. On several occasions his aggressive behavior caused other children in the program to be sent to the hospital. After several extensive conferences with the parent and attempts to modify his behavior, Peter was asked to leave the program to ensure the safety of the other children. Anyone who has worked with children has similar stories about bullies. They exist at every age and have low emotional intelligence. Male bullies tend to be more physical (punching, kicking, and pushing) while female bullies tend to be more verbal (Barone, 1997). Barone (1997) surveyed counselors, teachers, and administrators and asked them to identify effective strategies for dealing with bullies. The responses included tougher discipline, better supervision, and more counseling. We would like to add another strategy: encourage parent participation. We know that the interaction between the home and the child care early education center is very important in solving any problem involving children. Children need to know what the boundaries are and what is considered acceptable behavior. Therefore, we feel that *behavior management* is a better choice of terminology than is *tougher discipline*.

Educators need to speak about not only the physical damage but also the psychological damage that is caused when children live and play in hostile environments. A "No Tolerance of Physical Violence" policy should be adopted in every classroom. In a classroom that followed this policy, an argument erupted between three boys engaged in block building. The blocks became weapons, and the boys used them to strike each other. Before the teacher could get across the room to intervene, the boys, familiar with the "No Tolerance" Rule, started hugging each other and stating how sorry they were. Children can learn to understand and appreciate the feelings of others. These children also engaged in the last dimension of emotional intelligence—they used social skills.

Social Skills.   Clearly, the children in the previous scenario had social skills. Children, however, need to learn appropriate social skills—they do not just develop. Simply asking children to say, "thank you," "please," or "I am sorry," encourages the development of social skills. Old-fashioned manners are the first step toward having positive social skills. Children learn social skills from their family and educators, through direct instruction and modeling. We must always remember to use positive social interactions—particularly when we are around children.

To develop the highest emotional intelligence in children, we must encourage the development of self-awareness, positive handling of emotions, empathy, motivation, and social skills. Poor bonding, abuse, neglect, and certain societal issues can affect any of these building blocks of high emotional intelligence. We cover these obstacles to emotional intelligence next.

Oppositions to High Emotional Intelligence

This section covers problems or stumbling blocks that children, parents, and teachers face when developing emotional intelligence. We first discuss a lack of bonding with a caregiver followed by violence against children. Since children with special needs are more likely to suffer a lack of bonding and abuse, we discuss issues directly related to them.

Lack of Bonding.   The most important aspect of psychological safety is a secure attachment or bond with one or more caregiver(s). This means that the child will take initiative in seeking proximity and contact with an individual who is an active participant in her environment. Traditionally, during infancy the child's mother, who has the role of caring and protecting the child, is the first person with whom the child forms an attachment. The infant feels secure and protected in the care of the mother. Later as the child develops locomotion—during the toddler years—the attachment serves as a secure basis for exploration. This attachment and security has a correlation with attachments to other adults and peers. A child can have multiple secure attachments with other caregivers such as the father, extended relatives, and day care personnel without competing with or diluting the attachment with the mother (Cummings, 1980).

Ainsworth (1979) provided a framework of contrasting behaviors that may be used as a guide to assist in the development of a strong and secure attachment when working with infants, toddlers, and young children:

- Sensitivity-insensitivity: caregivers should be sensitive to the needs of the child and respond to the child's signals
- Acceptance-rejection: Caregivers should be positive and accepting of the child regardless of the mood of the child and/or the caregiver
- Cooperation-interference: cooperative caregivers permit the child to have autonomy and avoid exerting direct control
- Accessibility-ignoring: caregivers should be accessible to the child

The healthy child is raised in a sensitive, accepting, cooperative, and accessible environment. An attachment that has been built on these elements is beneficial for a lifetime.

A classic study by Dennis (1973) demonstrated the importance of psychological attachment in the young child. French nuns adequately fed and clothed children—from infancy through 5 or 6 years of age—who were housed in a Lebanese orphanage. During this time period, the nuns provided very little stimulation to the children and their interaction with the children was limited. The insensitivity and rejection that the children were subjected to resulted in extreme retardation of motor, linguistic, and intellectual development. Later these children were exposed to more stimulating environments and were able to overcome some of the deprivation. Infants and young children need to be in close proximity and contact with accessible adults who will interact with them in a sensitive and accepting manner. Children need to be raised in nurturing, permanent families, and receive child care free of abuse and neglect.

Violence Against Children: Abuse and Neglect.   Abuse is violence against children. A survey of state child protection agencies in 1996 by the National Committee to Prevent Child Abuse reported 969,000 children were abused and neglected (CDF, 1998). Many experts believe that this figure is low and that it may be three times this amount (CDF, 1998). We cannot raise children who have a high emotional intelligence if they are neglected and abused physically, emotionally, or sexually. The Child Abuse and Treatment Act of 1974, PL 93-247 defines abuse and neglect as "the physical or mental injury, sexual abuse, negligent treatment, or maltreatment of a child under the age of eighteen by a person who is responsible for the child's welfare under the circumstances which indicate that the child's health or welfare is harmed or threatened thereby" (U.S. Department of Health, Education, and Welfare, 1975, p. 3). Each state has a law that includes the federal law and additional state variations. Individuals can obtain the state law at local court houses or from legislature libraries. The effects of abuse and neglect are listed in Table 5.1 (Iverson & Segal, 1990).

A child raised in a violent environment suffers. Concerns about guns and children being victimized by guns and violence is increasing in schools throughout

TABLE 5.1   The Effects of Abuse and Neglect on Young Children

Infants and Toddlers
- Poor response to amicable approaches by adults
- Aggression toward adult care givers and peers
- Poor bonding characteristics

Preprimary
- Verbally and/or physically aggressive
- Angry and destructive behavior
- Immature with poor social skills
- Outsider play behaviors

School Age
- Angry and aggressive behavior

the United States, although children are far more likely to be killed by gunfire outside of the school (CDF, 1999). Nevertheless, we want our children to be psychologically safe in their educational environments. Schools have reacted to this problem by having drills (see the evacuation section of this chapter). Recently a second-grade classroom teacher in a rural school told a visitor that there was going to be a "Code Red" drill. The drill, when it occurred, consisted of locking the children in the room, closing the window coverings, and silently hiding under a table. During this process one of the second graders looked up and stated, "This is about me; I like to bring guns to school!" Children should bring teddy bears and blankets to school to feel secure, not guns.

The problem of violence in the schools needs to be discussed both with parents and school officials. Did this drill contribute positively or negatively to the children's emotional intelligence? Children need to feel secure and safe. But did this drill accomplish this? Or, did it frighten the children and encourage feelings of paranoia? Arguments can easily be made for both sides of this issue. The drill may have satisfied the legal liability issue for the school district but also raised the anxiety level of the children. On the other side of the argument, it could be noted that such a drill reassures the child that adults are concerned and are taking action to prevent problems.

Special Needs Population.   The special needs population, due to their unique characteristics, may suffer from poor bonding, abuse, neglect, and numerous other concerns. This group may have mental or physical disabilities and also includes homeless children and children living in poverty. Attention must be given to ensure that this population has positive bonding experiences and are not subjected to abuse. It is important that early childhood programs activate the anti-bias curriculum developed by Derman-Sparks and the ABC Task Force (Derman-Sparks, 1989). This curriculum provides an approach to assist children in developing acceptance and tolerance toward others, the avoidance of stereo-typing and biases, and the use of critical-thinking strategies.

Another way to help improve the emotional intelligence of children is to learn how to cope with the pressures they face. It is important that the child, family, and staff know how to cope with the stresses they face.

Stress Reduction.   Educators of young children are recognizing the fact that they must develop techniques to help children reduce stress. Infant massage is a technique that is used in many child care settings to relax the infants. As children get older, educators are teaching children self-massage techniques and meditation behaviors. In the latter, children sit quietly on the floor with their eyes closed. The children mentally focus on an imaginary light on their head or heart and are encouraged to have positive thoughts during this process. Wolf (2000) also suggests that educators maintain a quiet corner for the children so they may have self-initiated moments of quiet.

Clearly, Danny and Kyle felt secure in their child care arrangement to role-play a situation that held psychological danger for both boys. It is important to have a learning environment that provides psychological safety to the child. But in addition to psychological safety, children need to be provided with physical safety.

Physical Safety

According to information complied by the National SAFE KIDS Campaign, each year more than 4.5 million children age 14 and under are injured in the home and nearly two-thirds of the injuries requiring emergency room care involve children under the age of 3 (Facenda, 1999). Six out of ten children under age 6 need some form of child care (Children's Defense Fund, 2000). The Consumer Product Safety Commission says that at least 56 children have died in child care settings since 1990, but a state-by-state study by U.S. News (1996) recorded at least 76 deaths in child care facilities during that year alone (Rossellini, 1999). Many accidents occur because of a mismatch between the child's size and abilities and the equipment and activities. Care must be taken to purchase equipment and to plan activities that are developmentally appropriate for the size and ability of the children.

As the shift continues from home to child care settings, it is vital that parents and other involved individuals take precautions to ensure children live in safe environments and develop problem-solving skills to help them avoid unsafe situations.

Most childhood accidents can be classified into seven categories: poisoning, falls, burns, suffocation, drowning, cuts, and electrocutions. After we cover each of these categories we discuss precautionary methods to use in indoor and outdoor learning environments to help reduce such accidents. It is important to select appropriate and safe equipment and materials, to safely store and maintain the equipment and materials, and to use the equipment and materials appropriately at all times.

Poisoning

Substances that can cause poisoning are chemicals, medicines, and plants. All cleaning materials and other toxic materials should be kept in the original containers that clearly specify the contents of the toxic materials with clear warnings. The materials should be stored in a locked area that is inaccessible to the children. Additionally, the toxic materials should not be stored in food preparation areas or with food.

Medicines.   Prescription or nonprescription medicines should be treated as toxic materials. They should be kept in their original containers in a locked and child-inaccessible location. The staff of an educational center should only give prescription or nonprescription medication to a child after they have received written instructions from the doctor who has prescribed the medication and parental permission. When administering the prescription or nonprescription medication, the pharmaceutical directions on the container are acceptable to follow. The label should contain the name of the child for whom the medication is intended, the name of the medication, and the doctor prescribing the medication. Only the child

These taste the same! I don't
want either one.

listed on the container should receive the medication. A log should be kept of each administration of a prescription or nonprescription medication. The following information should be included in the log (Pennsylvania Department of Welfare, 1998):

- Name of the medication
- Name of child receiving the medication
- Storage requirements (refrigeration)
- Amount of medication administered
- Date of administration
- Time of administration
- Initials of staff person administering the medication
- Special notes related to administration

If Syrup of Ipecac is administered to induce vomiting upon direction from the poison control center, the following information should be recorded on an accident report and kept in the child's file (Pennsylvania Department of Welfare, 1998):

- Date and time instruction was received
- Name of the individual who issued the instructions
- Content of the information
- Time, date, and amount of Syrup of Ipecac administered

Plants.   Plants may brighten the child care setting, but it is important to check to see if the plant is poisonous. Plants are a leading cause of poisoning of young children (Kendrick, Kaufmann & Messenger, 1991). Some plants that are safe to have around young children are listed in Table 5.2.

Table 5.3 is a listing of poisonous plants that may be unintentionally taken into a home and/or child care setting. These plants may cause upset stomach, rashes, or even death.

When in doubt about the origin or name of a particular plant, consult your local nursery. When the circumstances are explained, the nursery staff is always willing to assist in the identification of the plant. If a child has swallowed any part of a poisonous plant, first remove any remaining pieces from the child's mouth,

TABLE 5.2   Safe Plants

■ African violet	■ Hen-and-chickens	■ Snake plant
■ Aluminum plant	■ Jade plant	■ Spider plant
■ Begonia	■ Peperomia	■ Wandering Jew
■ Boston fern	■ Prayer plant	■ Wax plant
■ Coleus	■ Rubber plant	■ Weeping fig
■ Dracaena	■ Sensitive plant	

TABLE 5.3   Unsafe Plants

■ Autumn crocus	■ Foxglove	■ Oleander
■ Azalea	■ Golden chain	■ Philodendron
■ Baneberry	■ Hyacinth	■ Poison hemlock
■ Belladonna	■ Hydrangea	■ Pokeweed
■ Black cherry	■ Jequirity bean	■ Privet
■ Black locust	■ Jessamine	■ Rhododendron
■ Buckeye	■ Jimson weed	■ Rhubarb leaves
■ Caladium	■ Lantana	■ Rosary pea
■ Caper spurge	■ Larkspur	■ Rubber vine
■ Castor bean	■ Laurel	■ Sandbox tree
■ Cherry	■ Lily-of-the-valley	■ Tansy
■ Chinaberry	■ Lupine	■ Thorn apple
■ Daffodil	■ Mistletoe	■ Tobacco
■ Daphne	■ Monkshod	■ Tung oil tree
■ Delphinium	■ Moonseed	■ Water hemlock
■ Dieffenbachia	■ Mountain laurel	■ White snakeroot
■ Duranta	■ Mushrooms	■ Yellow jessamine
■ False hellebore	■ Nightshade	■ Yellow oleander

and with plant in hand (for identification purposes) call the poison control center (Kendrick et. al., 1991).

Arts and Crafts Materials.   Materials that are used for arts and crafts projects can cause problems for young children when swallowed or inhaled. When purchasing and using art materials make sure they are labeled as follows (Kendrick et. al., 1991):

- Nontoxic item—will not cause acute poisoning
- Approved Product (AP)—item contains no materials in sufficient quantities to be toxic or injurious, even if eaten or swallowed
- Certified Product (CP)—item meets the same standards as AP, but also meets specific standards for quality, color, etc.

Kendrick et. al., (1991) provides guidelines on how to choose art supplies (given in Table 5.4). For additional information, contact Art Hazards Information Center (212-227-6231).

Poisonous materials can be present in a learning environment in other ways. For instance, items such as batteries and diapering materials need to be carefully monitored. Batteries are poisonous. The new button batteries are a concern as a poison and choking hazard (see the later section on suffocation).

Finally, diaper materials, lotions, creams, and talcum powder are potential hazards to young children. Children should not be permitted to play with these materials. Talcum powder should not be used with babies because the powder particulates can cause damage to the lungs when inhaled.

TABLE 5.4   Toxic Arts and Crafts Materials

- Avoid powdered clay. It contains silica that is easily inhaled and harmful to the lungs.
- Use wet clay that cannot be inhaled.
- Avoid glazes, paints, or finishes that contain lead.
- Use poster paints/water-based products.
- Avoid paints that require solvents, such as turpentine, to clean brushes and materials with fumes.
- Use water-based paints, glue, etc.
- Avoid cold-water or commercial dyes that contain chemical additives.
- Use natural dyes such as vegetables or onion skins.
- Avoid permanent markers that may contain toxic solvents.
- Use water-based markers.
- Avoid instant papier-mache that may contain lead or asbestos and use of color-print newspaper or magazines with water.
- Use newspaper (printed with black ink only) and library paste or liquid starch.
- Avoid epoxy, instant glues, or solvent-based glues.
- Use water-based white glue or library paste.
- Avoid aerosol sprays.
- Use water-based materials/pump sprays.
- Avoid powdered tempera paints.
- Use liquid tempera paint or any nontoxic paint.

Falls

Falls from a height or at ground level can cause additional injury to young children. Young children are developing their motor skills, and they possess a higher center of gravity than older children. Terrain, either indoor or outdoor, may hold enough variation that the child will be unable to process the terrain variations and consequently fall. Fortunately, the majority of times this occurs the child avoids injury, or only receives minor scrapes or bruises that can be handled with kind words, soap, water, and a kiss. Jill's parents bought her new shoes. Knowing that she was growing rapidly, they bought her shoes that were slightly too large. In trying out her new shoes, Jill ran down the hill. As she was running and gaining speed, the loose toe area of her shoe caught on a rock, causing her to tumble down the remainder of the terrain. Fortunately she rolled into a ball and was not injured. There are two points to this story. First, children are more likely to injure themselves when they have clothing or equipment that is inappropriately sized. Second, when moving in novel environments, educators need to be aware that this may pose a safety concern for young children.

Children need to explore uneven terrain to develop their motor skills, but the ground should be free from materials that may pose problems. Outside walkways should be free of ice, snow, leaves, equipment, and other hazards that may cause young children to fall. Steps should be designed for children whenever possible by providing treads and handrailings proportioned to the physical size of the children.

Riding Toys. Toys that children can ride on or in, such as tricycles and wagons, should be stable and balanced. Children should always wear impact-absorbing helmets when riding on tricycles, bicycles, or wagons. Riding should occur only in areas that are safe from vehicular traffic.

Walkers. Walkers have been a staple used for infants and toddlers for many years, but they are the leading causes of injury in children under 2 years of age (Consumer Product Safety Commission, 1993). Parents and caregivers are under the mistaken opinion that the use of walkers by infants and toddlers will result in the child walking sooner. Children need to follow the natural developmental progression through crawling, creeping, and pulling-up to an erect position to develop neuron-dendrite connections and lateralization that are vital for motor and cognitive development. They also need to crawl to develop depth perception, and here is the major problem with the use of walkers and the resulting injury. Crawling allows the child to gain depth perception. If children lack experiences with depth perception they might not be able to judge distances appropriately and when positioned in a walker, they may become unstable and consequently injure themselves. Children using walkers have fallen down stairs or tripped over thresholds or objects on the floor. Thus, we feel strongly that walkers should not be used. This is also a good way to save money in the child care budget!

Trampolines. Trampolines are another piece of equipment that should be avoided in child care centers. Trampolines have caused serious injury to children and this piece of equipment should never be purchased or used with young children.

High Chairs. High chairs are frequently purchased for young children. This piece of equipment is another source of injury. The theory behind the use of these chairs is that they place the child at the same level as the rest of the family during mealtime, and in theory this concept is good. However, young children are active and like to move around and explore their environment. They squirm and remove themselves from the chair, or push the chair away from the table. Both actions will cause the child and/or the chair to fall, resulting in injury. Additionally, the unoccupied chair may become a piece of climbing equipment. Parents and child care workers need to decide philosophically whether the high risk of injury is worth the convenience and bonding gains made by using high chairs. We recommend the use of child-sized chairs in child care centers. If high chairs are used, follow the following guidelines (U.S. Consumer Safety Commission, 1993):

- Chairs should have a broad base of support.
- Children should always be fastened into the chair with the safety straps.
- An adult should always attend to children who are in high chairs.
- Chairs should never be used as climbing devices.
- Chairs should be properly set up. All locking devises must be securely closed.
- Chairs should be placed away from surfaces that could be used to propel the chair.
- Children should not be permitted to stand in high chairs.

Cribs.   Cribs can also be the location of falls. To avoid this from occurring, the side latches should be functioning and securely latched when the child is in the crib. Check the child's standing height on the mattress against the height of the side rails. If the height of the rail is less than ¾ of the baby's height when the mattress is in the lowest position, it is time to obtain a larger crib or to move the child to a regular bed (Kendrick et. al., 1991). Additionally, any toys that a child could use for stacking and climbing should be removed from the crib. Stacking cribs and bunk beds should never be used in child care settings.

Playground.   Playground equipment is one of the leading causes of injury. Approximately 211,000 preschool and elementary children are evaluated in emergency rooms each year for injuries that occur on playground equipment. The majority of these injuries (nearly 70%) occur on public playgrounds while 67% of the deaths occur on home playgrounds. Approximately 9 to 17 children die each year in playground equipment-related accidents, and 31% of these deaths are the result of falls (National Program for Playground Safety, 1999). Most playground injuries occur on swings, monkey bars, climbers, and slides, and falls to the surface are the number one contributing factor in playground injuries (National Program for Playground Safety, 1999).

The majority of the injuries of young children occur to the head and face (60%), whereas older children between 5 and 14 years of age injure their arms and hands. Swings and slides are the most dangerous pieces of equipment for young children. Climbing equipment tends to injure older children more than younger children.

Indoor and outdoor climbing equipment should have impact-absorbing surfaces under the climbers which should extend at least four feet beyond the fall zone to assist in the prevention of fall-related injuries. Impact-absorbing surfaces include shredded bark, sand, gravel, and manufactured rubber mat material. The appropriate amount of each material is listed in Table 5.5 (U.S. Consumer Product Safety Commission, 1994).

Choice of material will depend on budget, age of the children, availability of assistance in maintenance, and the needs of children with disabilities. Some of the listed surfaces would make mobility difficult for children with disabilities.

TABLE 5.5   Loose-Fill Playground Surfacing Materials: Depth Needed

Height Type and Minimum Uncompressed Depth Point of Impact

5 Feet	6 inches of fine sand 6 inches of coarse sand 6 inches of medium gravel
6 Feet	6 inches of double-shredded bark mulch 6 inches of uniform wood chips 6 inches of fine gravel
7 Feet	6 inches of wood mulch 9 inches of uniform wood chips 9 inches of fine gravel
9 Feet	12 inches of fine sand
10 Feet	9 inches of wood mulch 9 inches of double-shredded bark mulch 12 inches of fine gravel
11 Feet	12 inches of wood mulch 12 inches of double-shredded bark mulch

Source: NAEYC, 1998, p. 61.

Rubberized surfaces are expensive and can double the cost of a playground. Gravel is a material that is enticing to toddlers; they practice the pincer grasp by putting gravel into body orifices—which is not a good idea! Sand needs constant maintenance, and raking, to keep the sand from packing. Each center and family who has outdoor climbing equipment must weigh all the choices and pick the best one for their situation, but some form of impact-absorbing equipment must be used. Indoor climbing devices also should have the same impact-absorbing surface as outdoor equipment. Early childhood educators should remind children when they are climbing to use the three-points of contact principle. Their bodies should have three parts in contact with the climbing equipment at all times.

Burns

Burns, as all injuries, can occur quickly and can be the result of thermal, chemical, radiation, or electrical causes. Whatever the cause, the burn results in one of three levels:

- Minor burn without blisters
- Deep burn with blisters
- Deep burn

Medical advice should be sought for deep burns with blisters and deep burns.

Thermal Burns. Thermal burns can be avoided by locating stoves and hot plates away from young children. Having a low barrier between the stove and the child can provide safety yet permit the child to view a cooking activity. If this is not possible, burner shields can be placed on the stove to prevent burns. All pots, when in use, should have handles turned inward, away from the grasp of children.

The temperature of water in areas accessible to children should not exceed 100 degrees Fahrenheit. Thermometers are available at hardware stores and should be used to periodically test the water temperature. Hot water pipes and other sources of heat should have protective guards or insulation to prevent burns.

Portable space heaters should not be placed in areas where children are present. They can cause injury through direct touching by the child or by accidental touching when the heater tips over onto the child. All stationary heaters should be insulated or have protective guards. Fireplaces and wood-burning stoves in child care centers are not advisable and may be against local ordinance. If such appliances are used, they should be securely screened or equipped with protective guards. Fireplace gas valve safety covers are also available and should be used when applicable. Children should never be around an open fire; sparks and wind shifts can result in injury.

Chemical Burns.   Chemical burns result when children are exposed to common household items (drain cleaners, oven cleaners, toilet bowl cleaners, bleach, pesticides, etc.) that should be kept in a locked cabinet. If children are exposed externally to chemical materials that are caustic with the potential to cause burns, the exposed area should be rinsed with flowing cold water for at least 20 minutes. The poison control center should be called.

The most common radiation burns that children are exposed to are the result of exposure to the sun. Parents and child care workers should avoid having children be exposed to prolonged periods in the sun. The sun's rays are most intense between 11 a.m. and 2 p.m., therefore, outdoor play should be avoided during these times. Shady areas should be available at all outdoor play spaces. If trees are not available, structures should be built to provide shade. Sunblocks can be used but should be handled the same as any medication. Parents should be asked to provide the sunblock with a written/dated consent for its use. Information outlining the application of the sunblock should be recorded, and it should never be placed on broken skin. Unfortunately, by the time sunburns are noticed it is too late! Treatment, other than cool compresses or baths, should not be administered without medical advice.

Electrical Burns.   Electrical burns result from exposure to uninsulated electrical current. If this should happen, disconnect the electrical power and call for medical assistance. Measures can be taken to reduce electrical burns by placing protectors on all electrical outlets, and placing the electrical outlets out of the reach of children.

Any of the above can cause a fire and children must be evacuated from the burning building. That is why it is important to maintain proper child/adult ratios even when the children are napping.

Suffocation

Suffocation occurs when the supply of oxygen is curtailed to the child by strangulation, choking, or by being smothered. A precursor to strangulation, choking happens when an object becomes lodged in the airway of an individual and suffocation follows. Young children should never be given toys or objects smaller than 1¼ inches in diameter. Toys that can be taken apart into small pieces should be avoided. This includes popular stuffed toys that many times have small pieces such as eyes and noses that can be removed by a child. Children are very talented at separating toys into parts so toys with small parts and equipment that can be taken apart should be avoided or carefully monitored. Devices are available to check objects for choking potential.

In addition to small toys, aquatic face masks are often purchased for young children taking part in aquatic activities. These can be a potential cause of suffocation and should be avoided.

Young children should not be served food in styrofoam plates or cups nor should they use plastic utensils. Pieces can easily break off of these materials and become a choking hazard. Prepackaged lunch box juices with small straws and crackers and cheese spreads should be avoided unless the straw and the plastic spreader are removed. Both of these small devices have been lodged in children's airways.

Strangulation causes many of the deaths that happen on equipment related to playground accidents. Clothing that children wear should be checked for long strings, hooks, or buttons that may become hooked on the equipment and cause strangulation. All equipment, indoor and outdoor, should be checked to determine if a space is present that could jam a child's head or piece of clothing. Indoors, the cords of blinds, shades, and drapes should be tied out of the reach of children. Never hang objects tied with string or ribbon in a child's crib.

Crib and Playpen.   The design of cribs and playpens is a leading contributor to strangulation. The strangulation of infants and toddlers in cribs is one of the leading causes of injury. Infants and toddlers can get their heads caught between the widely spaced slats of the crib, cutouts in the head/foot board of the crib, or in the space between the sides of the crib and a loose-fitting mattress. When purchasing a crib the following safety criteria should be followed:

- Space between slats should be no more than 2¾ inches
- No end-posts
- No cutouts or decorative knobs
- Must be a snug-fitting mattress (If you can fit two adult fingers between the mattress and the sides of the crib, the fit is too loose.) (Kendrick et. al., 1991)

Portable cribs have become a standard in most homes and in some child care centers. Unfortunately, they have also been the stage for the death of children by strangulation. When purchasing and using portable cribs, care should be taken to ensure that the mesh is a small weave (less than ¼ inch) and that the hinges are latched.

Strangulation can also occur under the same conditions in playpens and the top of a bunk bed and precautions should be taken to avoid injury. Children need to explore environments that are specifically designed for them. Playpens, while they may provide temporary security of the child for caregivers, inhibit movement. We feel strongly that children should be free to explore a child-appropriate and physically safe environment as much as possible. This should certainly be the case in child care centers designed for young children.

Bedding.   Bedding can be the cause of suffocation. If bedding is too soft or if stuffed animals that are large or heavy are placed in the crib, suffocation may result. All plastic wrapping materials should be removed from the child's environment. Trash bags and plastic bags should never be used as mattress pads.

Drowning

Drowning is one of the most common causes of death from injury. The location of drowning of children under 5 years of age varies according to age. Infants and toddlers tend to drown in the bathtub while 2- to 4-year-old children drown in swimming pools and large bodies of water such as lakes and oceans (Canadian Red Cross, 1994). The Consumer Product Safety Commission (CPSC) estimates that approximately 2,300 children under the age of 5 are treated in hospital emergency rooms each year as a result of near-fatal swimming pool accidents. Additionally, 69% of the children who were victims of swimming pool accidents were not expected by their caregivers to be in or at the pool, but they were still found drowned or submerged in the water (Facenda, 1999).

There is no substitute for adult supervision, but there are precautions that can be taken to prevent drowning at swimming pools. All swimming pools (in-ground, above-ground, or on-ground pools, hot tubs, and spas) should be provided with a barrier that is at least 48 inches above ground level, measured on the side of the barrier that faces away from the water surface. A barrier is defined as a fence, a wall, or a building that completely surrounds the water and obstructs access. Gates in the barrier should be self-latching and self-closing. Pool covers and pool alarms are reported to be unreliable and should not be used (Canadian Red Cross Society, 1994).

Children have drowned in natural bodies of water and open holes of water. Additionally, children, especially toddlers, who have mobility but a limited knowledge base and high centers of gravity, have drowned in toilets and 5-gallon, straight-sided buckets. Young children should never be left unsupervised around toilets and 5-gallon buckets should never be available to young children. Caregivers should make sure that water tables and wading pools are always supervised and emptied after each use. Empty containers of water should never be left unguarded. They are hazardous and also provide a breeding ground for bacteria.

Cuts

Children are easily injured—resulting in cuts, bruises, scrapes, splinters, bites, stings, and puncture wounds. A survey of both the indoor and outdoor learning environments for hazards will help minimize such injuries. Check all toys and play equipment for sharp edges, nuts, bolts, and screws that are not flush with the surrounding surface. All wooden equipment should be free of splinters and rough edges. Additionally, metal equipment should be free of rust and chipping paint. Joints should be checked to make sure that they cannot cause pinching or entrapment. All toys and equipment should be checked daily.

Electrocutions

Electrocutions can be avoided by making sure all electrical wires are not exposed and all receptacle outlets and power strips accessible to children 5 years of age or younger have protective covers. Whenever possible outlets should be positioned out of the reach of children. Avoid the use of extension cords and if they must be used they should be placed along the wall and never placed under carpets or rugs. Electrical wire should never be nailed to the wall nor should it be accessible to the young child who may mouth or bite the cord. All electrical appliances and cords should be stored out of the reach of the children when not in supervised use.

Injury Prevention

The first line of attack is to prevent injuries from occurring. Two important components of prevention are supervision and inspection of the environment and equipment.

Supervision

Child care programs can have indoor and outdoor equipment and materials that are safe and appropriate, but if children are not properly supervised all the efforts and expense to ensure a safe learning environment are in vain. Children must be supervised at all times—indoor or outdoor and when asleep or awake. This means that a staff person will be assigned to supervise a specific child and/or group of children. The designated staff person will know the names and whereabouts of the children under his supervision and will physically be present with the children in his group. The National Association for the Education of Young Children (NAEYC, 1998, p. 47) recommends the staff-child ratio and group size shown in Figure 5.1.

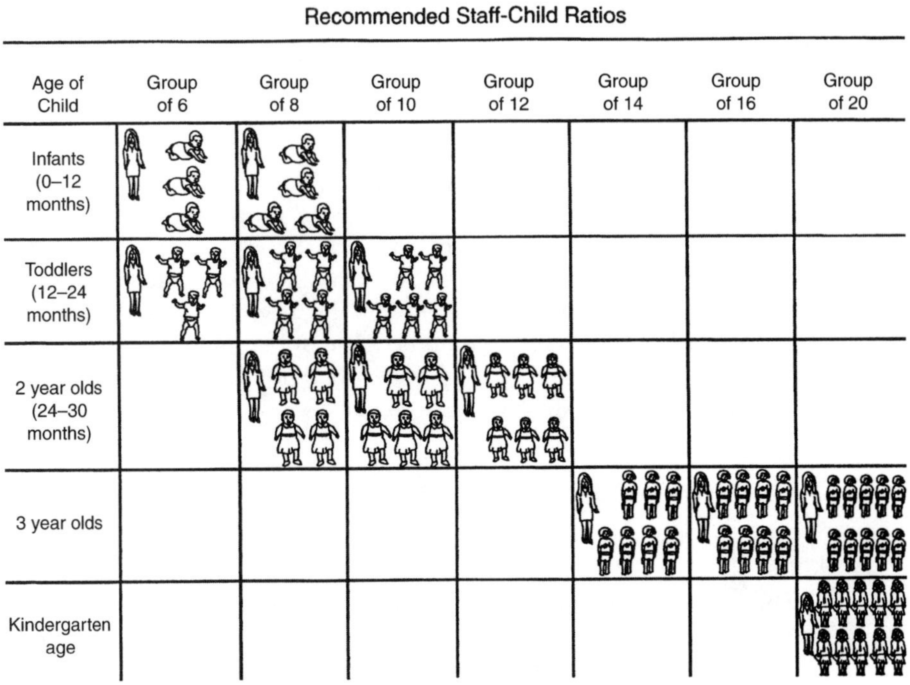

Recommended Staff-Child Ratios

Age of Child	Group of 6	Group of 8	Group of 10	Group of 12	Group of 14	Group of 16	Group of 20
Infants (0–12 months)	✓	✓					
Toddlers (12–24 months)	✓	✓	✓				
2 year olds (24–30 months)		✓	✓	✓			
3 year olds					✓	✓	✓
Kindergarten age							✓

FIGURE 5.1   Adult–Child Ratio

Equipment Inspection

The early childhood educator needs to inspect the environment and equipment. Of special concern for young children are problems related to entrapment; heights; pinch, crush, and sheering points; protrusions; sharp areas; suspended hazards; and protective railings.

Entrapment.   Entrapment is most prevalent with preschool children due to their small size. The size of any opening must be smaller than the width of the child's head and the distance from the top of the head to the tip of the chin. Typically that distance is thought to be from 3½ or 4 inches to between 8 and 9 inches. This distance should be applied to adjacent surfaces such as space between horizontal and vertical ladder rungs, open steps, and deck railings. Nets also need to be examined for entrapment problems.

Height.   The height of equipment is a concern. Protective surfaces need to be installed under equipment. The height of climbing equipment should not exceed several inches above the child's reach.

Pinch, Crush, and Sheering Points.   Points that can cause pinching, crushing, or sheering can be found on the bottom of rotating equipment such as merry-go-rounds and sea-saws. All equipment should be completely enclosed so children cannot insert their small fingers.

Protrusion and Sharp Areas.   Protrusion and sharp areas provide the probability to cut or puncture the child or catch clothing. Exposed bolts, tubing, and protrusions of support posts can potentially catch clothing and cause strangulation.

Suspended Hazards.   Suspended hazards such as cables, ropes, and wires cannot be suspended within 45 degrees off the ground and less than 7 feet above the ground. This does not eliminate cargo nets, guardrails, and climbing grids.

Protective Railings.   Protective railings are required at least 38 inches high around elevated walking surfaces over 30 inches in height. These heights, however, should be reduced for young children. The maximum rail height should correspond to the dimensions of elbow height, that is 26 inches for 5-year-olds and 38 inches for 12-year-olds.

Surfaces.   Surfaces need to be free of unmarked obstacles and broken glass or metal. In addition, all surfaces should be of non-slip material.

Additional Hazards

The learning environment needs to be checked for other hazards. In addition to poisonous plants and toxic materials, staff members should be diligent about checking electrical outlets, exposed air conditioners, electrical switch boxes and guy wires. All electrical equipment must be inaccessible to children. Signs need to be posted on playgrounds. The signs might indicate special features of the playground, curriculum promotion, regulations, etc.

Equipment must be marked with the name, address, and telephone number of the manufacturer. Installation and maintenance guidelines and inspection schedules need to be followed.

Emergency Procedures

Regardless of precautions, accidents do happen. When this does take place every step must be taken to ensure proper medical care for the child and to protect the staff and the child care center from liability. A written procedure for emergencies should be kept updated and staff should be trained accordingly (see Appendix C).

The safety criteria for selection and purchase of equipment should be well documented. The procedures for daily and weekly checks on the equipment must be recorded. Every center should have a written emergency action plan that is routinely practiced. The practice dates should be recorded as well as the individuals involved in the practice.

All parents and staff of a child care center should be trained in CPR for infants, toddlers, and children as well as first aid. A first aid kit should be present at all times, including when on field trips. We have found fannie packs to be wonderful carrying devices for travel first aid kits. Program administrators should post emergency phone numbers, and the staff should have quick and easy access to the parent's or emergency contact person's phone number. These emergency procedures should be practiced monthly. Finally, if an accident should occur, an accident report should be filed as soon as possible. The accident report form (Appendix D) should provide all the information about the injury including where in the learning environment the injury occurred, what part of the child's body is injured, what treatment was used, who administered the treatment, and when and by whom the parents were contacted. This form should be signed by both the parent and by the staff member present when the accident occurred.

We have heard a pediatrician state, "Child care workers are on the front-line. Accidents occur, and they are first on the scene to administer first aid and psychological care. It is a difficult role!" Quality care and maintenance should help to provide a safe environment for young children.

Emergency procedures for poisoning include having the telephone numbers of the local and national poison control centers posted by every telephone in the center and, if possible, programmed into the phone. An up-to-date container of Syrup of Ipecac should be available to induce vomiting if the poison control center advises its use. Do not induce vomiting unless recommended by the poison control center. If the child has swallowed a caustic material, inducing vomiting will cause additional damage as the vomitus material comes back through the esophagus.

At least one child care early educator on duty should have first aid and CPR training. This is a minimum requirement, and it is advisable to exceed the minimum. Just as emergency procedures are written down and practiced, the same is true for fire drills, disaster evacuation, tornado and hurricane drills, and violence control drills (Appendix E).

Many factors contribute to a safe environment for children like Danny and Kyle. Their psychological and physical safety must be ensured so children feel secure to explore their environment. Adults who are responsible for the safety and care of children must feel confident that every precaution has been taken to have a secure learning environment. Following these precautions, the early childhood worker can feel comfortable in letting the children explore the environment and develop to their fullest potential.

Summary

A child should be provided with psychological and physical safety. Psychological safety is important to develop feelings of security that allow the child freedom of exploration. Accidents are a major cause of injury and death to young children and are due to problems in the physical environment. Most childhood accidents can be classified into seven categories: poisonings, falls, burns, suffocation, drowning, cuts, and electrocutions. Parents and teachers should make every effort to ensure that the child care early education environment is safe for children. An important part of a safety routine is equipment inspection and practice of emergency procedures.

CHANGE AND ADVOCACY

1. Design a playground safety checklist and use it on various playgrounds in the area. Report inspection results to the appropriate agencies.

2. Design a puppet show that enforces positive appropriate social interactions.

3. Work with community agencies to improve local playgrounds.

4. Print a newsletter for parents informing them of recall items related to infants, toddlers, and young children.

REFERENCES

Accreditation Criteria & Procedures. (1998). Washington, DC: National Association for the Education of Young Children.

Afifi, A. K., & Bergman, R. A. (2000). *Window of opportunity.* University of Iowa, Virtual Hospital.

Ainsworth, M. D. S. (1979). Infant-mother attachment. *American Psychologist, 34,* 932–937.

Barone, F. J. (1997). Bullying in school, it doesn't have to happen. *Phi Delta Kappan, 79,* 80–82.

Canadian Red Cross Society. (1994). *Drowning.* Red Cross Canadian Provinces: Canadian Red Cross Society.

Children's Defense Fund. (1998). *The state of America's children yearbook 1998.* Washington, DC: Children's Defense Fund.

Children's Defense Fund. (1999). *The state of America's children yearbook 1999.* Washington, DC: Children's Defense Fund.

Children's Defense Fund. (2000). *The state of America's children yearbook 2000.* Washington, DC: Children's Defense Fund.

Crouchman, M. (1986). The effects of babywalkers on early locomotor development. *Developmental Medicine and Child Neurology, 28,* 757–761.

Cummings, E. M.(1980). Caregiver stability and day care. *Developmental Psychology, 16,* 31–37.

Dennis, W. (1973). *Children of the Creche.* New York: Appleton-Century-Crofts.

Derman-Sparks, L., & ABC Task Force. (1989). *Anti-bias curriculum: Tools for empowering young children.* Washington, DC: National Association for the Education of Young Children, Chp. 5.

Facenda, V. (1999). *Safe, not sorry. Bistol, 39* (5), 76–80.

Iverson, T. J., & Segal, M. (1990). *Child abuse and neglect: An information and reference guide.* New York: Garland.

Kendrick, A., Kaufmann, R., & Messenger, K. (1991). *Healthy young children.* Washington, DC: National Association for the Education of Young Children.

Karr-Morse, R., & Wiley, M. S. (1997). *Ghosts from the nursery: Tracing the roots of violence.* New York: Atlantic Monthly Press.

National Association for the Education of Young Children. (1998). *Accreditation criteria & procedures of the National Association for the Education of Young Children.* Washington, DC: National Association for the Education of Young Children.

National Program for Playground Safety. (1999). Cedar Rapids, IA. Retrieved August 20, 1999 from the World Wide Web: http:www.uni.edu/coe/playgrnd

Pennsylvania Department of Welfare, Child Care Division. (1998). Pennsylvania Code 55: 3270.

Pool, C. (1997). Up with emotional health. *Educational Leadership, 54* (8), 12–14.

Rosellini, L. (1999). The risks of day care. *U.S. News & World Report, 126* (16), 64.

U.S. Consumer Product Safety Commission. (1994). *Handbook for public playground safety.* Publication 325, p. 31. Washington, DC: U.S. Consumer Product Safety Commission.

U.S. Department of Health, Education, and Welfare, Office of Human Development/Office of Child Develoment, Children's Bureau/National Center on Child Abuse and Neglect. (1975). *Child abuse and neglect: The problem and its managment.* (DHEW Publications No. OHD 75-30073). Washington, DC: U.S. Government Printing Office.

Wolf, A. D. (2000). How to nurture the spirit in nonsectarian environment. *Young Children, 55* (1) 34–43.

6 Physical Fitness

CHAPTER OBJECTIVES

Knowledge

- The reader will understand the two types of physical fitness and what factors affect their development.

Skills

- The reader will plan developmentally appropriate physical fitness activities for children.

Dispositions

- The reader will value the importance of physical fitness across the lifespan.

CHAPTER SYNOPSIS

Importance of Physical Fitness

Types of Physical Fitness
  Skill-Related Fitness
  Health-Related Fitness

Health-Related Fitness
  Cardiovascular Endurance

Muscular Strength and Endurance
Flexibility
Body Composition
Temperature Regulation

Participation for a Lifetime
  Physically Educated Children

Scenario

As Denise was jogging around the block at 5:30 in the morning, she was reminiscing about her school days. Today was her 45th birthday and her friends had been commenting recently about how healthy she looked, and how she had not changed since high school. She watched what she ate and tried to do something physical every day. One day she might jog, another day bike with her children, and some days play soccer with her family. On days when she was not active, she didn't feel as well as usual. Many of her friends had put on weight and didn't seem to have much energy. As she was reflecting, Denise was so thankful that Mr. Wagner had been her elementary school teacher. He taught her the importance of physical activity and helped her to develop a love of movement. Although she never had the desire to be an athlete, Denise has always wanted to move. Many of her friends hated to sweat. She wondered why they did not like to be physically active and several said that all they ever did in gym class was exercise. They commented on how clumsy and uncoordinated they felt. Denise was glad that Mr. Wagner had made gym fun, and she always felt she had learned. Mr. Wagner never used running as a punishment.

Of increasing importance in today's society is the need for parents and teachers to help young children develop a love of movement and a lifetime commitment to leading a physically active, healthy lifestyle. Physically active adults are less likely to develop health-related risk factors and more likely to maintain independent function longer.

We want children to be intrinsically motivated to be physically active. Most young children love to move. They run throughout the house. Dad frequently states, "I wish I had Eliza's energy." Mom wants to quit throwing the ball for Travis to strike, but he continues to want to run the bases. Something, however, happens as children age. As they move into adolescence children are less likely to be physically active. Why does the child no longer enjoy moving, sweating, and being physically active? Why do they hate gym or drop out of playing soccer? The answer is not simple. One key to help young children maintain this interest in movement is to develop intrinsic motivation. We need to start activity programs early, ensure that the programs are developmentally appropriate, filled with interesting activities, child-directed, and that they incorporate play and spontaneity. The children should be successful and the activities fun. The purpose of this chapter is to provide the early child care educator with the knowledge of the importance of lifetime physical activity, the types of physical fitness, and how the components of physical fitness change across age. We conclude with factors that influence health-related fitness.

Importance of Physical Fitness

Physical fitness is receiving increased attention due to the health-related problems facing adults. Parents, teachers, and children themselves are becoming increasingly aware of the importance of achieving a base level of physical fitness. The benefits of achieving a level of physical fitness have been well documented in the literature. Regular exercise helps adults acquire stronger bones, muscles, ligaments, and tendons; reduce body fat and the risk of coronary artery disease and stroke; and improve flexibility. Proper physical exercise has demonstrated a reduction in mental tension, a relief from depression, improved sleep, and fewer symptoms of stress. In addition, physical activity also appears to reduce the risk of certain cancers, lessen the chance of osteoporosis, and extend life. Related benefits include improved sense of well-being, self-concept, and appearance (Corbin & Lindsey, 1991).

There is clear documentation for the importance of physical activity for adults—but what about physical activity and children? Two questions are important for child care-early educators. Does physical activity in young children prevent current and future health-related problems? Secondly, do physically active children become physically active adults? Although certain health risk factors are present and developing in childhood (Gilliam, MacConnie, Greenen, Pels, & Freedson, 1982), researchers have not been able to support the assumption that children who obtain acceptable levels of fitness evade serious health problems (Payne & Issacs, 1995). It is wise to assume that we will establish a lifestyle approach to health and fitness by encouraging physical activity in young children.

Types of Physical Fitness

Physical fitness can be categorized as either skill-related or health-related.

Skill-Related Fitness

Skill-related fitness affects sport performance and includes agility, reaction time, balance, coordination, speed, and explosive power. Agility is how quickly the child can change directions. The young child is quickly able to move out of the way of the swing she just noticed was about to hit her. Reaction time is how quickly the child can respond to a given signal. Teachers find reaction time important when playing memory games. Suzie rings the bell first after adding 3 + 6 in her head. Explosive power allows the individual to quickly produce a lot of force—as when performing a long jump. Justin runs the path and explodes to jump over the creek. He knows he cannot land in the water and get his new shoes wet.

Health-Related Fitness

Concerned with the components that lead to the reduction of health-related risk factors, health-related fitness includes cardiovascular endurance, strength and muscular endurance, flexibility, and body composition. Poor cardiovascular endurance has been related to heart disease in adults while limited abdominal strength and endurance in combination with low flexibility in the back have been related to lower back pain. Body composition with high levels of body fat is also related to heart disease.

For adults, increased physical activity leads to increased physical fitness as well as the following health benefits (Corbin & Lindsey, 1991; Ratliffe & Ratliffe, 1994):

- Stronger heart and improved cardiovascular fitness
- Lower blood pressure and heart rate
- Reduced risk of heart disease
- Stronger muscles and bones
- Improved flexibility

- More energy for daily activities
- Maintenance of normal body weight (greater lean body mass and lower percentage of fat)
- Greater efficiency for work and play
- Reduced stress and tension

Of concern to teachers of young children are health-related fitness, and how to encourage the development of an active lifestyle. This chapter, therefore, addresses the components of health-related fitness.

Developing physically active children is important due to the relationship between physically active lifestyles and reduced cardiovascular risk factors. Children's fitness levels are alarming. More than 40% of children show one coronary risk factor for cardiovascular disease: obesity, high blood pressure, or high cholesterol blood levels. About one in five children is considered overweight (Dietz, 1998). The prevalence of obesity varies by ethnic group: 5 to 7% of Caucasion and African-American children are obese while 12% of Hispanic boys and 19% of Hispanic girls are obese (Office of Maternal and Child Health, 1989). The increase of the most severe cases has doubled over the past 20 years while the increase in standard cases of obesity has increased by 50% (Gortmaker, Dietz, Sobol, & Webler, 1987). Overweight children tend to become overweight adults (Branddon, Rogers, Wadsworth, & Davies, 1986).

Some of the problems associated with cardiovascular diseases in adulthood are associated with problems in childhood. Problems with high levels of cholesterol, hypertension, and abnormal glucose tolerance are increasing in children (Dietz, 1998).

Children are showing increased health-related risk factors, perhaps because they cannot perform motor skills. Research funded by American Athletic Union and Planters Peanuts found that almost 66% of the nation's children were unable to pass simple, basic physical-fitness tests. Only 5% were judged outstanding in activities such as sit-ups, push-ups, and endurance running. From a sample of 19,000 boys and girls from 187 schools in 57 districts in Michigan, 40% of the boys between the ages of 6 and 12 could not perform more than one pull-up and 25% could not even do one. Seventy percent of the girls 6 to 17 years of age could not perform more than one pull-up and 50% of girls and 30% of boys could not run a mile in less than 10 minutes. The National Children and Youth Fitness Study II (Ross & Pate, 1987) indicate that approximately half of American youth do not reach the minimum weekly requirement of vigorous physical activity.

The remainder of this chapter focuses on the parameters of health-related fitness, and how it can be evaluated.

Health-Related Fitness

This section covers cardiovascular endurance, muscular endurance and strength, flexibility, and body composition. Each section provides a brief overview of the health-related fitness component.

Cardiovascular Endurance

Cardiovascular and cardiorespiratory endurance are used interchangeably in the literature. Cardiovascular endurance, a form of muscular endurance, is a person's ability to transport oxygen to the working muscles and remove waste products.

Body System Changes. The body systems related to cardiovascular endurance include the heart and circulatory system and the lungs and respiratory system. This first section addresses the maturational changes associated with heart rate and blood pressure. The second section covers respiration and breathing.

Cardiovascular System. As children grow, cardiovascular system changes are evident. The heart pumps the blood to the lungs to acquire oxygen. Blood contains hemoglobin that carries oxygen. Once oxygenated, the blood returns to the heart and is pumped to the working muscles. When the blood arrives at the capillaries, oxygen is transported into the working muscle. To understand cardiovascular fitness, we need to understand age-related changes in heart rate, blood pressure, and hemoglobin concentration. Heart rate and blood pressure are responsible for circulating the blood, while hemoglobin carries the oxygen. At the muscular level, we address how much of the oxygen is released to the working muscles (arterial-venous difference). The cardiovascular system is pictured in Figure 6.1.

Heart Rate. Heart rate is first detected about the fourth prenatal week. A newborn has a resting heart rate of about 140 beats per minute (bpm), but by the first birthday the heart rate has decreased to an average of 100 bpm. Around age 6, the resting heart rate of boys decreases to 86 bpm, while that of girls averages about 88 bpm. A steady decrease occurs up to adolescence, when boys average about 66 bpm and girls about 70 bpm. By late adolescence males have a heart rate of 57 to 60 bpm and females between 62 to 63 bpm (Malina & Bouchard, 1991). However by young adulthood (20 year olds), males and females have increased their heart rate and typically average 75 to 79 bpm with little change until about 60 years of age when the heart rate begins to decrease slightly.

Our heart rate changes from when we are at rest (resting heart rate) to when we move (exercise heart rate). The resting heart rate is measured when the individual is not involved in physical work such as walking or running. When lying down your heart rate is lower than when you are sitting and standing. Sitting requires more effort then when you are lying down. The resting heart rate decreases across childhood and early adolescence.

A linear relationship exists between heart rate, physical work, and stress. With increases in effort there is a direct increase in heart rate. For example, the fetal heart rate frequently exceeds 200 bpm during labor contractions. When crying, an infant's heart rate can increase from 140 bpm to over 170 bpm (Vaughan, 1975).

Maximal Heart Rate. Maximal heart rate is the highest heart rate attained during hard exercise. It demonstrates a 0.8 beats/minute/year decline with age (Bar-Or, 1983). Thus, the maximal heart rate of children and adolescents is between 195 to

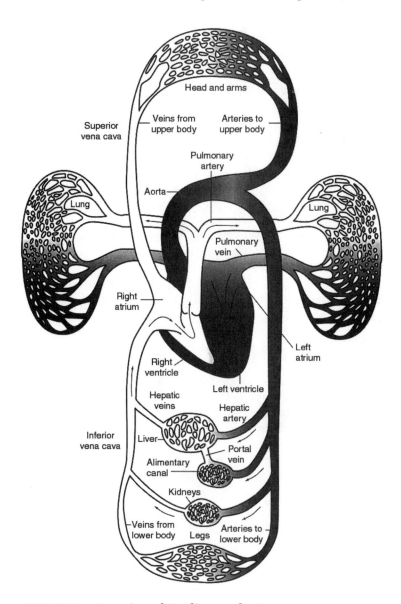

FIGURE 6.1   Drawing of Cardiovascular System

220 bpm. A 5-year-old's highest exercise heart rate is about 216 bpm. Young children have been known, however, to reach heart rates as high as 250 to 300 bpm during short bursts of activity, but when the activity is sustained the rates are significantly lower (Shephard, 1994). After maturity the predicted maximal heart rate attained is determined by the following formula (Astrand & Rodahl, 1986): Maximal HR = 220 – age (years).

Blood Pressure.   Blood pressure is a measure of how hard the heart is working and includes systolic and diastolic pressure. Systolic pressure is the maximum pressure immediately following a heartbeat and increases with age from about 108 to 115 Hg. Hg is the symbol for mercury that is read on the blood pressure gauge. Diastolic pressure is the minimum pressure just before a heartbeat and measures the ease of blood flow. Diastolic pressure ranges from about 72 to 83 millimeters mercury at rest and changes only slightly with exercise. Girls tend to be about 5 to 10 millimeters Hg lower than boys of the same age. Through adolescence, blood pressure demonstrates a slight decrease.

Hemoglobin.   Hemoglobin is another factor that changes with age and fitness level. The oxygen-carrying component of the blood, hemoglobin, increases with age. Even though young children have low hemoglobin concentrations they are more efficient at extracting the oxygen that is in the blood. They have a higher arterial-venous difference in oxygen extraction than do adults.

Respiratory System.   Changes in the respiratory system are also important when understanding cardiovascular endurance. Respiration or ventilation is the process of taking oxygen in through the nose or mouth and delivering it to the lungs, where it is transferred to the blood. The weight and capacity of the lungs doubles in the first 6 months postnatally and triples by the first year. At maturity, the lungs increase approximately 20 fold. The airways increase two to three times in diameter. The bronchial tubes double by age 6 while the trachea doubles by age 15. The air sacks (alveoli) increase in number up to age 8 and increase in size after that. A newborn can inhale about 3 milliliters (ml) of air per gram of tissue while an adult can inhale about 8 to 10 milliliters per gram of tissue.

Breathing increases during exercise in order to provide more oxygen to the blood and muscles. Children's breathing is shallower with more rapid respiration. During exercise children may even appear to hyperventilate.

Maximal Oxygen Consumption.   This is a measure of the maximal amount of oxygen that an individual can use at the tissue level during effort and is used as a measure of the individual's ability to sustain physical work for extended periods of time. Research has provided clear information about maximum oxygen consumption in older children and adults but relatively little data exists on children younger than 6 years of age. For children 6 years and older, the data indicate that maximum oxygen consumption for boys is constant during childhood and adolescence with a sharp increase during the adolescent growth spurt—which appears to be directly related to body size. Girls, on the other hand, are comparable to boys when body weight is accounted for but experience a decrease in maximum oxygen consumption around 10 years of age. Much of this decrease is due to an increase in body fat. Young children are comparable to adults in maximum oxygen consumption when body weight is taken into account.

Gender differences in maximum oxygen consumption are minimal in childhood (1.5%), increase during the adolescent growth spurt (32% at age 16 years), and level to 20% during adulthood (Gabbard, 2000). Maximum oxygen consumption is related to body fat during the adolescent growth spurt. Females increase in percentage of body fat, thus accounting for much of these differences.

Response to Exercise and Training.   Children respond to exercise similarly to adults with no differences between males and females. With increased exercise, heart rate increases directly proportional to the intensity of the exercise. Systolic blood pressure goes up while diastolic pressure does not change. Respiratory rate and volume increase up to about 50 to 65% of the maximum oxygen consumption. After this point, respiration increases rapidly because the body cannot keep up with the oxygen demands or removal of the waste products, and fatigue sets in rapidly.

Aerobic Training.   Aerobic training is becoming increasingly popular. A major question today is whether children benefit from aerobic training similarly to adults. Adults who are training aerobically notice decreased heart rate and blood pressure and increased maximum oxygen consumption, in addition to improved extraction of oxygen at the working muscle. As children age these differences are also evident with the exception of a decrease in extraction of oxygen at the working muscle. Consequently, it is difficult to separate the improvements due to training from those due to growth. Studies fail to show strong effects of training in prepubescent children (Haywood, 1993). Several factors may contribute to these findings. Since children have higher heart rates, their training heart rate might need to be higher. Children are physically active on a daily basis; they play outdoors and raise their heart rates. Haywood concluded that it appears that prepubescent children do not respond to aerobic training similarly to pubescent children, adolescents, and adults. Based on this research it is not advisable to have children run long races. In addition, training can lead to injury. Repeated forceful contractions can cause early closure of the growth plates on the bones causing the specific bone to stop growing.

Training programs designed for adults are not recommended for children. However, we do recommend that children are physically active, at a level sufficient to raise their heart rates, for approximately 20 to 30 minutes a day. This means the children should participate in gross motor activity such that they notice increases in heart and breathing rates. If the staff member notices that a child has difficulty in maintaining this level of physical activity, further assessment should be made.

The child care early educator should allow time for children to run around and be active. Children always love to play tag or be chased. On the playground and in the gross motor room, equipment should be set up to encourage large muscle activity. The equipment should be reorganized and changed frequently to keep the environment novel. Ropes to swing on, ladders to climb, horizontal bars to swing across, and beams of varying widths stimulate the vestibular system and aid in the development of balance.

Muscular Strength and Endurance

Muscle strength is the maximum force that can be generated by a muscle or muscle groups while muscle endurance is the capacity of the muscles to continue to work over an extended time. To understand strength, we will first review muscle development.

Muscle Development. The infant increases in number of muscle fibers for a short time after birth, but thereafter the increase in the size of a muscle is almost exclusively due to a massive increase in the size of the fibers (Lang & Luff, 1990). Children increase in muscular strength during childhood and adolescence with minimal gender differences prior to puberty. At puberty, males increase in testosterone levels and consequently have a sharp increase in muscular strength. Strength increases are due to the cross-sectional size of the muscle; consequently gender differences relating to strength are due to a size difference, not a difference in the nature of the muscle fiber.

Exercise, Strength, and Endurance. Exercise can produce strength gains in boys and girls as young as 6 or 7 years of age (Sewall & Micheli, 1986; Weltman, 1989). During puberty large gains in strength can be seen in boys. Prior to puberty increased strength does not accompany an increase in muscle size but does lead to improvements in ability to exert force in the intended direction and to activate the contracting and lengthening components of the muscular contraction. The child is better able to isolate the required muscles and not contract two opposing muscles at the same time.

Anaerobic Training. In contrast to aerobic exercise, anaerobic (without oxygen) exercise is the maximum rate at which the muscles can work without additional oxygen. This type of activity is vigorous, intense, and of short duration. The response to short, intense bursts of activity require different physiological responses. Children differ from adults in anaerobic performance whether measured relative to body size or in absolute terms. Relative measures take into account the body weight of the individual.

Preadolescent and adolescent boys demonstrate improvement in anaerobic capacity with training (Haywood, 1993). Much of this difference is due, however, to improved skill levels. A major part of determining either aerobic or anaerobic efficiency is in performing the skill. If a child can perform the skill efficiently then she is also conserving energy and will improve her score. For example, when asking a child to jump up, the skilled performer efficiently times muscle contractions and uses muscle force appropriately. The young child, however, contracts more muscles than are necessary and uses more force in the muscles. Therefore, he cannot last as long.

Weight training for prepubescent children is not advisable. Children's bones are still growing and are susceptible to injury—especially at the growth plates. Children should never attempt single maximal lifts. Alternative modes of training children are to use stretch tubing or self-supporting movements that do not place the child at a high level of risk (Siegel, Camaione, & Manfredi, 1989).

Children completing repeated forceful contractions can cause injury to the growing bones. Little League officials noticed an injury problem in children training extensively in baseball. A pattern of children with elbow problems resulted from damage to growth plates at the elbow. Due to these injury patterns, Little League officials initiated rules that restricted the numbers of games a child can pitch, the amount of time a child should spend practicing, and the amount of rest required between games. This rule drastically reduced the number of injuries.

Males, at puberty, have a distinct advantage in strength training due to increased levels of testosterone. However, prior to puberty strength gains are limited. We do not recommend strength training programs for normally developing children with the exception of a very weak child. Strength is not a factor in movement and sport for the young child; skill level makes the difference. After puberty, strength training programs can produce strength benefits in both males and females.

Even though we do not expect strength improvement, we still need to encourage children to participate in strength activities. On the playground, vertical ladders are great to hang from. Developmentally appropriate climbing equipment can be fun. Pushing and pulling activities can also be used as strength activities.

Flexibility

Flexibility refers to the range of motion around a given joint and is joint specific. Tasks that require flexibility are daily tasks such as tying shoes, rising from a chair, and bending to pick up an object. Flexibility is important to complete daily tasks and for injury prevention.

Flexibility is not related to the length of the limbs and does not have to be restricted by increased muscle strength. Females tend to be more flexible than males.

Across the lifespan there is a limited amount of data available on the development of flexibility. Clarke (1975) indicated that flexibility increases throughout childhood, but males start to loose flexibility around 10 years of age and females at about 12 years of age. Activity level, however, is a better indicator of flexibility than is age.

Fitness tests typically measure flexibility of the back, hip, and hamstrings via the sit-and-reach test. This is chosen due to the high frequency of lower-back pain in adults.

To improve flexibility, the individual must move the joint regularly and systematically through an increasingly larger range of motion. Static (slow and gradual) stretching is recommended rather than ballistic (bouncing) stretching. The stretch should go beyond the typical muscle length but not to the point of pain. Adults should not move a child's limbs through her range of motion because they can easily push the child beyond her normal range of motion and cause injury to the joints.

Body Composition

Body mass can be divided into lean and adipose tissue. Lean tissue consists of bone, muscle, and organs while adipose tissue is body fat. Knowing an individual's body composition (percentage of lean body tissue and fat) is important because excess fat is related to increased health risk. In addition to influencing the health risk, body fat also has an influence on the individual's self-concept. Obesity can negatively contribute to self-concept and make it difficult for the obese child to relate to others. Children as young as 6 years of age are aware of prejudice against obese people (Wadden & Stunkard, 1985).

Body Fat. Body fat appears in the fetus about the seventh prenatal month. At birth body fat is approximately 16% and increases to 24 to 30% at 1 year of age. Body fat tends to decrease from the onset of walking until approximately 6 years of age—when it is about 14% (Sinclare, 1985). Some children increase in body fat percentage between 5 and 7 years of age. After this time, males cease to increase in body fat but females continue to do so throughout the adolescent years. Females have more body fat than males at all ages, with greater differences during and after puberty.

Fat cell number increases threefold throughout the first year of life and gradually increases until the onset of the growth spurt—at which time the number of cells increases significantly. Research suggests that fat cells are prone to over-multiply if overfeeding occurs during the early stages of life (Hager, Sjostrom & Arvidsson, 1977). The number of fat cells becomes fixed by adulthood and increases in size with the exception of extreme obesity (Brooks & Fahey, 1985).

Body weight is not an accurate indication of body composition. Muscle weighs more than body fat. Two individuals can weigh the same but have very different body compositions. One can have a high percentage of lean body mass and low body fat while the other can have a significantly greater proportion of body fat and be classified as obese.

Obesity is increasing at an alarming rate. It is important for the child to understand body composition and its relationship to physical activity and nutrition. Not only does obesity increase health risks, but it also affects motor performance. Shirley (1931) discovered that heavy babies demonstrated greater delays in walking than did lighter babies. Jaffe and Kosakov (1982) found that 29% of the fat babies and 36% of the obese babies demonstrated motor development delays. Only 9% of the normal weight infants demonstrated motor development delays. These results must be interpreted cautiously since the body mass index (height/weight ratio) was used to determine obesity—not body composition.

Body fat is related to cardiovascular endurance. Pissanos, Moore, and Reeve (1983) found that, for 6- to 10-year-olds, the sum of the skinfolds was the best predictor of cardiovascular performance. Body fat percentage is quantified by pinching the skin at various body sites (i.e., triceps, subscapular, calf) and measuring the thickness. The total of the various sites is then compared to the norm. Children with higher levels of body fat ran slower in the mile and 600-yard run than did leaner children (Slaughter, Lohman, & Misner, 1977; Slaughter, Lohman, & Misner, 1980).

Of concern to child care early educators is whether fat children become fat adults. Tracking research has investigated this issue. Unfortunately, the research shows that the fattest children at age 6 have a greater risk of becoming fat adults. Obesity occurs when the energy intake (calories from food) exceeds the energy expended through normal daily activities and growth. Throughout this book we refer to appropriate nutrition and sufficient physical activity to maintain a healthy weight. As educators of young children we must understand obesity and work to prevent children from becoming obese and possibly growing into obese adults.

Next we address issues related to temperature regulation. Understanding how environmental temperature affects children differently than adults, we address issues of children working, playing, and exercising in hot and cold environments.

Temperature Regulation

Children are exposed to all types of environments, ranging from the hot and humid climates of the south to the extremely cold climates of the north. It is important to understand that children and adults do not respond to hot or cold climates in a similar way. Children's sweat glands are not fully developed and consequently do not dissipate heat as well as those of adults. Children also dehydrate rapidly. This means that they feel overheated before the teacher does and also lose water faster. In addition, children do not acclimatize to heat as well as adults. When there is a rise in temperature it takes the child longer to adjust to the hot environment. Consequently, a child can suffer heat-related problems much quicker than an adult.

Children also have a greater problem in colder climates. When exposed to the cold, they loose their body heat quicker, especially young infants. Children need to be clothed in layers; as the temperature rises they can shed clothing and not run the risk of overheating.

Sweating is not a good predictor of exercise intensity or effort for either adults or children. We tend to sweat more in hot and humid climates than on hot, low humidity days. The evaporation mechanism is what is important. The evaporation of sweat from the skin cools the blood in capillaries near the skin's surface—which in turn helps to maintain optimal temperature level. If the adult is hot, the child probably feels the heat to a greater degree since his sweat glands are not completely developed. Thus it is extremely important for the staff in direct contact with the children to allow frequent water breaks and, when necessary, time to rest and cool down in the shade. Water should be available in the classroom and on the playground. Children should be encouraged to drink frequently, and teachers need to watch for signs of dehydration. These signs include muscle cramping, non-resiliant skin, and problems with movement.

In cold environments, especially when swimming in cold water, we need to listen to the child. We should not think, just because we are not shivering, that the child is fine. We need to look for signs of temperature loss (blue lips and shivering).

Throughout this section we have presented the research underlying the development of health-related fitness throughout childhood. The final section provides recommendations for helping young children to develop an understanding of physical fitness and its importance across the lifespan.

Participation for a Lifetime

The National Children and Youth Fitness Study (Dotson & Ross, 1985; Pate & Ross, 1987) attempted to find factors that influence a child's performance on a physical fitness test. The age range of the children studied was from 5 to 18 years. The results indicated that those children who did better on fitness tests tended to participate in more community-based activities, watch less television, have physical education instruction from a specialist, be exposed to more types of activities, and be in a family that was more active. This research indicates that children need to be exposed to physical activity early and be able to choose a physical activity at which they feel successful. Teachers and parents need to be good role models. Children need to see their parents engage in physical activity because the **family that participates together stays healthy together!**

In a survey of children, over 75% exceeded the standard recommended (Blair, Clark, Cureton & Powell, 1989) to achieve fitness. This is important since some suggest that activity levels exhibited during childhood may influence adult levels of activity (Armstrong, 1992). If this conclusion is upheld, it underscores the importance of encouraging children to be physically active.

Physically Educated Children

We first need to understand who is the physically educated individual. The American Alliance for Health, Physical Education, Recreation, and Dance published a document that defined the Physically Educated Person (Franck, Graham, Lawson, Loughrey, Ritson, Sanborn, & Seefeldt, 1991). The definition includes four aspects related to being physically educated: Is, Does, Knows, and Values. To be physically educated (IS) individuals need to be physically fit and know how to design appropriate programs. They are physically active (DOES). They have developed the knowledge about physical fitness (KNOWS). And finally they value the feelings attained from achieving fitness and understand its importance in a healthy lifestyle (VALUE). The definition of a physically educated person helps to determine a developmental sequence.

When planning lessons, the teacher needs to consider knowledge, skills, and dispositions. We need to develop concepts as we acquire the skills to achieve fitness. In addition, developing a value system that includes the importance of achieving fitness is critical. Young children need to love to move. Once the door is open to the outdoors, children are much more likely to run than walk. They enjoy telling each other how sweaty or strong they are. Infants and toddlers enjoy the rush of air on their faces when being held by a rapidly moving parent. They laugh and giggle. We need to reward this initial movement passion so that children continue to enjoy a lifetime of physical activity and fitness.

Summary

Participating in physical activity is important for a lifetime of health. Early childhood is an important time to develop intrinsic motivation for children to move. We need to realize, however, that young children are not miniature adults. Children are psychologically and physiologically different from adults. We need to understand the physical changes that occur with age and how these changes affect motor performance and fitness measures. Even within a given age, children are very different. Emphasizing the importance of physical activity, providing time during the day to be physically active, exposing children to a variety of activities, and being a good role model are essential for the promotion of a healthy lifestyle.

CHANGE AND ADVOCACY

1. Contact state and federal legislators to provide mandatory movement programs in child care early education programs.

2. Design a puppet show for young children emphasizing the importance of exercise and fitness in a healthy lifestyle.

REFERENCES

Armstrong, N. (1992). Are American children and youth fit? Some international perspectives. *Research Quarterly for Exercise and Sport, 63,* 449–450.

Astrand, P. O., & Rodahl, K. (1986). *Textbook of work physiology* (3rd ed.) New York: McGraw Hill.

Bar-Or, O. (1983). *Pediatric sports medicine for the practitioner.* NY: Springer-Verlag.

Blair, S. N., Clark, D. G., Cureton, K. J., & Powell, K. E. (1989). Exercise and fitness in childhood: Implications for a lifetime of health. In C. V. Gisolfi, & D. R. Lamb (Eds.), *Perspectives in exercise science and sports medicine: Youth, exercise, and sport.* Indianapolis: Benchmark.

Braddon, F., Rogers, B., Wadsworth, M., & Davies, J. (1986). Onset of obesity in a 36 year birth cohort study. *British Medical Journal, 193,* 299–303.

Brooks, G. A., & Fahey, T. D. (1985). *Exercise physiology: Human bioenergetics and its applications.* New York: Macmillan.

Clarke, H. H. (Ed.). (1975). Joint and body range of movement. *Physical Fitness Research Digest, 5,* 16–18.

Corbin, C. B., & Lindsey, R. (1991). *Concepts of physical fitness with laboratories* (7th ed.). Dubuque, IA: Brown.

Dietz, W. (1998). Health consequences of obesity in youth: Childhood predictors of adult disease. *Pediatrics, 101,* 518–525.

Dotson, C. O., & Ross, J. G. (1985). Relationships between activity patterns and fitness. *Journal of Physical Education, Recreation, and Dance, 56,* 86–89.

Franck, M., Graham, G., Lawson, H., Loughrey, T., Ritson, R., Sanborn, M., & Seefeldt, V. (1991). *Physical education outcomes: A project of the National Association for Sport and Physical Education.* Reston, VA: National Association for Sport and Physical Education.

Gabbard, C. (2000). *Lifelong motor development* (3rd ed.). Boston: Allyn and Bacon.

Gilliam, T. B., MacConnie, S. E., Greenen, D. L., Pels, A. E., & Freedson, P. S. (1982). Exercise programs for children: A way to prevent heart disease? *Physician and Sports Medicine, 10,* 96–109.

Gortmaker, S., Dietz, W., Sobol, A., & Webler, C. (1987). Increasing pediatric obesity in the United States. *American Journal of Disabled Children, 141,* 535–540.

Hager, A., Sjostrom, L., & Arvidsson, B. (1977). Body fat and adipose tissue cellularity in infants: A longitudinal study. *Metabolism, 26,* 607–614.

Haywood, K. M. (1993). *Life span motor development.* Champaign, IL: Human Kinetics.

Jaffe, M., & Kosakov, C. (1982). The motor development of fat babies. *Clinical Pediatrics, 21,* 619–621.

Lang, G. J., & Luff, A. R. (1990). Skeletal muscle growth, hypertrophy, repair, and regeneration. In E. Meisami & P. S. Timiras (Eds.), *Handbook of human growth and developmental biology: (Vol. 3).* Boca Raton, FL: CRS Press.

Malina, R. M., & Bouchard, C. (1991). *Growth, maturation, and physical activity.* IL: Human Kinetics Books.

Office of Maternal and Child Health. (1989). *Child health USA '89.* Washington, DC: U.S. Department of Health and Human Services, National Maternal and Child Health Clearinghouse. ED 314–421.

Pate, R. R., & Ross, J. G. (1987). Factors associated with health-related fitness. *Journal of Physical Education, Recreation, and Dance, 58,* 71–73.

Payne, V. G., & Issacs, L. D. (1995). *Human motor development: A lifespan approach.* Mountain View, CA: Mayfield.

Pissanos, B. W., Moore, J. B., & Reeve, T. G. (1983). Age, sex, and body composition as predictors of children's performance on basic motor abilities and health-related fitness items. *Perceptual and Motor Skills, 56,* 71–77.

Ratliffe, T., & Ratliffe, L. M. (1994). *Teaching children fitness: Becoming a master teacher.* Champaign, IL: Human Kinetics.

Ross, J., & Pate, R. (1987). The national children and youth fitness study II: A summary of findings. *Journal of Physical Education, Recreation, and Dance, 56,* 51–56.

Sewall, L., & Micheli, L, J. (1986). Strength training for children. *Journal of Pediatric Orthopedics, 6,* 143–146.

Shephard, R. J. (1994). *Aerobic fitness & health.* Champaign, IL: Human Kinetics.

Shirley, M. (1931). *The first two years: A study of twenty-five babies.* Minneapolis: University of Minnesota Press.

Siegel, J. A., Camaione, D. M., & Manfredi, T. G. (1989). The effects of upper body resistance training on pre-pubescent children. *Pediatric Exercise Science, 1,* 145–154.

Sinclare, D. (1985). *Human growth after birth* (4th ed.). Oxford: Oxford University Press.

Slaughter, M., Lohman, T., & Misner, J. (1977). Relationship of somatotype and body composition to physical performance in 7- to 12-year-old boys. *Research Quarterly, 48*(1), 159–168.

Slaughter, M., Lohman, T., & Misner, J. (1980). Association of somatotype and body composition to physical performance in 7–12 year-old-girls. *Journal of Sports Medicine and Physical Fitness. 20*(2), 189–198.

Vaughan, V. (1975). The cardiovascular system. In V. Vaughan & R. McKay (Eds.), *Nelson textbook of pediatrics* (10th ed.). Philadelphia: Saunders.

Wadden, T. A., & Stunkard, A, J. (1985). Social and psychological consequences of obesity. *Annals of Internal Medicine, 103,* 1062–1067.

Weltman A. (1989). Weight training in prepubertal children: Physiologic benefit and potential damage. In. O. Bar-Or (Ed.), *Advances in pediatric sport science: Vol. 3.* Champaign, IL: Human Kinetics.

PART THREE

Movement Issues Concerning Infants, Toddlers, and Young Children

Movement Development

CHAPTER OBJECTIVES

Knowledge
- The reader will comprehend the steps in conducting a movement task analysis.

Skills
- The reader will analyze a movement skill to determine a developmental sequence of instruction.

Dispositions
- The reader will value the importance of designing a learning environment that permits the child to achieve success while challenging the development of movement skill.

CHAPTER SYNOPSIS

General Intertask Developmental Sequence
    Reflexes and Reactions
    Rudimentary Movement
    Movement Concepts
    Fundamental Motor Patterns
    Proficiency Barrier
    Transitional Skills

    Sport-Specific Skills and Fitness
Intratask Sequences
    Classical Stage Theory
    Probability Theory
    Component versus Whole Body Analysis
Skill Progression, Task Complexity, and Task Analysis
    Task Analysis

Scenario

Watching the children in his class practice kicking, Mr. Ladewig was pleased that all the children were actively involved. Each child had a ball to kick into his or her own crate. Every time they were successful in reaching the target they took a step back to increase the difficulty of the task. Everyone was laughing, having fun, and was successful at his or her own level of skill. What Mr. Ladewig saw in his class was different from what he observed in Ms. Smith's class. She felt that the children would learn fundamental motor patterns and sport skills by playing a game of kickball. At the start of the game, Ms. Smith told the children where to stand and what positions they were playing. Half the children were spread out in the outfield and half were clumped around home plate. Ms. Smith had the best athlete pitching the ball. Even though the 4-year-old was good at rolling, getting the ball across the plate was difficult for her. When the pitcher was able to get the ball across the plate, it was rare that the kicker could make contact with the ball. Sometimes the kicker would kick before the ball arrived, sometimes he would fall on top of the ball. On the rare instances that the kicker did make contact with the ball, he didn't know what to do! Ms. Smith had to instruct him to run to first base. The outfielders, if paying attention, would watch the ball roll by them and then start chasing the ball. As they got close, they would bend down to get the ball but instead their feet would hit the ball and cause it to shoot away. Eventually they would retrieve the ball and run to home plate. Tired of standing in the outfield and bored at watching one child kick at a time, Gail decided to practice her skipping. Most of the other children in Ms. Smith's class were also bored. Mr. Ladewig realized that the children in Ms. Smith's class did not have the prerequisite skills to play kickball. The children needed to learn how to roll, throw, catch, and kick prior to attempting to put the skills together.

Mr. Ladewig realized the importance of young children acquiring motor skills, and he also knew that until children have learned the movement skills required to play a game, they are not ready to play the game. Without these skills, children will be unsuccessful in playing the game and may become bored and frustrated. How many T-ball games have you watched where the children are playing with their caps, making a whistle with the grass between their two thumbs, or entertaining themselves watching insects in the grass?

Relating to the windows of opportunity discussed in Chapter 2, an opportune time to acquire gross motor skills is during the early childhood years. Children optimally acquire motor skills at very young ages. However, for optimum learning to occur, an appropriate progression of activities must be designed for the child. To determine this, the skills that the child can already perform must be analyzed. Matching the child's level of performance to a developmental progression of the skill assists the teacher in guaranteeing success during the learning process.

The purpose of this chapter is to develop the knowledge to analyze or break down a skill to teach using developmentally appropriate guidelines. In order to do this, first we discuss the two types of sequences, intertask and intratask. Next we create a general developmental intertask sequence followed by giving specific examples of intratask sequences. Finally, we examine how to complete a task analysis.

To help the teacher in planning a lesson in which all children are successful it is important to understand the two types of sequences covered in this chapter—intertask and intratask. An intertask sequence is a progression of skills in which the new skill is based upon movements acquired when learning previous skills in the sequence. Another name for an intertask sequence is developmental sequence. As the child progresses through the intertask sequence, complexity increases. An example of an intertask sequence for jumping was included in Chapter 2. An example of an intertask sequence for an infant would be the development of walking. Children will initially push up to balancing on their hands and knees. As they develop this skill they will rock back and forth. This then leads to crawling and creeping. After developing the skill of creeping, they start to pull to a stand. They need to hold onto an object in order to balance themselves. As they continue to explore and develop their gross motor skills, they start to move while holding onto something. Eventually they will let go of the support, stand for a few moments, and then fall. Next they are able to stand unsupported and, later, walk without support.

Intratask sequences are changes that occur within a specific movement, or the qualitative changes in a skill from the first attempts through the attainment of skilled behavior. When children first start to run, their steps are short and wide. The teacher can hear the children running because they contact the ground with a flat foot. As the skill of running is developed, the arms gradually move down and swing in opposition to the legs, the stride length increases, the base of support decreases, and a heel-toe roll appears. The next section provides an overview of the timing of skill development throughout childhood.

General Intertask Developmental Sequence

Adapting Seefeldt's (1980) general progression of skill attainment, we have included another level. Starting with reflexes and reactions and moving to rudimentary movement, we next include movement concepts (see Figure 7.1). This is the language of movement and is important when learning the skills at the next level—fundamental motor patterns. Between fundamental motor patterns and transitional skills a proficiency barrier exists. The top of the progression includes sport-specific skills, dance, and fitness. The next sections explain a general intertask sequence.

Reflexes and Reactions

Reflexes are involuntary, subcortically controlled movements and are elicited by a particular sensory stimulus such as light, sound, touch, or pressure. Reflexes and reactions allow the infant to gain information about the immediate environment and learn more about the relationship between the body and outside world. Reflexes and reactions are important for survival (e.g., sucking, rooting), perception (e.g., depth perception, object constancy), and maintaining posture (e.g., tonic neck, head righting). The absence or presence of a reflex is used to test the neuromotor maturation of newborns. If a reflex is absent, irregular, uneven in strength, or prolonged, neurological dysfunction is suspected. Within the first five minutes after

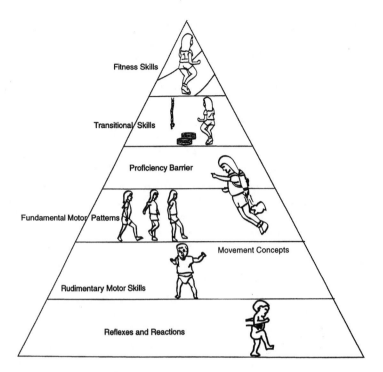

FIGURE 7.1   Developmental Pyramid

birth, the newborn's reflexes are tested and an Apgar score is given (Apgar, 1953). On a ten-point scale infants are given ratings from 0 to 2 for heart rate, respiratory effort, irritability, muscle tone, and skin color—with a higher number indicating complete neuromotor maturation. If the child is given a score of 7 or better he is deemed to be in good physical condition. A score between 4 and 6 indicates that the baby requires special help in establishing breathing and other vital signs. A score below 4 denotes that the infant is in serious danger and immediate medical attention is required.

Types of Reflexes

Primitive Reflexes.   Reflexes are categorized as primitive, postural, or locomotor. Primitive reflexes are for nourishment and protection and typically last from birth into the first year of life. Initially these reflexes are strong and then gradually weaken with advancing maturity until they are no longer stimulated. The primitive reflex of rooting (search) is elicited when there is stimulation in the mouth area, and the infant responds by turning her head toward the source of stimulation. This reflex is strongest during the first three weeks of life, but the infant gradually gains control and becomes purposeful in bringing the mouth into contact with the nipple. The sucking reflex is elicited most easily when the child is hungry, sleeping, or in the normal feeding position. Touching of the lips, gums, tongue, or hard palate elicits the sucking reflex.

Postural Reflexes.   Postural reflexes coordinate movements of the head, trunk, and limbs so that the body can automatically adjust its posture according to changing environmental conditions. They generally appear after the second month and decline late in the first year or early in the second year. Examples of postural reflexes are pull-up, parachute, and propping reflexes. The pull-up reflex is an involuntary attempt of the infant to maintain upright posture. If an infant who is sitting upright with one or both hands held is tipped backward, she will flex her arms in an attempt to remain upright. If tipped forward a similar response occurs. This reflex usually appears around the third or fourth month and continues through the first year. The parachute and propping reactions are elicited for protection. They occur in response to a sudden force or when balance cannot be maintained. These reflexes depend on visual stimulation and cannot be elicited in the dark. When held vertically in the air and tilted toward the ground, the infant will extend the arms downward in an apparent attempt to cushion the anticipated fall. Pushing the infant off balance from a sitting position stimulates the propping reflex. These postural reflexes begin to appear around the fourth month and persist beyond the first year. These are necessary before the infant can learn to walk since they protect the child in the case of a fall.

Locomotor Reflexes.   Locomotor reflexes appear to be actions related to the voluntary behaviors from which they take their names. They typically disappear weeks before the infant actually attempts the voluntary locomotor skill. The crawling reflex generally exists at birth and disappears around the third or fourth month. This reflex is stimulated when the infant is in a prone position (on her stomach) and pressure is applied to the sole of one foot. The infant will reflexively crawl using both arms and legs. The swimming reflex is similar to the crawling reflex. Infants are capable of locomotion in the water.

Certain primitive reflexes must disappear or become inhibited, and certain postural reactions must appear before specific voluntary motor acts can be attained. As an example, there must be inhibition of the asymmetric tonic neck reflex for derotative righting to occur. The asymmetric tonic neck reflex is elicited when the infant is on his back and his head is turned toward either side. The arms and legs assume a fencer's "on guard" position. The arm and leg on the side of the body that the head is facing are extended and the other arm and leg are flexed. If the asymmetric tonic neck reflex is still apparent when the child turns his head to initiate the roll, his arm toward which he turns is extended and blocks the roll. A voluntary roll cannot occur if a tonic neck reflex exists. Derotative righting occurs when the head is turned to the side and the body follows. The child appears to have rolled over. Derotative righting is necessary prior to voluntary roll. The infant gains experience in turning the pelvis and spine sequentially during derotative righting.

Photo of asymmetric tonic neck reflex.

In order for upright stance and ambulation to occur, the child must not demonstrate the plantar grasp reflex. If the bottom of the foot is stimulated and the toes curl under, the infant's foot will not be in complete contact with the ground and standing will be difficult (see Figure 7.2).

Plantar Grasp   Stepping Reflex   Leads to Walking

Controlled

FIGURE 7.2   Plantar Grasp Reflex Controlled, Stepping Reflex Leading to Walking

Rudimentary Movement

Rudimentary movement involves stability movements such as gaining control of the head, neck, and trunk muscles; the manipulative tasks of reaching, grasping, and releasing; and the locomotor movements such as creeping, crawling, and walking. Many of the motor milestones (sitting, crawling, creeping, standing) are developed during this phase of development and can occur only after the infant has gained control of a series of body parts. The average age of attainment of the motor milestones are well-documented (Bayley, 1935; Shirley, 1963) and are fundamental to skilled performance.

Rudimentary movements are the beginning combinations that excite parents and increase their anticipation concerning their child's impending motor milestones, but more importantly these combinations provide the infant with the ability to practice emerging motor skills. We see this practicing when the infant is on all fours and rocks back and forth in rhythm to her cooing. Another example is when the infant, who has just gained the ability to ungrasp an object, will drop a toy to the ground repeatedly.

Movement Concepts

Previous general developmental pyramids are based on the development of motor skills. A component that has been missing from the pyramids but critical to learning motor skills is the development of movement concepts. To learn motor skills, the child must understand the concepts that underlie motor skill performance. The learner initially needs to develop a movement vocabulary prior to being able to understand, analyze, and modify motor skills. Movement concepts should be developed in early childhood. In this chapter we briefly discuss movement concepts but cover them in depth in Chapter 8. Concepts can be divided into:

- Body Awareness—What the body can do
- Space Awareness—Where the body moves
- Movement Qualities—How the body moves
- Relationships—To whom and what the body relates

Body Awareness.   Body awareness includes a knowledge/awareness of the body and how it is controlled and moved. Concepts that are included in body awareness are the shapes that the body can make (wide, narrow, stretched, curled, twisted), on what body parts the body can balance, and how weight is transferred from one body part to the next.

Space Awareness.   Space awareness includes where the body moves. It is important for young children to understand their relationship in space. Concepts included are general and self-space, direction (forward, backward, sideways, diagonally, and up and down), pathways (straight, narrow, zig-zag), and levels (high, middle, low).

Movement Qualities.   Movement qualities include speed, force, and flow. Flow can be broken into bound and free. Bound flow occurs for movements that the individual can stop at any given time. Free movements are continuous and cannot be stopped once initiated.

Relationship Awareness.   Relationship awareness includes to whom and to what the child's body relates. It can include body parts with objects and people, and people with people. One of the first concepts that must be developed in early childhood is the child's relationship to other people and objects. A child needs to understand, for example, where he is in relation to other children and the swings to avoid getting hit by a swing.

Movement concepts are used to develop the range and efficiency of skilled movement. Once children have an understanding of movement concepts, they can increase the range and repertoire of their movement abilities.

Parents and educators are constantly developing movement concepts when they are interacting with children. The simple challenge to stretch up to the sky or to roll across the room helps to develop relationship awareness. Children will also develop this relationship on their own. Eighteen-month-old Colby was grocery shopping with her mother. While in the produce section, her mother was momentarily distracted, and Colby climbed on a pile of potato sacks. From her lofty position Colby gained a different perspective of the world and of her mother frantically looking for her.

Fundamental Motor Patterns

As children gain strength and develop postural control and balance they start to acquire fundamental motor patterns classified as locomotor (e.g., running, skipping, hopping), non-locomotor (e.g., bending, twisting, pushing, pulling), and manipulative (e.g., catching, throwing, kicking). During this phase (typically the preschool and early elementary school years), children develop skills such as running, jumping, catching, and throwing. The level of performance that a child develops is directly related to experience.

Seefeldt and Haubenstricker (1982) have documented age-related attainment of the various levels of fundamental motor patterns. Boys and girls display an immature overhand throw for force around the age of 3 years and acquire a more efficient pattern around 5 years of age for boys and 8.5 years of age for girls. Mature catching develops before 7.5 years of age for girls and after 7.5 years for boys (see Figure 7.3). These age-related guides should be used to determine the ages at which most children are likely to have demonstrated the mature skill pattern and are ready to begin to adjust the skill for sport-specific movement. More importantly, these guides emphasize the importance of teaching the fundamental motor skills. Remember, if an 8-year-old child displays an immature running pattern—his foot lands flat—he is not wrong, that is simply the level he has achieved.

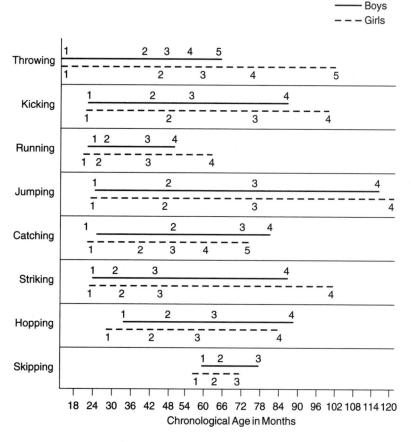

FIGURE 7.3   Age of Attainment of Fundamental Motor Patterns

Reprinted with premission of John Wiley & Sons, from Seefeldt, V., & Haubenstricker, J. (1982). Patterns, phases, or stages: An analytical model for the study of developmental movement. In J. A. S. Kelso & J. E. Clark (Eds.) *The development of movement control and coordination* (p. 314).

After reading the last paragraph you might have noticed gender differences in movement. The question is, "Are these differences between boys and girls genetic or are they due to practice?" The basic answer is practice! French and Thomas (1985) analyzed 64 previous studies on gender differences in motor skills. They found that gender differences were related to age for balance, catching, dash, grip strength, long jump (jumping for distance), shuttle run (run between two lines), sit-ups, tapping speed, and the vertical jump (jumping up). The males were typically somewhat ahead of the females but the gender differences were minimal until the adolescent growth spurt (where males gain a distinct size advantage). French and Thomas attributed these gender differences to environmental factors such as encouragement, practice, and parental and peer expectations. However, for throwing, they found that the boys were very different from the girls. There was minimal overlap in the throwing outcome scores and the average boy's distance throw was greater than the 99th percentile for girls. The question remains as to why gender differences in throwing performance are much greater than those for other tasks. Are they due to mechanical differences in throwing form or are they due to early encouragement? Needless to say, we need to have equally high expectations in all areas of movement for both boys and girls.

Fundamental motor patterns are the building blocks that allow the child to successfully develop more complex movements. It is essential that early movement experience begin with exposure and instruction in fundamental skill development. The teacher of young children can develop skill themes to enhance the development of fundamental motor patterns and apply movement concepts to learning fundamental motor patterns. Skill themes can be categorized into locomotor, manipulative, and nonmanipulative skills. Locomotor skills are walking, running, hopping, skipping, galloping, sliding, chasing, fleeing, and dodging. Manipulative skills include throwing, catching, kicking, punting, dribbling, volleying, and striking. Non-manipulative skills include turning, twisting, rolling, balancing, transferring weight, jumping and landing, stretching, and curling.

Proficiency Barrier

Between fundamental motor pattern and transitional skill development a proficiency barrier commonly exists. If the child has not learned prerequisite fundamental skills, combinations of fundamental motor patterns will not occur. For example, if a child has not learned how to efficiently walk and hop he will not learn a combination of these patterns to form the skip.

Transitional Skills

Commonly occurring during the late elementary and middle school years, the transitional period includes what traditionally has been viewed as lead-up games that begin to combine the fundamental motor patterns into game-like situations. It is important to recognize that lead-up games are structured to permit success without the level of skill or complexity of the environment that are required in the adult versions of the games. Once children have learned to throw and catch they can play a game of "three player keep away." The purpose of this game is to practice the skills of throwing and catching under changing conditions. The throws are no longer easy to catch, and the catcher must move to catch the ball.

Sport-Specific Skill and Fitness

The final level of skill progression is the specialization of sport skills, dance, and the maintenance of fitness. Early learning and sport achievement do not automatically lead to successful performance. Clarke (1967) demonstrated a low correlation for prediction of future success based on sport performance. Only 25% of the boys deemed outstanding athletes during both the elementary and junior high school years were considered outstanding during the senior high school years. Since physical size and coordination advantages may disappear, childhood athletes and their parents should understand that continued practice and skill development are essential for continued success. Additionally, they should understand that biological maturity may bring another athlete to prominence and that less success does not indicate lack of effort. Caution must be taken that a prepubertal child not overspecialize in any one sport activity.

The general intertask sequence of motor skills should be used to develop a general progression of skills. The teacher must understand that preschool children are moving between reflexes and reactions, rudimentary movement and fundamental motor patterns while developing movement concepts. Understanding quality of movement by reviewing intratask sequences is covered next.

Intratask Sequences

Intratask sequences focus on changes that occur within a given task until the task is mastered. The components of the skill are analyzed to determine levels of progression. This sequence describes the change from an immature motor skill to an advanced mature pattern. For example, recall how young children first attempt to throw a ball (see Figure 7.4). When Salli first attempted to throw the ball, she merely flexed and extended her arm at the elbow (Figure 7.4a). Sometimes it was even hard for her to let go of the ball or she let go too soon and the ball would fall

Level 1	Level 2	Level 3	Level 4
Arm Motion	Adds Trunk	Unilateral Step	Contralateral Step

FIGURE 7.4   Development of a One-Hand Overhand Throw for Force

to the side. As she gained experience, Salli began to add some trunk motion by bending backward and forward at the waist (Figure 7.4b). With continued practice, Salli added trunk rotation, her shoulders and hips would turn sideways, and she added a unilateral step (step with same foot as the throwing hand, Figure 7.4c). The next level included stepping with the foot opposite the throwing hand and rotation forward with the hips followed by the shoulders (see Figure 7.4d).

The initial theory underlying intratask skill development was the classical stage theory. The current theory posits change using the probability theory.

Classical Stage Theory

Classical stage theory states that there is a universal, invariant sequence of motor skill development. Skills develop in a staircase fashion with a child completing one stage prior to progressing to the next stage. Thus it would seem that each time we watch Micki throw she should look the same. Sometimes, however, Micki looks as though she just stepped off the baseball diamond and other times she seems to have never held a ball in her life. Children are extremely variable in their performance. They can produce fairly skilled behavior one day and the next day appear as though they are practicing for the first time. This may also be true on a given day depending on whether the child is fatigued, bored, or frustrated. Consequently, classical stage theory has not proven practical and probability analysis was developed (Roberton & Halverson, 1988).

Probability Theory

Roberton and Halverson (1988) adapted the classical stage model to include the inherent variability of children. A probability value estimates the possibility of any level of performance occurring at a given time. Practically, the child will sometimes appear to have learned a skill while at other times he will have difficulty in performing that same task. Under well-practiced conditions, the child will demonstrate a higher level of performance. Under novel conditions, however, the child reverts to a lower, more comfortable level of skill performance. As an example, after much practice with his teacher, Todd demonstrated a mature catching pattern. As he was waiting to catch a large, soft ball, his hands were relaxed and at his sides. As he saw the teacher initiate the throw he brought his hands up, reached for the ball in front of him, contacted the ball with his hands, and bent his elbows to absorb the ball's force. The ball did not touch his chest. Noticing that Todd had performed a good throw, the child care worker wanted to challenge him. She selected a smaller ball. This time instead of reaching and giving with the ball, Todd circled the ball with his arms and trapped it against his chest.

The child moves from one level of skill performance to the next by using a greater range of movement around the force-producing points; adding more rotating joints; displaying greater flow or less interruption of the movement timing; and positioning the body for maximum production of forces (Seefeldt, 1980). Movement becomes more efficient and effective with the incorporation of more mature patterns or sub-routines into the total movement. For example, returning to the throw, Salli initially demonstrated limited motion and used few body parts. As she increased in skill she added trunk rotation and included a step. Improving her skill further she separated her trunk rotation by having the hips rotate first followed by the shoulders, upper arm, and finally, forearm. The movement also became smoother and less choppy.

Progress from one level to the next can be curtailed by not having the prerequisite movements, performing in a novel situation, or the presence of limiting conditions (Seefeldt, 1980). If a child does not have a flight phase (both feet off the ground) when running he does not have the antecedent or prerequisite movements to perform a jump. Even though Barrett can easily catch a large softball thrown by her aunt, she has great difficulty when her brother throws the ball. Her brother's throw puts her in a novel situation, and she has to adjust her catch. If a child has learned critical antecedents poorly, he is limited in his ability to progress to the next level of performance. When Chip works on twisting and turning, he locks his hips and shoulders. Consequently, when throwing he experiences a limiting condition in that he is limited to block rotation instead of the more efficient segmental rotation of the hips and shoulders.

Two approaches to describing the changes from one level of skill performance to the next are the component and whole body analysis. The component and whole body analysis are two ways of describing the quality of the movement as the child increases in skilled performance.

Component versus Whole Body Analysis

When analyzing the fundamental motor patterns, the teacher of young children can look at the body as a whole or can evaluate the component parts (trunk, legs, arms).

Whole Body Analysis.   The whole body analysis views the body in its entirety and combines the changes in the various body parts into the separate levels or stages. For example to reach a level 1 of hopping (Haubenstricker, Branta, Seefeldt, Brakora, & Kiger, 1989), the thigh of the nonsupporting knee is parallel to the ground and held stable with the foot in front of the body for support. The body is upright with arms bent at the elbows and hands near shoulder height in a stabilizing position. Little height or distance is achieved in the hop. A child demonstrating a level 4 of hopping would swing the nonsupporting knee back and forth like a pendulum to aid in force production. The arms are relaxed and held close to the sides of the body with the elbows bent. The use of the arms diminishes as the nonsupporting leg is used more.

Component Analysis.   The component model predicts that individuals differ in rates of body segment development, and thus each body segment passes through developmental steps individually. For hopping, the leg and arm are analyzed separately (Roberton, 1984). Level 1 of the leg action has limited flight while the supporting knee and hip flex quickly with a pulling of the foot from the floor rather than a projection. The swing leg is held high and is not moved. The arm action for a level 1 has the arms held high, out to the side, and motionless.

Both types of analysis are valuable. For the purposes of young childhood, when children are in the early learning phase, and child care early educators are analyzing the skill, a whole body analysis is sufficient. After understanding how skills develop, the child care early educator needs to produce a developmental progression.

Skill Progression, Task Complexity, and Task Analysis

The difficulty of learning tasks is directly related to the nature of the movement and the conditions in the environment (Gentile, 1972). Skills may be classified according to whether the performer's interaction with the environment is consistent and whether the body is stable or requires transport. Skill classification can generally be simplified and thought of as a continuum from a stationary (the child throws the ball to a stationary target) to a moving environment (children are continually moving during a game of tag) and from requiring no manipulation of an object (skipping) to object control (kicking a soccer ball). This classification is commonly called a continuum of closed to open skills, respectively (see Figure 7.5).

The environmental requirements of a skill vary. A forward roll differs from batting a pitched ball in two ways. First the environment is stable for the forward roll, and the child tries to repeat the skill the same way each time. Body stability (balance) is required without the manipulation of an object. Skills of this type are termed *closed skills* and are generally considered to require a consistent pattern of response on each movement attempt. In addition to repeating the skill, the indi-

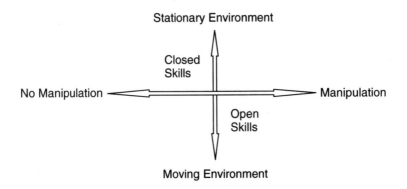

FIGURE 7.5   Environmental Demands

vidual is able to choose when to initiate the movement; in other words the skill is self-paced.

Batting a baseball differs from the forward roll in that the child must match her movement to the demands of a changing environment. When batting a pitched ball the child is not free to arbitrarily choose how to swing. The swing of the bat must occur neither too high nor too low. This type of skill, termed *open,* requires the child to develop an understanding of how to modify the swing to accommodate the changing environment. She must adjust the level of the swing to the level of the ball. In addition, the skill is externally paced. The child must time her movement to the flight of the ball. She can be neither too soon nor too late.

For skill learning, the nature of the performance environment dictates the successful patterns that will be developed by the child during practice. Successful performance of a closed skill requires development of highly consistent movement patterns (Higgins & Spaeth, 1972). Effective performance in open skills requires the child to adapt the movement to each specific situation. Most movement skills are considered to be open skills.

Relating to task complexity, performing in a moving environment is typically more difficult than in a stationary environment. A child must attend to the important aspects of the environment (flight of the ball, speed, etc.) and quickly choose the appropriate skill to use (e.g., whether to swing). Developmentally it has been thought that the child should learn a skill in a fixed environment prior to practicing the skill in a moving environment. For example, young children initially play T-ball (closed environment), move to having coaches pitch (a highly predictable environment), and finally play ball with a peer pitching (open environment). However, learning any skill requires that the child practice the skill in as close to the game situation as possible. If the child practices an open skill in a closed environment for too long, subsequent difficulty performing in a changing environment may occur. When teaching side arm striking with a bat, success at hitting must be weighed against striking different pitches. Consequently, the progression from T-ball to peer pitching is appropriate as long as the child is able to progress to the next level once early success is achieved. Moving to the next level can be embedded in practice.

For each skill within the developmental sequence a skill progression can be developed and task complexity modified. An example of a skill progression for a young child is crawling, creeping, walking, and running—followed by jumping. If a child can successfully run she has the prerequisite strength and balance for jumping. Associated with skill progression, task complexity is important in modifying the skill. Factors that can be varied to increase task complexity in a skill such as catching include ball size, speed, color, and trajectory in addition to striking surface, length of handle, and weight of implement (Roberton, 1984). These factors can be progressively modified to help the child's skills improve. The novice would catch a large, light ball thrown at chest height. As the child becomes more successful, the teacher can decrease the size of the ball and throw the ball so that the child has to reach to catch the ball. Continuing to increase complexity, the ball can be thrown from different angles and at different speeds. Finally, the child must move to catch a small and forcefully thrown ball.

Task Analysis

A task analysis is important when determining what skills to practice in each day's lesson. A combination of intertask and intratask sequences aids the teacher in determining the learning hierarchy. First, the teacher reviews the general inter-task sequence presented earlier in this chapter. What general skills are the children able to perform? Are they new walkers, or are they racing from room to room? Do the infants still exhibit reflexes and reactions that prohibit the development of locomotion?

Once a general developmental level (e.g., rudimentary movement, funda-mental motor patterns) is determined, the specific concepts and skills are chosen. One of the first movement concepts we develop with 3-year-olds in our Kinder Kinetics Program is space awareness. We have refined a learning hierarchy to develop the concept of where they can move (see Figure 7.6). Young children con-gregate together; they move close to other children. When they are close to other children, the probability of bumping into each other is high, and the likelihood of getting into trouble is increased. To avoid this, we want the children to understand the concept of movement in space. To accomplish this goal, we first have the chil-dren understand the concept of self-space: How do their bodies change shape and require more or less space? After several lessons exploring how to change their self-space, we next concentrate on developing an understanding of general space. We spread 15 large hoops within the boundaries, one hoop for each child. The

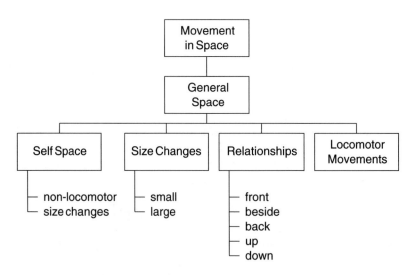

FIGURE 7.6   Learning Hierarchy for Space Awareness

children move from hoop to hoop with the rule that only one child can be in a hoop at a time. Once they move among the hoops with relative ease and spacing, we increase task complexity by increasing speed of movement or by requiring different locomotor skills. Finally, all hoops are removed—making the task more abstract. (This complete lesson is included in Chapter 8.)

For motor skill learning to occur, the child must receive adequate amounts of practice. Therefore, games of exclusion (e.g., musical chairs) and games with limited participation (e.g., duck, duck, goose) should be avoided. It is the role of the teacher to ensure that the practice of a skill is monitored so that efficient movement patterns develop. In addition, practice of the individual skill should be performed under conditions that closely match situations in which the skill will be performed. The practice environment and required skills must be adjusted to meet a child's changing body size, level of motor skill, and self-perception (self-esteem, self-concept).

Summary

Movement is important for young children. Early childhood educators need to understand how movement develops in children and use creative and fun learning activities that allow children to develop the concepts and skills necessary for an active life. When working with children we emphasize moving from simple, concrete lessons to more advanced, complex, and abstract lessons.

Intertask sequences provide the understanding of the relationships of one skill to another. Intratask sequences assist the teacher in understanding quality of movement, or what a skill should look like.

CHANGE AND ADVOCACY

1. Organize a workshop for parents and volunteers to make them familiar with the developmental pyramid and how to apply the concept to their child.

2. Design a pamphlet for youth sport coaches describing the importance of following a developmental sequence.

REFERENCES

Apgar, V. (1953). A proposal for a new method of evaluation of the newborn infant. *Current Research in Anesthesia and Analgesia, 32,* 260–276.

Bayley, N. (1935). The development of motor abilities during the first three years. *Society for Research in Child Development Monograph, 1,* 1–26.

Clarke, H. (1967). Characteristics of the young athlete: A longitudinal look. In *AMA Proceedings of the Eighth Annual Conference on the Medical Aspects of Sport—1966.* Chicago: American Medical Association, 49–57.

French, K. E., & Thomas, J. R. (1985). Gender differences across age in motor performance: A meta-analysis. *Psychological Bulletin, 98,* 260–282.

Gentile, A. M. (1972). A working model of skill acquisition with application to teaching, *Quest, 17,* 3–23.

Haubenstricker, J., Branta, C., Seefeldt, V., Brakora, L., & Kiger, J. (1989). *Prelongitudinal screening of a developmental sequence for hopping.* Paper presented at the annual convention of the American Alliance for Health, Physical Education, Recreation, and Dance. Boston, MA.

Higgins, J. R., and Spaeth, R. K. (1972). The relationship between consistency of movement and environmental conditions, *Quest, 17,* 61–69.

Roberton, M. A. (1984). Changing motor patterns during childhood. In J. R. Thomas (Ed.), *Motor development during childhood and adolescence* (pp. 48–90). Minneapolis, MN: Burgess.

Roberton, M. A., & Halverson, L. E. (1988). The development of locomotor coordination: longitudinal change and invariance. *Journal of Motor Behavior, 20*(3), 197–241.

Seefeldt, V. (1980). Developmental motor patterns: Implications for elementary school physical education. In C. Nadeau, W. Holliwell, K. Newell, & G. Roberts (Eds.), *Psychology of motor behavior and sport.* Champaign, IL: Human Kinetics Publishers.

Seefeldt, V., & Haubenstricker, J. (1982). Patterns, phases, or stages: An analytical model for the study of developmental movement. In J. A. S. Kelso and J. E. Clark (Eds.), *The development of movement control and coordination* (pp. 309–318). New York: Wiley.

Shirley, M. (1963). The motor sequence. In D. Wayne (Ed.), *Readings in child psychology.* Upper Saddle River, NJ: Prentice-Hall.

8 Movement Programs for Infants, Toddlers, and Young Children

CHAPTER OBJECTIVES

Knowledge

■ The reader will understand the steps required in planning movement programs for infants, toddlers, and young children.

Skills

■ The reader will plan a developmentally appropriate movement lesson.

Dispositions

■ The reader will value the importance of being physically active across the lifespan.

CHAPTER SYNOPSIS

Scenario

On her way home from a day of observing student teachers, Dr. Polkis was excited about what Ms. Luxbacker taught that day. One of the major concepts she emphasized in the elementary methods class was the importance of planning, setting the class climate, and ensuring that all children are active throughout the class. When Dr. Polkis arrived at the class, Ms. Luxbacker handed her a well-planned developmentally appropriate lesson on the different ways to jump. The next test was to see how she interacted with the 5-year-olds. The first hurdle was passed, the movement room was set up with the equipment spread throughout the room. The environment was exciting. Outside the area where the children initially worked (boundaries), there were boxes to jump off, balloons to play with, hoops to jump into, and wands on cones to jump over. As the children walked into the class, Dr. Polkis noticed that Ms. Luxbacker called each child by name. During the introduction to the lesson, she asked the children how many ways they could jump. The children were spaced around the area, and she had them try all the ways they knew how to jump. Ms. Luxbacker asked the children what a jump was, and she helped them to understand that their feet had to be in the air in order to jump. She then asked the children how many feet they could take-off from and how many they could land on. The focus of the day's lesson was to understand how to land when jumping. To understand the concept of landing, she had the children jump up and land stiff-legged, then she had them jump up and land but bend their knees when they landed. She asked them which one felt better. Bending the legs was of course the answer. To help the children understand the concept of absorbing force she threw a ball against a thick mat hanging on the wall, and the children watched it fall to the ground. She then asked the children to tell her why the ball dropped when it hit the mat yet bounced back when it hit the wall. The children compared the difference between the mat and the wall and concluded that the mat took the movement (energy) out of the ball. They needed to take the energy out of the jump so their teeth did not rattle when they landed. When the children went through the obstacle course and practiced all the different ways to jump, they decided that the key words for the day were "jump, bend." In closing the lesson, Ms. Luxbacker assessed the children's landing skills and recorded that the majority of children landed with a knee bend. She also noted the children who did not land with a knee bend so that she could provide developmentally appropriate instruction. Dr. Polkis wished that all her students planned lessons that were as developmentally appropriate as this and that they were also able to interact with the children and provide developmentally appropriate feedback.

Planning Learning Activities

The "earlier the better" idea is entrenched in parents and children (Elkind, 1990; Payne & Issacs, 1995). We continually see pictures of Tiger Woods learning golf at the age of 3 and of children starting their training for baseball at the age of 6. We see infant swimming programs, programs that teach the violin to 4-year-olds, and even soccer programs for 3-year-olds. Parents think that early stimulation is important and that if they do not expose their children to these programs they will not develop to their fullest potential. Limited research has been conducted on the benefits of these programs and some research has even indicated that early stimulation may have long-term deleterious effects (Gardner, Karmel & Dowd, 1984). On the other hand, new research is focusing on the importance of early stimulation to enhance the brain development of young children. What is a parent and caregiver to do?

Movement programs for young children are important if they follow developmentally appropriate guidelines. The purpose of this chapter is to briefly cover the two types of existing programs for young children and then integrate the knowledge gained in earlier chapters for the child care early educator to develop skills in planning developmentally appropriate movement programs for children.

The types of early childhood programs fall into two categories (Payne & Issacs, 1999): programming and no-programming. Those that have programming incorporate skills for future development while the no-programming type avoid specific training and practice of future movements. Gymboree, Prudden Infant Fitness, and Infant Swim programs are examples that use programming. Programs that are included in the no-programming group might be the community "play group" or the exploration equipment at a children's museum.

Parents need to avoid programs that claim excessive improvements in the infant's future motor or intellectual development. The American Academy of Pediatrics has a clear policy statement concerning infant exercise programs indicating that there are no known benefits for infant exercise programs for healthy infants. They suggest that parents should seek "safe, nurturing, and minimally structured" play situations.

The American Academy of Pediatrics (1985), the YMCA (1984), the American Red Cross (1988), and COPEC have published guidelines to follow in evaluating early childhood movement programs. Important considerations for child care programs include reviewing the adult-child ratio, commitment to a developmentally appropriate philosophy, and an appreciation of the child as an individual. One of the best indicators that we use to evaluate our Kinder Kinetics Program is for the children to love to come to the program. We are happy when parents tell us that their children were up early in the morning because they were so excited about coming to the program!

Too often early childhood teachers believe that a child's motor skills develop on their own or that the young child is too young to learn motor skills. Many early childhood educators do not consciously plan for developmentally appropriate motor skill learning as they plan for learning in other areas. Planning for young children to acquire motor skills is a complex process but can and should be done by the early childhood educator. The rest of this chapter addresses issues with planning and teaching developmentally appropriate learning activities to young children. Initially, the teacher must understand the learning assumptions.

Learning Assumptions

NAEYC (1990) provides six basic assumptions about the interactive processes of learning and teaching. The process is interactive between the learner, teacher, and environment; the teacher does not mechanically provide information to the child. First, children learn best when their physical needs are satisfied, and they **feel safe and secure** psychologically (NAEYC, 1990). We have provided guidelines for what the early childhood educator needs to do to assist the child in feeling psychologically secure in Chapter 5. Maslow's hierarchy of basic human needs also addresses components of feeling safe and secure. Maslow first discusses physiological security, including such things as hunger, thirst, and pain avoidance. His next level of the hierarchy includes providing a safe, secure, and stable environment. It is important for the teacher to establish a class routine and to maintain a calm, steady environment where the children understand expectations. A feeling of belongingness is the third level of the hierarchy. Children need to feel included in the class; they need to be part of the class. Games that exclude children should not be used. In addition to undermining the feeling of belonging, games of exclusion do not allow the child who needs the most practice the chance to practice. The poorest-skilled child is the first to be excluded. The next level of Maslow's hierarchy includes esteem needs, meaning that the child needs to gain self-respect. It is important that we provide the child with a majority of successful experiences. When planning we need to understand what the child can do and then select the next level of skill that the child can acquire. The top of the hierarchy is self-actualization. At this level the individual cherishes his strengths and understands his weaknesses.

The second basic learning assumption is that children **construct knowledge.** Children learn by interacting with the environment, as discussed in Chapter 1; they experiment with objects and discover knowledge. Making errors is part of learning that allows a child to form concepts and understand relationships. For example, when Chris was 18 months old he saw his mother stub her toe. His mother sat in a chair to wait for the pain to subside. Seeing the blood, Chris went into action. He immediately went to his mother, bent over to kiss her toe and said, "Mommie make it feel better." Subsequently he traveled to the bathroom, picked up a dirty tissue from the waste basket, returned to his mother and began administering first aid!

Learning is a cycle of **becoming aware, exploring, inquiring, and finally utilizing and applying.** As learners, children become aware of the environment or what they want to learn. Curiosity stimulates interest. During **exploration,** children interact with the environment and attempt to figure out the components of what is being learned. Hands-on experience is important and children typically use various senses to gain awareness. Moving to **inquiry,** children start to analyze and compare their own concepts to what is observed and attempt to more closely match the conventional patterns. Finally, through **utilization** children are able to apply what they have learned and adapt it to new situations. This process is not linear. Children can explore and inquire simultaneously. It is critical that children interact with the environment since they learn by doing.

Children **learn through play** by analyzing the learning cycle. Spontaneous play provides opportunities to interact with and manipulate the environment while exploring and experimenting. Play provides the child with an environment in which she can try new skills and practice in a variety of situations without pressure of evaluation. Yale's teacher was trying to teach him to run. Miss Irene would give him feedback on how to hit the ground with his heel and roll to his toe. She would try to also point out to him to listen to his movement because he could hear himself running. Try as she might, Miss Irene was not making a difference. During free play that day, Miss Irene watched Yale, when he was playing hide-and-seek with the other children. His running form was good. Yale knew that he could not be heard or "IT" would know where to look!

Children are motivated to learn through their **interests and inquisitive nature.** Teachers should select content that engages children to figure things out. We need to understand what motivates children and plan environments that introduce new and stimulating objects, people, and experiences.

NAEYC purposes that children learn through **social interaction** with other children and adults. This is critical not only for intellectual development but also for competence and self-esteem. Katie and Robert are 2½-year-old twins. Their mother was having difficulty getting Katie dressed until Robert leaned over and said, "Cute." Katie immediately finished dressing. Even at a young age, Katie was socialized by feedback from her sibling.

Finally, **individual variation** cannot be stressed enough. Children develop and learn at their own pace. A wide range of individual variation is normal and expected. Experiences and cultural backgrounds vary, as do genetic makeup and maturation rate.

Once the principles of learning are understood, the next step is to determine the philosophy of the program and then, using the philosophy as a guide, plan the program.

Philosophy of the Program

The first step in planning developmentally appropriate lessons for young children is to develop a philosophy statement based on the most current and appropriate theory of development and learning. One's personal philosophy must be incorporated into the philosophy of the program. The philosophy set forth in this book is that movement is important for a lifetime, and that all children need to develop a healthy lifestyle. Being physically active is a critical component of a healthy lifestyle. Children are not in competition with each other but need to develop their movement skills to their fullest potential to maintain participation in physical activity for a lifetime. We know that having a positive attitude toward physical activity and developing a feeling of competence in physical activity is related to being physically active (Biddle & Armstrong, 1992; Fegruson, Yesalis, Pomrehn, and Kirkpatrick, 1989).

Long-range goals that will produce social/emotional, cognitive/language, and physical/movement development need to be determined. The concepts and skills to be learned need to follow a developmental sequence and can be abstracted from the developmental pyramid presented in Chapter 7.

Included in the philosophy statement can be a definition of the physically educated individual. Modifying NASPE's statement (Franck, Graham, Lawson, Loughrey, Ritson, Sanborn, & Seefeldt, 1991) to apply to infants, toddlers, and young children we might include:

A Physically Educated Child:

IS   learning the concepts and skills needed to be physically active for a lifetime.

DOES   participate daily in physical activity.

KNOWS   why movement is important.

VALUES   the importance of moving and how it relates to a healthy lifestyle.

This definition of a physically educated person was used as a guideline to establish content standards for children from kindergarten through grade 12. The content standards (Rink, Dotson, Franck, Hensley, Holf-Hale, Lund, Payne, & Wood, 1995) include:

A Physically Educated Person:

1. Demonstrates competency in many movement forms and proficiency in a few movement forms
2. Applies movement concepts and principles to the learning and development of motor skills
3. Exhibits a physically active lifestyle
4. Achieves and maintains a health-enhancing level of physical fitness
5. Demonstrates responsible personal and social behavior in physical activity settings
6. Demonstrates understanding and respect for differences among people in physical activity settings
7. Understands that physical activity provides opportunities for enjoyment, challenge, self-expression, and social interaction

As stated, the NASPE content standards were developed for children kindergarten through grade 12 but can be adapted for infants through age 5.

A Physically Educated Infant, Toddler, or Young Child:

1. Participates in a wide variety of movement activities at their developmental level
2. Develops an awareness of others during movement activities
3. Engages in movement activity to raise the heart rate
4. Participates with family in a physical activity setting

For each of these content standards, specific developmentally appropriate motor/physical, cognitive/language, and social/emotional objectives need to be developed.

After setting the philosophy of the program, the teacher needs to understand the learner in order to select developmentally appropriate content. The lessons must be child-centered with the lesson matched to the child's level of development.

Planning Developmentally Appropriate Movement Programs

The first step in planning is to understand the learner's physical, cognitive, and emotional maturational levels. After the learner is understood, the teacher can determine the content that matches the characteristics of the learner. As the teacher determines the criteria for the lesson and the environment, she also develops learning cues. The last part of the interactive model of teacher thinking involves working with the children and matching their behavior to the criteria. Figure 8.1 illustrates this process.

Understand the Learner

To plan developmentally appropriate lessons, the early childhood educator must understand the learner physiologically, cognitively, and emotionally. An understanding of the child's growth and maturation status is important in setting expectations for the child while cognitive developmental level aids us in determining how to present the information to the child. Emotional intelligence is important in maintaining motivation to participate for a lifetime.

Physical Maturational Level.   During early childhood the child is changing rapidly. There is a wide range in body height and weight, and perceptual-motor abilities change rapidly due to neural maturation and maturation of the kinesthetic, visual, and auditory apparatus. The infant relies on kinesthetic information (touch) to learn about the environment. Everything goes into the infant's mouth. The toddler switches to a reliance on vision to gather environmental information. Visual acuity improves up to about 10 years of age. The 1-year-old child has a visual acuity of about 20/100 to 20/50 while the 5-year-old child has a visual acuity of about 20/30. With age and experience the visual apparatus and the other sensory systems improve in discrimination and in sensory integration. The child is more able to integrate sound with touch and vision. The child can gather more

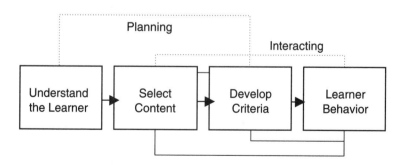

FIGURE 8.1   Model of Teacher Thinking

information about the turning rope through sound, vision and feel. Ovande sees the rope turning, hears the rope hit the ground, and feels the breeze of the rope. This information helps him decide when to jump.

Laterality, an awareness of the two sides, develops with age. By about 4 to 5 years of age the child is aware of right and left, and it is at adult levels by age 10. Lateral dominance develops around age 4.

Closely related perceptual abilities that improve with age are size constancy, figure-ground perception, and whole-part perception. With age the child is able to understand that distance does not make the object smaller. Young children overestimate the space between two objects that are placed farther and farther away. Size constancy is fully developed by 11 years of age. Figure-ground perception develops to adult levels by about 8 years of age. This enables the child to see the figure separate from the background. Catching requires the child to see the ball apart from the background. Whole-part perception allows the child to see the parts that make up the whole. The child first perceives the whole object, followed by focusing on either the parts or the whole and concluding development by integrating the parts that make up the whole. This is important in understanding the action of the different body parts that constitute a skill. For example, understanding a throw includes looking, stepping, reaching, and follow-through. Spatial orientation, recognition of an object's orientation in space, fully develops by about age 8. By age 3 to 4 years the child is able to understand over/under, high/low, and front/back. The next concept to develop is near-far perception. The child is initially able to organize near space. They can perceive complex details and build up complex spatial relationships in space near them and then they are gradually able to extend this concept into far space. This is an explanation why the child continually moves toward the pitcher prior to striking the ball, or why the thrower should stand close to the catcher.

Related to spatial orientation is the ability to track objects—follow movement in space. The child can first gather information about objects that move vertically. Horizontal motion is developed second followed by diagonal and circular motion. Thus a developmental sequence for catching would include drop-catch (vertical motion), roll-catch (horizontal motion), and throw-catch with a partner (diagonal motion). The first two sequences allow the child to gather movement information about the oncoming ball and develop success with catching. By age 8, the child has developed the ability to track.

Knowledge of a child's physical maturity is important in setting expectations for the child. For example, understanding maturational and growth differences aids the teacher setting distance expectations. The infant who displays the palmar grasp reflex is developing an awareness of hand-eye coordination. A 5-year-old who demonstrates the same throwing pattern as a 7-year-old would not be expected to throw as far. A small child would not be expected to kick as far as a larger child. A 3-year-old child would not be able to run the same distance as his larger older sibling. A knowledge of perceptual differences helps one understand why Rose wants to move closer to the pitcher. If the pitcher stands far from her, she has difficulty focusing on and following the ball so she knows when to strike.

Near-far perception indicates that the child first organizes space near him before he is able to do so with an object at a distance. The adult on the other hand has slowed reactions and is unable to keep from getting hit in sensitive areas of the body if the child does strike the ball!

Cognitive Maturational Level. Children are increasingly able to express thoughts and ideas verbally. Their imaginations are extensive, and they demonstrate little concern for accuracy or proper sequencing of events. Play is important for the child to develop the how and why of her actions.

The task of learning a movement is complicated by the inability of the child to manageably reduce the quantity of information needed to perform the movement. When thinking and learning the child needs to observe the environment, select an appropriate movement, perform the movement, and then reflect on that movement to see if it matched what was intended. On the next trial the child needs to integrate feedback from the teacher, the environment, and herself to modify the skill for the next attempt. Typically children learn to walk on a specific surface whether it is a hard floor or carpeting. However, when they switch to a different type of floor, a different surface, you can see their motion slowly change as they adapt their pattern to the new movement.

Maximum attention demands are placed on the beginning learner because the child does not have the experience to accurately pinpoint essential information. Characteristics of the beginning mover that increase the difficulty of learning are (1) lack of knowledge about what elements of the movement on which to focus, (2) longer time to monitor perceptual input from the visual system and the body, and (3) difficulty in performing simultaneous movements. As children grow older they become faster at processing information (Gallagher & Thomas, 1980). Prior to age 11, the speed of the child's decision making is considerably slower than that of older children or adults. However, practice at a skill will reduce the information processing demands associated with the task and eventually certain aspects of the skill will be automatic. Children need to be cued to think about their next move. Dr. Vollmer, a first/second-grade teacher, helped her class develop rules, but they were having difficulty remembering them and communicating them with each other. The children decided to match the rules to hand movements (cues). The first rule for the class was to sit straight and tall, the cue was showing the pointer finger. Rule number 2 was to walk quietly in the halls, the cue was to use the pointer and index finger to simulate the walking motion. The students loved to use these movements to help the other children remember the rules!

Information processing factors may slow the rate of learning motor skills for young children. However, increased practice of the skills and appropriate instruction by the teacher can reduce the effects of the young child's lack of using strategies.

The learner's cognitive maturational level is important when structuring the lesson. Many motor skills require a rapid response to external factors in addition to rapid movement. A child not only performs the movement slowly but also thinks and makes decisions slowly.

When learning, the young child approaches the learning situation with different strategies. Typically a young child does not have the experience of an older child and consequently does not think the same way. Deani was excited about what she had learned in preschool one day. As her dad was reading the paper she was telling him that she had learned to count. Her dad subsequently asked her how high she could count. After thinking and looking around the living room, Deani climbed the cushions of the couch, stepped onto the arm rest, raised her hands in the air, pushed up on her toes and started saying, "1, 2, 3 . . . ". She was showing how "high" she could count. Deani processed the word *high* differently than her father. They did not think the same way. They did not have the same experiences.

Emotional Maturational Level.   Children at this age are egocentric and believe that everyone thinks the way they do. Sharing and getting along with other children can be difficult. Children tend to be shy, self-conscious, and fearful of new situations. They frequently are unwilling to leave familiar surroundings. The ability to distinguish right from wrong begins and this aids the development of a conscience.

During the early childhood years two important social-emotional tasks are developing: sense of autonomy and a sense of initiative. Autonomy develops through a growing sense of independence. During this time of development, a child expresses an ability to manipulate some factors in his environment rather than act as being directed. We can see the 2-year-old saying "no" to almost every question; a child might even say "no" to getting ice cream. Therefore, it is important to give children numerous situations in which they can express their autonomy appropriately. You can ask a child to select a ball to throw or catch. They can choose to throw to a target on the wall or to a partner. They can choose between galloping or running. Children need to make decisions.

Based on Erikson's (1950) psychosocial model of development, children first learn to develop trust. This develops mainly from basic needs being met. The second stage, autonomy vs. shame/doubt, develops between 18 months and 3½ years. If children are not encouraged to develop autonomy, they develop shame and doubt. Children need to develop a sense of independence (knowing that they are capable of doing things on their own). Eighteen-month-old Charlotte wanted to sit in the same chair that her parents used. At the same time, she wanted to climb onto the chair by herself. The technique she used was to lay her chest prone on the seat, grab the back of the seat and wiggle until her body was on the seat. Charlotte then stood up and promptly sat down on the seat of the chair. This entire procedure was designed by Charlotte and showed a highly developed sense of autonomy. As Charlotte develops, she will move onto the next stage of Erickson's theory, initiative vs. guilt. During this stage children must be free to take initiative, to create and take risks. If they are not able to do this, they develop a sense of guilt. The final stage, industry vs. inferiority, develops between 6 and 12 years of age and is based on development of competence in skills that are valued by society (Trawick-Smith, 2000).

Select Developmentally Appropriate Content

After understanding the learner, the early childhood educator is ready to determine what experiences to provide the child. The first step is determining general content followed by determining expectation levels or criteria.

To select the general content the teacher can review the developmental pyramid presented in Chapter 6. Young children are between rudimentary movements, movement concepts, and fundamental motor patterns.

Developmentally appropriate physical education includes development of concepts, movement skills, and fitness applied to dance, games, and sports that lead to a physically active lifestyle (see Figure 8.2). Concepts provide the foundation for understanding movement while skills provide the means to be physically active. Increased levels of physical activity lead to physical fitness. Appropriate attitude fosters the motivation that is important for maintaining physical activity across the lifespan.

Concepts.   The major emphasis of movement programs for young children is the development of concepts. Concepts provide the language to learn movement skills and are categorized as movement, skill, and fitness (see Figure 8.3). Linking movement concepts and fundamental motor patterns, Laban and Ullmann (1963) described movement focusing on body awareness, space awareness, movement qualities, and relationships. Skill concepts include an understanding of what skills the body can perform, and when each skill is appropriate. Fitness concepts are the health- and skill-related components of physical fitness.

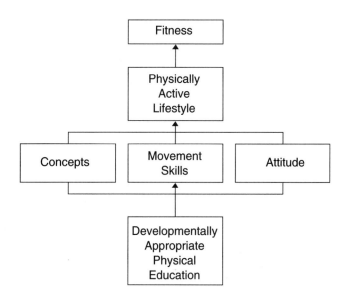

FIGURE 8.2   Content of Developmentally Appropriate Physical Education

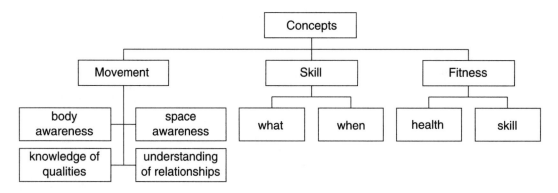

FIGURE 8.3   Concepts in Developmentally Appropriate Physical Education

Movement Concepts.   Movement concepts include body awareness, space aware-ness, knowledge of qualities, and understanding relationships (see Figure 8.4). An understanding of movement concepts is the foundation of all skill development.

Body Awareness.   Identification of body parts followed by an understanding of the skills the body can perform is part of developing an awareness of the body. In learning the parts of the body, the child is first able to identify the body part. If the parent says, "Eyes," the child points to the eyes. Subsequently the parent is able to

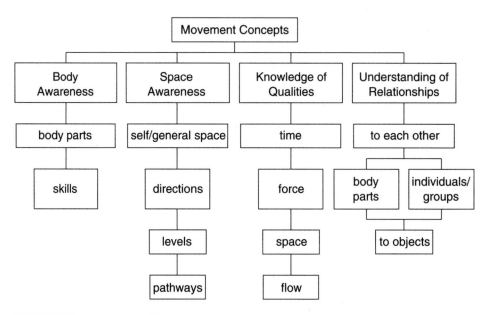

FIGURE 8.4   Movement Concepts

point to the eyes while the child names the body part. The child's ability to name body parts is mainly due to practice. Every time Cyrus responded with the word *chin* when his mother pointed to her chin, Cyrus was rewarded with smiles and excitement from his mother!

Learning the **skills** that the body can perform is also included in body awareness. The skills are traditionally divided into non-locomotor, locomotor, and manipulative movements. When the child is not moving from one place to another, the movements are non-locomotor. Bending, twisting, turning, and stretching are examples of non-locomotor movements. Locomotor movements would include walking, running, galloping, hopping, and skipping. A developmental sequence for learning locomotor movements is presented in Appendix F.

Manipulative movements can be either force-producing or force-absorbing. Force-producing movements send objects away, as in the skills of throwing and striking, whereas force-absorbing movements include catching. To help a child understand what occurs with force-absorption, bounce a ball on the floor and see what happens. Then bounce a ball at a thick mat. Ask the children what happened to the ball when it was bounced at the floor and the mat. Obviously, a child needs to be like the mat in order to catch the ball; if she is stiff like the floor the ball will bounce away. This demonstrates how the teacher can assist the children in learning a concept and skill by interacting with the environment.

Manipulative skills also include moving while controlling an object with the feet or hand. Dribbling a ball is a manipulative skill. The child has to maintain control of another object with different body parts.

Space Awareness.   Space, directions, levels, pathways, planes, and extensions are part of space awareness. A key concept to develop during early childhood is space awareness. The child needs to understand self-space (personal space) and general space. Infants and toddlers begin to get the concept of space awareness by crawling under tables of different sizes. For some tables they do not need to alter their motion while to get under other tables they need to be much lower. An example of a space awareness lesson is included in Box 8.1. During this lesson the children explore self-space to determine how it changes shape. General space is presented using concrete examples. Large hoops are spread throughout the area and children move from one hoop to the next with the requirement that only one child be in a hoop at a time. Children are frequently stopped and asked if they are using good self-space. The next step is to remove all the hoops. Moving in space without visual aids requires abstract understanding. Finally, the children apply the concept to "lining up" and other areas where space utilization is important.

Other key concepts to develop during early childhood include directions, levels, and pathways. Directions include forward, backward, up, down, and sideways. Levels relate to high, middle, and low. We crawl in the low level but jump into a high level. Pathways can be either straight, curved, or zig-zag. Shapes are made of combinations of pathways.

After individual lessons and experiences such as development of directions, levels, and pathways, integration of the concepts is important. For example, it is

BOX **8.1**

Lesson on Space Awareness

Grade Level
Kindergarten, First Meeting
10 children/8 males, 2 females

Equipment
10 hoops, 10 beanbags, 5 cones

Space Organization
Children spread in general space

General Objective
While moving within boundaries in the multipurpose room, the child will demonstrate a knowledge of and ability to use self and general space as measured by completing a task sheet and successfully playing.

Objective	*Activity*
While seated the child will review the concepts of self and self-space by appropriately responding to 5 of 5 questions.	Point to yourself. *Yourself* is made up of two words, what are they? What is self? What defines self? When we put the word *space* with *self*, what do we mean?
Spaced evenly throughout the gym, the children will demonstrate the variables that affect self-space in 4 of 4 activities.	low/high wide/narrow big/small Where will their self spaces fit?
Spaced evenly throughout the gym, the children will be able to locate objects and people in reference to their self-space.	Side Up Down Front Back
While seated in self-space in the gym, the children will review general space by answering 5 of 5 questions.	What is general space? How does it compare to self-space? What can we do in general space that we cannot do in self-space? What do we have to be careful of when moving in general space? Why is good use of general space important?
In the gym the child will demonstrate the ability to make use of general space such that all children are spaced throughout the gym.	With hoops Change modes of travel Change speed

Culminating Activity

In the gym the child will demonstrate the ability to make use of general space such that all children are spaced throughout the gym.	Without hoops, change modes of travel Change speed, remove eyesight Reduce size
While seated in a circle the child will review self-space and general space by answering questions on the task sheet.	Task sheet (see Box 8.2)

Culminating Activity Format

Name of Activity
General Space Fun

Objectives
While moving in the gym the child will demonstrate the ability to make use of general space such that all children are spaced throughout the gym. If the children are not spaced when "frozen," they will move into position such that appropriate general space is used.

Equipment
Cones

Organization
The children are spread out in good general space.

Directions
The children move about in general space, on the command "freeze" they evaluate whether they are in appropriate general space. If not, they move into good general space. The speed of the movement is increased and the boundaries are decreased to increase task complexity.

Teaching Points
After freezing, the children determine whether they are appropriately using general space. Check to see if touching others while moving.

---

important for the child to know he is moving backward at a high level in a curved path. The teacher asks the children to drive on the road (lines on the floor). As the children drive, they need to be aware of the space in which other children are moving. Sometimes when the children park their cars or trucks (themselves), and return, they need to back out of their parking space. To do this the children know they are moving backward in a high level.

Movement Qualities. The components of time, force, space, and flow are concepts that relate to the quality of movement. Time refers to the speed of movement and can range from slow to fast. A turtle creeps slowly, whereas the rabbit moves quickly. Force is the amount of energy used to complete the movement. We impart force to a throw but absorb force when catching. Space used is the flexibility in the movement ranging from direct to indirect. A direct movement would have little flexibility and a rigid, straight path. An indirect movement is more flexible, and the path can meander. Flow, a more advanced concept, relates to the level of control of the movement. Flow can range from bound to free. The mover has complete control of a bound movement and can stop the movement instantly. These are constrained and cautious movements. Walking while balancing a beanbag on the head would be an example of bound flow. A free movement is continuous and cannot be stopped once initiated. A child running down a hill is an example of free flow.

Movement Relationships.   Movement relationships focus on the relationships of body parts to each other and of the individual to other individuals or groups and objects. Relationship awareness covers concepts such as *over, under, around,* and *through.* The child can jump over the obstacle on the floor, go under the bridge, around the mulberry bush, or through the door.

Skill Concepts.   The children are developing a knowledge of what their bodies can do and when they should perform a given skill. This knowledge is developed as part of skill concepts (see Figure 8.5). For example, children learn the concept of a jump, and when they should use the jump. The child can jump off the chair, jump up to hit the pots and pans, or jump across the brook. They should not jump down the steps.

Fitness Concepts.   Fitness concepts cover the knowledge related to how to develop and maintain physical fitness (see Figure 8.6) and also include understanding the

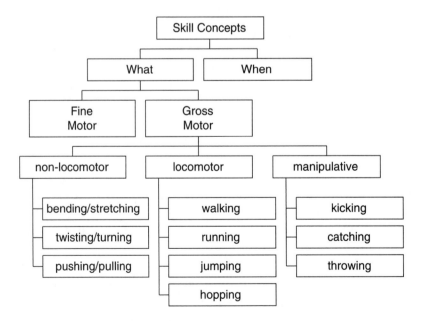

FIGURE 8.5   Movement Skill Concepts

benefits of physical activity. We specifically think that it is important for the child to understand health-related fitness concepts. Children learn to take their heart rate and learn the relationship between heart rate and level of physical activity. On her developmental level, a 3-year-old can put the heart-o-meter on her wrist and see that it does not move when she is quiet. However, when she has been running, the toothpick in the playdough that is placed on her wrist moves back and forth! An understanding of how strength differs from endurance is important. Children can understand the concept of flexibility and range of motion, how far they can bend without pulling. They can certainly see what happens when a rubber band is stretched too far. Finally, understanding body composition—knowing that a body is composed of lean body mass and body fat is important.

Movement Skills. Returning to Figure 8.2, we just covered material that included movement, skill, and fitness concepts. Next we cover development of movement skills such as catching and throwing (see Figure 8.5). As the child starts to understand the language used to learn movement, she also acquires movement skills and learns how to modify those skills. Movement skills are categorized into fine motor and gross motor skills. Fine motor skills use small muscle groups. An example of what may require fine motor skills is drawing or coloring. The muscles of the foot are used in fine motor control of the ball when dribbling. Although fine motor skill development is important, we do not cover its development in this book. Gross motor skills use large muscle groups such as the muscles of the leg, trunk, and arm when throwing, or the trunk and leg when kicking for distance. To raise the heart rate and promote a healthy lifestyle, gross motor movements are emphasized in this book.

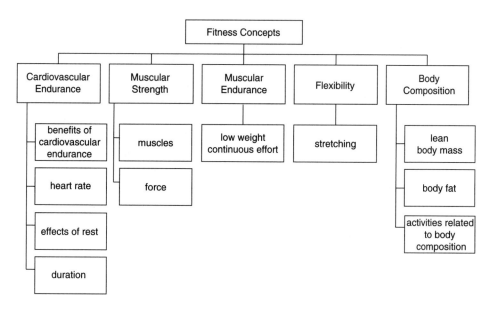

FIGURE 8.6 Fitness Concepts

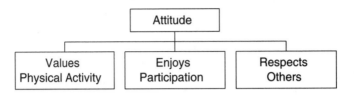

FIGURE 8.7   Movement Attitude

Movement Attitude.   In addition to learning movement skills, we need to be concerned with the child's attitude. Each child needs to value physical activity, appreciate individuals for who they are, and develop socially appropriate behaviors (see Figure 8.7). Next we more thoroughly evaluate the content to develop a learning hierarchy.

Learning Hierarchy

Once the general skill or concept is selected, the teacher then needs to determine a learning hierarchy or a developmental sequence and determine criteria. For example, for the child to have a thorough understanding of space, she needs to understand the space that her body requires, how she can change her shape, and subsequently how her space relates to others.

The learning hierarchy includes all the variables involved in the performance of the skill, sequences the skill from simple to complex, and aids the teacher in planning the lesson. Expanding the discussion of learning hierarchy from Chapter 7, we need to include an analysis of environmental conditions of open/closed and externally/self-paced. Recall that in the closed skill, the environment is relatively constant not only throughout the performance of the skill but also on different occasions of performing that skill. The performer's task, once the skill is performed correctly, is to attempt to replicate that movement or series of movements time after time. Thus, in an open skill, flexibility and diversification are desirable, whereas a closed skill demands exact replication of a successful movement pattern.

Externally and self-paced dimensions refer to the initiation of the movement. When performing a self-paced skill, the individual initiates the movement when desired, whereas in an externally paced skill, anticipation timing is involved. The learner is not able to initiate the response when desired, but must respond to a set pace or rhythm.

The parameters of open and closed skills and of self- and externally paced dimensions are not discrete but rather are opposite ends of a continuum. These factors are important when planning task difficulty. The young child can develop the idea of an overhead strike by hitting a suspended ball without having to deal with the complexity of timing the strike to a moving ball. The next section provides a sample lesson for developing the concept of space awareness. The skill is open since the child moves in an ever-changing environment, but we initially teach the concept in a closed environment where the child does not have a wealth of choices to make as he or she moves.

Sample Lesson. The space lesson presented in Box 8.1 first provides the children with experiences on what defines their self-space and how their self-space can change. After developing an understanding of how their self-space can be large, small, high, low, wide, or narrow, we then work on how to move in general space. To develop an understanding of moving in general space, the children first need to understand the concept of boundaries. Boundaries define the area in which we move. The first part of the lesson should provide concrete examples followed by abstract application. Initially the children move from hoop to hoop with the restriction that only one child can be in a hoop at a time. The number of hoops matches the number of children. After they complete this task, the hoops are removed and the task becomes more abstract. They are forced to look where everyone is moving and find the "open spaces." To increase the difficulty of the lesson the size of the space can be reduced or they can be required to move more quickly. We have even had the children move with their eyes closed! As the children are moving, the teacher needs to evaluate the children's understanding of self and general space. Is Tammy moving close to other children, does Rick continually bump into others either accidentally or on purpose? A final activity measures their cognitive understanding. The child completes a task sheet by drawing a line to the space the fish should occupy.

Develop Criteria

Assessment and evaluation are important for the teacher of young children for two reasons: learning and accountability. We test children to measure if they are progressing toward some goal. Assessment aids us in understanding what the child can do and in identifying the next step in the learning process. Secondly, assessment and evaluation allow us to establish accountability. Is the teacher effective? In this section we cover assessment as it relates to developing the criteria.

For learning to occur when teaching and developing motor skills, both the teacher and child must be able to analyze the skill to determine corrections. Assessment can be summative or formative and process- or product-oriented. *Summative* and *formative* refer to the time at which testing occurs while process and product testing address the type of testing conducted. Any test can be given in a formative or summative manner.

When assessing children we use both summative and formative assessment. Throughout the learning experience we use formative assessment to determine what the child has learned and what the child needs to learn. Thus it occurs frequently. Summative assessment is used at specific points typically at the end of a time period. It describes where the child is at that specific point in time. Teachers of young children use both types of assessment. Formative assessment guides learning, whereas summative assessment describes the individual at a specific point in time. Thomas and Thomas (1984) recommend that summative assessment is used to determine physical growth (height, weight, body fat) and physical fitness (cardiovascular endurance, muscular strength and endurance, and flexibility) to determine if the child is within normal bounds. Formative assessment is used to determine whether the child is reaching the learning goals and objectives. If the child is not meeting the goals and objectives, the assessment is used to determine what the child is ready to learn, or where he is in the learning hierarchy. Formative assessment also helps the teacher evaluate and modify his lessons. We use formative assessment to develop the criteria.

Formative assessment is used to measure movement concepts, movement skill, attitudes, and values. For all areas knowledge and behavior need to be evaluated. Measuring the child's knowledge of self and general space can be completed by use of a task sheet (see Box 8.2). Drawing a line around each animal's self-space provides an insight into what the child understands. Moving the fish to general space shows the child's knowledge of appropriate use of space. This could be made more concrete for younger children by having them place cars on a highway. In addition to the cognitive assessment, the child's behavior needs to be measured during the learning time, and how he applies the concept to other areas should be monitored. For example, the teacher can see if the children understand general and self-space as they move in the gym. Are they spread out moving in a variety of directions or are they clumped together moving as a unit? Applying general and self-space to other areas, the teacher can evaluate children when lining up. Do the children push and shove, or are they using the limited space appropriately?

The second component that needs to be evaluated is movement skills. Measuring movement skills can be completed by product or process assessment, also referred to as quantitative or qualitative testing. Product assessment measures outcome: how far, how fast, or how many. Process testing evaluates form. Factors that can influence quantitative performance of individuals are developmental factors such as weight, strength, motivation, maturation, and physique. Travis can throw the ball farther than Chip, not because Travis has better form but merely because he is bigger, stronger, and maturationally advanced compared to Chip. We use process testing to develop the criteria.

Using an observational checklist can aid process testing of motor skills. To develop an observational checklist for a skill (see Figure 8.8 on page 174), the teacher needs to first list the important elements of skill. Once these are identified, developing cues to aid in observation of the elements is critical. The cues that the teacher uses are also beneficial to the child in helping to focus attention on the important components. For example, to measure rhythmic jumping, the critical elements to observe would be "jump, bounce." Rose needs to jump a little, bounce to absorb the force, and then jump a little, bounce again. The key words "jump, bounce" need to have rhythmic tempo in which "jump" is emphasized and "bounce" is a follow-through.

For instructional purposes qualitative assessment is more appropriate since it indicates not only the instructional sequence but also provides feedback for both the teacher and the learner. After reaching a mature form, quantitative measures may chart a child's progress and allow comparisons to norms for children of the same age and gender.

BOX **8.2**

Self-Space and General Space Assessment

Self-Space

Draw a line around self-space.

General Space

Draw a circle around the fish that use good general space.

CREATIVE MOVEMENT 3- TO 4-YEAR-OLDS

Name_____   Instructor _____

_____ Quick balanced stops on signal
_____ Firmly held freezes
_____ Quick starts on signal
_____ Purposeful movement to solve
      problems (Does child understand
      problems?)
_____ Uses a variety of movements to
      solve problems
_____ Listens while moving
_____ Continuous exploratory movement
      from starting/stop signal
_____ Demonstrates understanding of
      self-space
_____ Controls body parts while moving
_____ Demonstrates understanding of
      own areas of high, medium, and low

_____ Moves near to and far from
      others without collisions
_____ Demonstrates knowledge of
      names of all large/small
      body parts
_____ Accurate meeting and parting
      of specific body parts
_____ Thinking and moving
      simultaneously
_____ Twisting the body in a variety
      of ways
_____ Demonstrates ability to change
      speed of movements
      abruptly
_____ Duplicating an imposed speed
      of beat in movements
_____ Moves in wide variety of ways
      to a moderate pulse beat
_____ Creates new movement
      responses which fit the beat

MOTOR DEVELOPMENT 3- TO 4-YEAR-OLDS

Name_____   Instructor _____

JUMPING
_____ Two feet to two feet
_____ Control with soft landing
_____ One foot to two feet
_____ Over obstacles
_____ Run and jump

THROWING
_____ To self
_____ Step w/opposite foot
_____ Uses body parts to increase force
_____ Follow through
_____ To stationary target
_____ To partner

CATCHING
_____ To self at different heights
_____ Bounce to self & catch
_____ From a partner
_____ At various levels
_____ Look, reach, give
_____ Catch yarn ball/scoop

KICKING
_____ Stationary ball
_____ Stationary ball on run
_____ Ball rolled by someone
_____ Kicking at a target
_____ Dribbling the ball
_____ Different parts of the foot

BALANCING
_____ One leg
_____ Different body shapes
_____ Walk on low beam
_____ Variety of tilt boards

Key: * = Proficient
            ✓ = Control
            + = Improving
                (Pre-Control)

FIGURE 8.8   Observational Checklist

A variety of assessment techniques can be used. It is important, especially with young children, that we obtain a true measure of their skills. For example, Robert was being evaluated to determine whether he was ready for kindergarten. The psychologist asked him to draw a man. When she looked at his drawing all she saw was scribbling so she concluded that he was not ready to enter kindergarten. The parents, hearing this news and knowing their child, were concerned and asked the director of the child care early education center to test him. The director also asked him to draw a man and he drew the same thing, scribbles. From observing Robert in the center, she knew that Robert was able to draw a man so she asked him to tell her about the picture. Robert then told her that he drew a picture of a man in a snow storm. The director then asked him to draw a picture of a man on a sunny day! Robert went to kindergarten.

Assessment can include: student projects and journals, parental report, interview, peer observation, self-assessment, group project, portfolio, role playing, observation-teacher/student, and audio and video tapes.

Structure the Learning Environment

The final component that needs to be addressed prior to working with the children is learning environment structure. During movement programs all children need to move most of the time. They do not need to sit or stand and watch the other children practice the skill. Likewise, they do not need to have the pressure of performing in front of the other children. Thus, it is imperative that equipment is provided for all the children. If the class is working on throwing and catching, there is a ball for two children. If the class is working on throwing a large ball at a target, then each child needs his or her own ball and a target at which to throw.

In addition to all children being active, we must also plan for a range of skill levels. Within one class, we can have children who are good at balancing and those who are not. It is important to use the "slanty rope" technique. When working on balancing, some children can walk on a wide line on the floor while others walk on the narrow line. Some children walk on a wide, low balance beam, while others walk on a narrow elevated balance beam. Use of this technique allows all children to be successful at their own level of skill development.

Elimination games are never appropriate. With elimination games, the child who needs to practice the skill the most is the one who practices the least. In addition, the poorly skilled child looses motivation; he does not want to be the first to sit out so he quits trying.

Interaction with the Learner

Thus far, the teacher's thinking has been done before interacting with the children. During the lesson both the teacher and learner must analyze the learner's performance to determine whether it is meeting the criteria that were developed during the planning phase. The performance is evaluated to determine any error that is made. Young children tend to ignore relevant information and, therefore, respond immediately without using feedback or developing subjective reinforcement. The teacher must require the children to evaluate their performances to determine future behaviors. The cues used to focus a child's attention on the criteria of the concept/movement should be used to develop subjective reinforcement and prescriptive feedback. For example, criteria for throwing for a younger child might be "look, step, throw." If the teacher notices that the child is not stepping, she can ask the child what the cues for throwing are and whether she followed the cues. If the child did not follow the cues, the teacher can ask the child to try the throw again as she says the cue words.

After the child understands the proper positioning in relation to the target mentioned above, the next step is to improve the form of the throw. As the children increase in skill level and understanding, the key words change also. The appropriate sequence for throwing would be a large step with the foot opposite the throwing hand. Next is sequential rotation with the hip leading the shoulders. As the shoulders rotate forward, the upper arm lags behind the shoulders. The forearm lags behind the upper arm. The throw is completed by the follow-through as the arm rotates across the body. The new key words might be "step, hips, shoulders, follow-through."

A widespread discrepancy between performance and criteria might indicate that the abilities and experiences of the learners were inappropriately assessed and that the teacher initiated instruction on a level too advanced for the learners' developmental levels. Therefore, the criteria need to be revised for a more developmentally appropriate level in the sequence.

Summary

Developmentally appropriate movement programs for young children are important to the attainment of a healthy lifestyle as an adult. Early childhood educators can provide movement programs for the young children in their care. First, a philosophy statement of the purpose of the program is important. Providing the children with opportunities to move and learn successfully will assist motivation to move for a lifetime. After establishing the philosophy, the teacher needs to select developmentally appropriate content that is appropriate for the physical, cognitive, and emotional maturational levels of the learner. The last step in program development is to assess the child and the teacher. Assessment of the children should be as realistic as possible in the natural setting. The teacher evaluates the learning of the children to determine if they have been successful. In addition, reflection of the situation is important. Teaching physical activity to children should be fun and relaxing for everyone.

CHANGE AND ADVOCACY

1. Design a poster describing and advocating for a physically educated child. Distribute the poster to local child care centers and head start programs.

2. Encourage child care center regulatory agencies, state and federal Head Start agencies, and K–3 programs to provide developmentally appropriate movement activities for children.

REFERENCES

American Academy of Pediatrics. (1985). Policy statement: Infant swim programs. *American Academy of Pediatrics News, 1,* 15.

American Academy of Pediatrics. (1988). Policy statement: Infant exercise programs. *Pediatrics, 58,* 800.

American Red Cross. (1988). *American Red Cross infant and preschool aquatic programs: Parent's guide:* American Red Cross.

Biddle, S., & Armstrong, N. (1992). Children's physical activity: An exploratory study of psychological correlates. *Social Science and Medicine, 24,* 325–331.

Elkind, D. (1990). Academic pressures—Too much, too soon: The demise of play. In E. Klugman, & S. Smilanky (Eds.), *Children's play and learning: Perspectives and policy implications.* NY: Teachers College Press.

Erikson, E. (1950). *Childhood and society.* NY: Norton.

Ferguson, K. J., Yesalis, C. E., Pomrehn, P. R., & Kirkpatrick, M. B. (1989). Attitudes, knowledge and beliefs as predictors of exercise intent and behavior in schoolchildren. *Journal of School Health, 59,* 112–115.

Franck, M., Graham, G., Lawson, H., Loughrey, T., Ritson, R., Sanborn, M., & Seefeldt, V. (1991). *Physical education outcomes: A project of the National Association for Sport and Physical Education.* Reston, VA: National Association for Sport and Physical Education.

Gallagher, J. D., & Thomas, J. R. (1980). Effects of varying post-KR intervals upon children's motor performance. *Journal of Motor Behavior, 12,* 41–46.

Gardner, J., Karmel, B., & Dowd, J. (1984). Relationship of infant psychobiological development to infant intervention programs. *Journal of Children in a Contemporary Society, 17* (1), 93–98.

Laban, R., & Ullmann, L. (1963). *Modern educational dance* (2nd ed.). London: Macdonald & Evans, Ltd.

National Association for the Education of Young Children (1990). *Guidelines for appropriate curriculum content and assessment in programs serving children ages 3 through 8.* Washington, D.C.: NAEYC.

Payne, V., & Issacs, L. (1999). *Human motor development: A lifespan approach.* CA: Mayfield Publishing Co.

Rink, J., Dotson, C., Franck, M., Hensley, L., Holt-Hale, S., Lund, J., Payne, G., & Wood, T. (1995). *Moving into the future: National standards for physical education.* St. Louis: Mosby.

Thomas, J., & Thomas, K. (1983). Strange kids and strange numbers: assessing children's motor development. *Journal of Physical Education, Recreation and Dance, 54* (8), 19–20.

Trawick-Smith, J. (2000). *Early childhood development.* Upper Saddle River, NJ: Merrill.

PART FOUR

Programmatic Development

9 Developing Healthy Lifestyles

CHAPTER OBJECTIVES

Knowledge
- The reader will understand the assessment, planning, and implementation required to develop a healthy lifestyle.

Skills
- The reader will plan developmentally appropriate learning activities to develop a healthy lifestyle for infants, toddlers, and young children.

Dispositions
- The reader will value the importance of children developing a healthy lifestyle.

CHAPTER SYNOPSIS

Play
  Types of Play
  Social Role of Play

Decision Making
  Developing Appropriate Decision Making

Meal and Snack Planning
  Eat a Variety of Foods

  Prepare Foods Safely
  Maintain a Healthy Weight

Disease Prevention

Safety Promotion

Activity Planning

Teacher and Parent Physical Activity Plan

Scenario

A conversation took place between Barrett and Sara. Barrett was telling Sara that she was excited because on Saturday they were celebrating her great-grandmother Moma's 80th birthday. Barrett told Sara how much she loved doing things with Moma. Moma took her to the park, climbed through the obstacles at Discovery Zone, and pushed her on the swings. They went fishing together, and even built things together. Often Moma would chase her. Sara was surprised because her grandmother did not do those things! Sara told Barrett about her Grama. Grama loved Sara, but she did not do much with her; she was always sick. She had to stay in bed a lot and could not go outside. Barrett and Sara then started to determine what they needed to do to grow up like Moma. Their list included: eat vegetables instead of candy, move around a lot, be careful crossing the street, don't light matches, and stay away from dogs you don't know. Barrett was glad that her Moma was able to play with her!

Moma was able to do things with her great-granddaughter because she had maintained a healthy lifestyle. Maintaining a healthy lifestyle is important. Why? First, many of the leading causes of death in adulthood are related to lifestyle. The top two causes of death are heart disease and cancer, both directly related to lifestyle choices. High fat, high salt, high sugar, and low fiber diets—in addition to stress, lack of exercise, smoking, and use of alcohol and drugs are major factors in the development of these two diseases. When children reach high school, the spontaneous physical activity that is so apparent in young children is no longer evident (Glover & Shepherd, 1989).

During childhood a major cause of death is unintentional injuries. Avoiding risk and promoting safety can prevent many of these deaths. However, developing a healthy lifestyle that includes physical activity, eating habits, disease prevention, and safety promotion is critically important during the early childhood years. During this time young children are more flexible and willing to exhibit positive health behaviors that lead to good habits in adulthood. The closer the child is to adolescence the more difficult change becomes.

One of the best ways to influence the development of a healthy lifestyle and maintenance of these behaviors is through play. We cover the types of play and how play develops next.

Play

Play is spontaneous and self-imposed and always involves movement—whether fine or gross motor. In addition, when children are asked what play is, children describe play as being pleasurable and self-selected (Monighan-Nourot, 1997). Children use play to become organized and comfortable with their world. They learn to adapt to the various circumstances and experiences in their lives through play and begin to understand symbolic thought necessary for cognitive development. Play is the vehicle used to build social relationships between peers and adults.

During infancy and early childhood, motor skill development is related to the development of play, learning, experiences, and thinking. Manipulative play is important since it sets the stage for cognitive thought by helping the infant make connections between objects and actions. The child begins to play not only with objects but also with his parents and other caregivers. Fourteen-month-old Kara attended a high school Spanish banquet with her older siblings and parents. After eating Kara entertained herself for over an hour during the entire Spanish dance program by transferring globe key chains from one drinking cup to another. Kara was involved in spontaneous and self-imposed manipulative play. Stimulation of these play initiatives will help to stimulate development. Children need objects to manipulate and caregivers to encourage the stimulating activity. Kara had all of these characteristics to develop her play skills.

Play is very important in the development of children, and one that adults should take very seriously. In addition to providing functional practice for motor skills, play can help build knowledge and develop social skills and feelings. Children are intrinsically motivated to play; they do not have to be forced to play. We enjoy our jobs because we get to play all day!

An important aspect of play is that it must be spontaneous and self-directed. Adult-chosen and -directed motor activities for young children can overburden the children and become too demanding. However, with play we can facilitate physical activity and the acceptance of health behaviors by designing the environment to provide the opportunity and stimulus for play in these roles. Imitation and structuring of the environment should develop the motor abilities of young children. If children see their parents, teachers, and caregivers engaged in physical activity and healthy behaviors, they imitate these actions.

A primary environment that supports play is the key to the total development of a healthy child. In order to fully understand play and how to structure the environment to enhance play behaviors, we next discuss the types of play and when they develop, and conclude with the social role of the player.

Types of Play

Play can be categorized as functional, symbolic, and games with rules.

Functional Play. Functional play is termed *practice* or *sensorimotor play* by Piaget. Children repeatedly practice an action or schema with objects, people, or language. Functional play is evident when the infant opens his hand holding a spoon, and permits the spoon to drop to the floor. A caregiver picks the spoon up, gives it to the infant, and, as you guessed, the infant drops the spoon again. Functional play is common during the first 2 years of life, but it resurges whenever a child is mastering a new skill. Kirk cut up every piece of paper in the house when he was developing his skills with the scissors.

Symbolic or Representational Play. The second type of play, symbolic or representational play, begins around the 18th month and continues into adulthood. Symbolic play helps the child develop mental representations and can be categorized into constructive play and dramatic play.

Constructive Play. Constructive play, the first type of symbolic play, emerges as a transition between functional play and the more sophisticated forms of symbolic play. The child uses materials and objects to make representations of things. For example, Jake lines up blocks to represent the plants in his garden.

Dramatic Play.   Developing from constructive play, dramatic play is characterized by the creation of imaginary roles and situations by the child. Jake pretends to water and weed his garden. If the play involves the negotiations of roles with others, the play is termed *sociodramatic* (Smilansky, 1968). Jake enlists Mark and Janice to be farmers. A discussion takes place as to who will water and who will weed.

Games with Rules.   The third type of play, games with rules, emerges around school-age and continues into adulthood. To engage in games with rules, the child must understand and agree to prearranged rules and must posses social skills. Exposing children to games before they posses logical thinking and social interaction skills frustrates and confuses the child. This is a major argument against organized youth sport for children.

As children participate in different types of play their social role changes. We cover how their social role changes next.

Social Role of Play

The player's social role changes on a developmental continuum with the child. As the child matures and gains new knowledge and skills, the social role changes. The child takes on different social behaviors depending on age, personality, and her social, motor, and cognitive skills. Parten (1932) described the social stages of play:

- Onlooker behavior
- Solitary behavior
- Parallel behavior
- Associative group play
- Cooperative play

During onlooker behavior a child will watch the other children engage in play. At this time the onlooker is developing knowledge about play. The child who is playing by herself without any interaction with other children or adults is engaged in solitary play. Parallel play denotes that several children may be playing next to each other and/or sharing materials without agreement. They are not making any attempt to connect their individual play with other children. Associative group play is the beginning of formal group play, and the hierarchical extension of parallel play. Children play next to each other and agree to share materials. Finally, cooperative play is the second form of group play. During this play the children interact and discuss play themes and roles.

Now that we understand the role of play and how it develops, we move into what needs to be developed during play situations. The first skill we discuss is decision making. The child must understand how to make healthy decisions and then acquire the knowledge on which to base those decisions.

Decision Making

To develop a healthy lifestyle children need to learn how to make appropriate decisions. Health information is constantly changing; we cannot teach children everything they need to know. Historically, health education emphasized development of specific knowledge with little emphasis on skills and attitudes. But today health educators spend the majority of time developing healthy lifestyle attitudes and skills. As a result, children are developing decision-making skills that lead to the development of healthy behaviors and attitudes. The remainder of this chapter focuses on how to develop decision-making skills followed by application to nutrition, principles of hygiene and infection control, safety, and physical activity programs. We provide examples of how to incorporate play to develop these skills. Since it is important for the early childhood educator to be an appropriate role model, we conclude the chapter with recommendations for physical activity programs for adults.

Developing Appropriate Decision Making

Health habits are established in early childhood. During this time, the child needs to develop appropriate decision making processes. Acquiring knowledge is important, however, as we all know we can have a broad knowledge base but still make incorrect decisions. Health education historically focused on developing children's knowledge. Today, however, health educators focus on developing skills and behaviors. By developing skills and behaviors, there is greater likelihood for carryover into adulthood. An emphasis needs to be placed on developing life skills that promote health literacy, maintain and improve health, prevent disease, and reduce health-related risk behaviors. Health literacy is competency in critical thinking and problem solving, responsible and productive citizenship, self-directed learning, and effective communication (Joint Health Education Standards Committee, 1995).

Children continually grow and develop and are exposed to a variety of environmental influences that affect health. Under these conditions children must make decisions. Appropriate decision making is a learned process and should start during the early childhood years.

The National Health Education Standard 6 states that children will demonstrate the ability to use goal-setting and decision-making skills to enhance health. Performance indicators for kindergarten through the fourth grade include:

1. demonstrate the ability to apply a decision-making process to health issues and problems
2. explain when to ask for assistance in making health-related decisions and setting health goals
3. predict outcomes of positive health decisions
4. set a personal health goal and track progress toward its achievement

Although these goals were developed for children 5 years of age and older they are relevant for children from birth through 4 years of age. Children need to be taught how to think rather than what to think; our knowledge about healthy behaviors is constantly changing. Individuals taught about childhood participation in physical activity in the 1930s would have been afraid to allow their children to exercise. Researchers discovered that the child's heart was not proportional to the blood vessels. If children followed this adult theoretical model, then vigorous exercise would strain their hearts. Thus, intense physical activity would need to be avoided during childhood. Karpovich (1937) was the first to dispel the child's heart myth. Once the myth was dispelled, however, changes were not automatic. Not until the 1950s with the initiation of the President's Council on Physical Fitness did we observe increases in physical activity for children. Even then, most of the fitness testing measured skill-related fitness rather than health-related fitness. The 1980s introduced the concept of vigorous physical activity for everyone throughout life.

Not only do teachers need to evaluate current knowledge and make appropriate decisions, but children must also do this. Steps in decision making include the following five steps: analyze the situation; determine potential actions and share actions with others; evaluate each of the actions; determine the most appropriate action; and evaluate the outcome of the action. Initially, the child needs to describe the situation where a decision needs to be made. This should be completed in the child's own words. The adult can assist the child by asking probing questions.

The second step of decision making is to determine potential actions. The child can generate possible alternatives with the assistance of others. Involving others in the decision-making process helps the individual to determine all possible alternatives. One way to determine all possible actions is brainstorming. Children generate as many possible alternatives concerning the issue. Freedom of expression and creativity are encouraged and precise instructions are given about how and what is to be brainstormed. For brainstorming to be effective, the problem must first be well defined. During the session all ideas should be accepted—not criticized—and evaluated objectively when the session is over. During Dr. Vollmer's first-grade class on conflict resolution, the children were given a story of Nina and Jen lining up to go to lunch. Nina lined up as expected, but Jen cut in line in front of her. Initially the class described the problem and then brainstormed possible actions that Nina could take. Nina could cry; tell the teacher, other adults, or her friends; hit Jen; or tell Jen her feelings. All possible actions were written on the board (Vollmer, 1999). This same activity can also be done with younger children using dolls and puppets. The advantage to this is that the teacher can tell a story about a situation (common to the classroom) that happened to the doll or puppet. The children can then brainstorm solutions.

After determining all alternative actions, each action needs to be evaluated to determine which actions best fit the situation. Meeks, Heit, and Page (1996) suggest that alternative actions need to be evaluated on whether the actions promote health, protect safety, protect laws, show respect for self and others, follow guidelines set by responsible adults, and demonstrate good character (Meeks et. al., 1996). Once the action is selected and initiated, the outcome of the decision needs to be evaluated based on these criteria. The children in Dr. Vollmer's class evaluated the alternative actions. For each action, consequences were determined. As a group the class felt the best action for Nina was to explain her feelings to Jen and tell her that she needed to go to the end of the line.

Decision-making patterns can serve as valuable clues to the way individuals perceive themselves, their relationships with others, and the world around them (Anspaugh & Ezell, 1998). Children's actions provide information about their value systems that mediates many of the decisions related to healthy lifestyle choices. Four-year-old Charles was not yet potty-trained. Every time his mother would try to work on potty-training, he would counter with, "No, I don't have time right now." When his mother would successfully have him sit on the potty-chair he would say he needed his newspaper. Soon Mrs. Royal was pregnant with her second child and she knew that Charles had to be trained. Not taking "no" for an answer, she sat him on the toilet. As she was waiting outside the bathroom she could barely contain herself. She heard Charles chanting over and over:

> "Man, I have to swish my pants;
> Man, I have to wipe myself;
> Man, I have to flush!"

Clearly, Charles had the skills and knowledge to be potty-trained. He had made the decision he did not want to use the toilet; he did not want to grow up! A sample lesson on decision making is featured in Box 9.1.

Meal and Snack Planning

One of the major goals of developing a healthy lifestyle is to increase the child's lifespan. It is well documented that good nutrition is one of the pathways to a long, healthy life. Proper nutrition can reduce the chances of developing cancer, heart disease, obesity, and some types of diabetes. Proper eating habits begin at birth but the effects of positive or negative maternal nutritional habits affect the lifespan of the child long before the child is born.

Parents and early childhood educators should practice food management from the time the infant is born. Breast-feeding and delaying the introduction of solid food may decrease the chances of an infant developing into an overweight child and an overweight adult (Moran, 1999). The Food Guide Pyramid should be followed when preparing meals and snacks for children.

Food should never be used as a reward or for comfort, nor should the child be rewarded for eating. This behavior places the wrong emphasis on food. Unfortunately we see this behavior frequently. Supermarkets give children cookies when they shop with their family. Parents encourage this behavior because the cookie comforts the child thus making shopping easier. We also see rewards given

---

BOX **9.1**

Sample Lesson on Decision Making

Objective:
The child will develop the skills to make good decisions.

Activity:
Stage a puppet show in which two puppet friends have to make a decision. One puppet wants to go outside and play and the other puppet wants to watch TV. Ask the children how they can decide what the puppet should do.

1. The children will analyze the situation. Restate what the problem is.
2. The children will determine all the possible choices.
   a. one puppet watches TV and the other puppet goes outside
   b. both puppets watch TV or both puppets go outside
   c. they both watch TV for a little while and then they both go outside and play
3. The children will analyze which choice is best.
   a. choice a means that they do not play together
   b. choice b means that one has to give up what he or she wants to do
   c. choice c means they get to play together and they each get to do what they want for a little while
4. The children will decide which choice is best for them.
   a. if they are not good friends and do not want to play together, they can choose what they want to do
   b. if they want to be with their friend, they either give up what they want to do or they can do both things
5. The children will make a choice.
6. The children will evaluate the consequences.

Closure:
What sorts of decisions do you have to make?
Play the decision-making game. Count the decisions you make today.

Evaluation:
Make a chart with different types of decisions children make. Each time a child makes a decision, have him or her mark it in the appropriate box.

---

to children for eating. Many fast food restaurants use an inexpensive toy to sell food high in fat content. Intermixing food and rewards can lead to behavior problems. As a young child John Larkin was typically a terror when his family went out to eat. At restaurants where toys or entertainment were not provided, he would climb out of his high chair, play with his food, and generally create havoc for his family and other patrons. However, at a local fast food restaurant, where there were toys and other children, he was perfectly well mannered!

Providing the child with a developmentally appropriate diet is important. Sensitive periods exist in the development of food preferences. During the first 2 years of age children are the most willing to eat a variety of foods, but interest declines around 4 years of age (Parizkova, 1996). This implies that, during the first few years of a child's life, adults have the ability to influence the lifespan of the developing child with long-term, positive or negative consequences. As an adult Jerry only eats meat, peas, and potatoes. Those were the foods he ate as a child. He was not encouraged to eat a variety of foods and consequently he continues to eat only those foods today.

The U.S. Department of Agriculture and the Department of Health and Human Services developed the Dietary Guidelines for Americans (discussed in Chapter 3) which are recommendations for diet choices for individuals two years of age and older. The guidelines are simple and include: eat a variety of foods; maintain a healthful weight; choose a diet low in fat, saturated fat, and cholesterol; choose a diet with plenty of vegetables, fruits, and grain products; use sugars only in moderation; use salt and sodium only in moderation; and if you drink alcoholic beverages, do so only in moderation. The first six guidelines are important for the teacher of young children to use when selecting snack foods for the children in their care.

Eat a Variety of Foods

Children can benefit from snacking, however, snacks cannot be used as a substitute for regular meals. Snacks should be served at least two hours before the next mealtime. Frequently, children repeatedly eat the same foods for snacks; they also eat a lot of junk food. This can not only spoil the child's appetite for a regular meal but can also contribute to tooth decay and obesity. Young children should be exposed to the Food Guide Pyramid and be allowed to select snack foods that fit each category. Lunches and snacks can be evaluated in relation to the Food Guide Pyramid.

Snack time serves several functions. Not only do snacks have a nutritional purpose, but snack time also has a social objective. Snack time should be a fun and informal learning experience. It is also a wonderful time to work on language skills. A wide variety of foods should be served during snack time, and children should assist in choosing the snacks (see Table 9.1 for suggestions). Snacks such as popcorn, seeds, nuts, and some raw vegetables are healthy snacks, but children should be supervised when eating these foods since they can cause choking. Snack time provides an excellent opportunity to introduce children to foods and customs of other cultures. Teachers can organize "taste testings" where parents bring in healthy foods from a variety of cultures.

Teachers need to take a positive approach in presenting nutritional concepts. Children should continually be exposed to a variety of foods, and be allowed to taste the foods without being required to eat large portions. Some children are slow eaters, and they typically are also finicky eaters. These children tend to eat better when other children are also eating.

TABLE 9.1 **Suggested Snack Foods for Children**

- Crackers
- Half a toasted bagel with cheese
- Vegetables cut into bite-sized pieces
- Celery with cheese on top
- Fruit cut into bite-sized pieces
- Dried fruit (raisins, cranberries, apricots)
- Soup
- Low-fat microwave popcorn
- Pretzels
- Muffins with milk or juice
- Slice of pita bread
- Dry low-sugar cereals

Suggestions for snack time are to set up routine times for eating and to allow the child to make the decisions whether to eat and what to eat. A specific area should be designated for eating. The child can help to set up the eating area and prepare the snacks. Portion sizes for children are different from those of adults, and "clean-plate clubs" are inappropriate. Leeds (1998) recommends 1 tablespoon of each food for each year of life. A 2-year-old would have 2 table-spoons each of potatoes, cubed chicken, and beans. The children should be given small portions when introducing a new food and food should never be used as a bribe or reward.

Prepare Foods Safely

A healthy lifestyle means eating nutritional foods from the Food Guide Pyramid, but it also means that the food must be prepared safely. Basic steps to follow to prevent foodborne illness are:

- Persons who are ill, or who have skin infections should never handle food
- Wash hands with soap and water, for at least 15 seconds, before touching the food
- Thaw frozen food by placing in refrigerator at 33–38° Fahrenheit, or by microwaving
- Clean all knives and cutting boards when working with raw and cooked foods
- Keep hot foods at an internal temperature of 140°F or higher
- Keep cold foods at an internal temperature of 45°F or less (Iowa Health Book, 1997)

These practices should help to reduce the number of cases of salmonella. Salmonella is a bacteria that causes an infection in the gastrointestinal system (stomach and intestines) in humans and animals, and is one of the major causes of gastrointestinal infections. Certain foods such as eggs, meat, poultry, and unpasteurized dairy products are susceptible to salmonella infection. Individuals who prepare foods for child care early education programs should take special care to avoid contaminating food and causing illness.

Maintain a Healthy Weight

The epidemic of childhood obesity that has been growing over the last two decades must be stopped. Anyone who has tried to lose weight knows how difficult it is to accomplish this task. The best attack is to prevent obesity in the first place. More than one in seven American children, between the ages of 6 and 17, are now considered obese (Smith, 1999). A major concern about childhood obesity is that it tends to develop into adult obesity. Once a child is over 3 years of age, the likelihood that obesity will persist into adulthood increases (Moran, 1999). The chance that an obese child will become an obese adult increases each year after age 6.

A small percentage of weight gain is caused by genetic or hormonal causes, but generally a person gains weight when the energy input (food) exceeds the energy output (exercise). The food pyramid turned upside down is a major problem. Children are eating large amounts of fat, oil, and sugar. **Choose a diet low in fat, saturated fat, and cholesterol; use sugars only in moderation; use salt and sodium only in moderation.**

Experts at the Center for Science in the Public Interest determined that foods marketed for children closely resemble junk foods. Commercials played during cartoons for young children advertise foods with excessive amounts of fat, sodium, and sugar, which can contribute to heart disease, cancer, and high blood pressure in later life (Bruess & Richardson, 1994).

Recommendation for foods differs depending on age group. Chapter 3 provides information on the amount of calories required for each age group and when foods should be introduced. As soon as the infant is skilled at reaching, grasping, and bringing things to her mouth (around 8 months), the child should be allowed to feed herself. Examples of snack foods that are good at this time are Cheerios and overcooked spaghetti without sauce. Around 7 months children can have teething crackers. Recommendations for children above 2 years old are similar to those of adults with the exceptions being caloric intake and recommended dietary allowances. See Box 9.2 on page 192 for a sample lesson on snack planning.

Disease Prevention

Early childhood educators and young children can reduce the risk of disease and keep the immune system healthy. Keeping the immune system healthy requires proper nutrition and physical activity, in addition to adequate sleep. Reducing the risk of disease relates to cleanliness of the individual and the environment. The

BOX **9.2**

Sample Lesson on Snack Planning

Objective:
The child will develop knowledge and skills in planning and making a healthy snack.

Activity:
The children will make healthy muffins for their snack using a graphic recipe.

1. The children will discuss what ingredients should be in muffins.
2. The teacher will show the children the graphic recipe (see Figure 9.1).

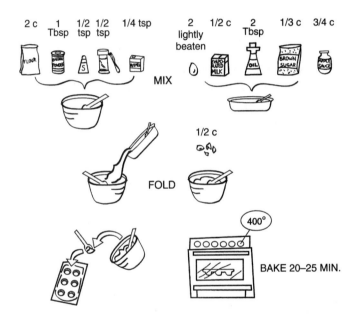

FIGURE 9.1   Graphic Muffin Menu

3. They will analyze the ingredients to determine if they are nutritious and healthy.
4. The children will make the muffins following the graphic recipe.

Closure:
The children will eat the muffins while discussing the ingredients and why the muffins are healthy and nutritious.

Evaluation:
Draw the healthy ingredients of muffins, modified to the developmental level of the children.

children need to develop knowledge of appropriate grooming behaviors while the teacher of young children needs to evaluate the environmental conditions. Eliza's godmother gave her her first set of fingerpaints for Valentine's day. The next day her mother put plastic down and art paper over the plastic. With the paint set, there was a trowel to stir the paint. Eliza initially dipped this into the blue color and began to spread the paint on the paper. Her mom then told her these were finger paints, and she could use her fingers to spread the paint. Eliza responded, "Oh no mommie, I will get messy!"

Clean air and water are critical in addition to appropriate storage of food and personal items such as the children's toothbrushes. Appropriate disposal of waste products such as diapers and used tissues helps to reduce the spread of disease. See Box 9.3 on page 194 for a sample lesson on washing hands and Box 9.4 on page 195 for a sample lesson on appropriate clothing.

Safety Promotion

The elements of safety education are knowledge about accident prevention, promoting positive attitudes, and developing proper behavioral practices (Miller, Telljohann, & Symons, 1996). A positive approach to safety is more likely to influence a child's behavior. Decision making is important in safety education because accidents are caused by the risk involved in an activity, in combination with human error. The child needs to analyze the risks involved in the activity, and what can be done to lessen those risks.

The School Safety Program should include the following components: Instruct faculty, staff, and students on:

1. Planning and implementing safety procedures
2. Providing safe transportation (taking the bus, walking, and riding a bicycle)
3. Establishing accident reporting and recordkeeping procedures
4. Obtaining liability insurance protection (for staff)
5. Providing emergency health care
6. Creating a safe environment
7. Checking equipment daily

Box 9.5 on page 196 provides information on bicycle safety.

Activity Planning

Keeping children active is essential to keeping children healthy. Increasing physical activity is also important in the prevention of overweight children, but unfortunately the trend is toward decreasing physical activity. National surveys in the United States and Canada suggest a downward trend in childhood physical activity (Hill & Trowbridge, 1998). Children are spending less time outdoors in

BOX **9.3**

Sample Lesson on the Importance of Hand Washing

Objective:
The child will discover what happens when they do not wash their hands.

Activities:
1. Discuss the importance of hand washing. Germs and dirt get on our skin if we do not wash our hands. The germs and dirt can then get into our bodies and make us sick.
2. Use two identical plastic dolls. Have the children wash one doll each time they are supposed to wash their hands. Do not wash the other doll. Play with the dolls throughout the day.
3. At the end of the day or week, compare the two dolls.
   How dirty is the doll?

   clean   ok   dirty

   How does the doll smell?

   good   ok   bad

4. Ask the children: Which doll do you want to be? If they choose the unwashed doll, what would their friends think of them? Should we wash our hands and our bodies? Why?

Closure:
Draw a picture of a clean person and a picture of a dirty person.

Evaluation:
Have children make a chart to record when they wash their hands.

---

physical activities and more time indoors watching television and playing video and computer games. There is a decline in physical education in the public school curriculum as well as physical education taught by trained professionals. Unfortunately many teachers use recess as punishment; children learn to link physical activity to punishment. In some early childhood classrooms, teachers will deny a child recess as punishment because of her negative behaviors. This type of punitive action may result in the child linking physical activity to punishment; psychologically the child links physical movement with negative thoughts and behaviors!

BOX **9.4**

Sample Lesson on Appropriate Clothing

Objective:
The children will develop skills and dispositions for selecting clothing that is appropriate for the season of the year and the weather conditions associated with the seasons.

Activity:
The children will discuss the season of the year. They will be guided by the teacher in understanding temperature, precipitation, sun, and wind differences.

1. The teacher will ask the children what the weather is like on the day of the activity.
2. When all the key weather terms have been mentioned, the teacher will guide the children toward determining the season of the year.
3. The children will discuss the four seasons of the year and the weather conditions associated with the seasons.
4. The teacher will show the children the seasons of the year chart (see Figure 9.2) and the clothing chart (Figure 9.3).
5. The children will decide the appropriate clothing to go with the season and give reasons for their choices.

Closure:
The children will discuss what clothing they wore today, and how it is appropriate for the season of the year.

Evaluation:
Through observation of the discussion and matching activity, the teacher will determine if the children have grasped the concept of appropriate clothing and weather conditions.

FIGURE 9.2   Seasons of the Year Chart

FIGURE 9.3   Seasons of the Year Clothing Chart

BOX **9.5**

Sample Lesson on Bike and Trike Safety

Objective:
The child will develop an understanding of the importance of following road signs when walking or riding a bicycle.

Activities:
1. Have the children discuss all the different road signs that they know.
2. Have the children draw and color the different road signs.
3. Set up a "bike" pathway in the movement room using lines to indicate streets and the children's signs posted.
4. Have the children move through the path and not follow the signs.
5. Have the children move through the path and follow the signs.
6. What happened when following the signs and what happened when they did not follow the signs.

Closure:
Why is it important to follow the signs on the road?
Play red light—green light.

Evaluation:
Have signs set up around an obstacle course. As the children go through the obstacle course they mark down the signs they follow.

Despite the barriers of participating in physical activity, there are many ways in which adults can encourage children to be physically active. Most importantly, adults should be good role models of how to lead a physically active lifestyle. The early childhood educator can incorporate developmentally appropriate physical activity in a variety of ways. Children should be active daily as part of play, games, learning, transportation, physical education, planned activities, etc. Children must enjoy moving and being active in order to promote skill, confidence, and knowledge. Physical activity is FUN! Box 9.6 is a lesson on helping children to develop a sense of balance.

The early childhood educator can make learning a physically active process. Children should be active throughout the daily learning activities. The teacher can reduce the amount of time spent in sedentary activities. Children need to have the opportunity to develop movement skills and an adequate level of fitness. Throughout the lessons we need to keep the following key points in mind:

- Equipment for all
- No exclusion
- No fitness as punishment
- No team selection in front of others

BOX **9.6**

Sample Lesson on Balance

Objective:
The child will develop the skill of balance while performing the fundamental motor pattern of walking, running, and hopping on a balance beam.

Activities:
1. The teacher will place a narrow strip of tape and a wide strip of masking or duct tape on the floor.
2. The children will be asked to walk the wide tape balance beam.
3. The children will walk the wide tape balance beam again while holding a pretend umbrella.
4. The children will move to the narrow tape and repeat the sequence.
5. Depending on the developmental level of the child, the task can be repeated using running and hopping locomotor patterns.

Closure:
The children will discuss the two types of balance beams to determine which was more difficult.

Evaluation:
The teacher will observe the individual children as they do the tasks and determine the next task level.

Teacher and Parent Physical Activity Plan

As has been mentioned throughout this book, adults are role models for children and need to model a physically active lifestyle. Even if you have never been physically active, it is never too late to start. You do not need to join expensive health clubs or purchase fancy equipment. You already have the equipment to begin being physically active at your individual level of development. However, the first step to becoming physically active is to see your doctor for "the ok" to begin.

The easy way to incorporate physical activity into your lifestyle is to give up electronics. Forget the car; forget the elevators and escalators; use those legs and walk. Walk the dog, the cat, and the children. You do not have to sweat and be uncomfortable, but you do need to move! Recent research indicates that in order to develop an appropriate level of fitness, activity throughout the day counts. It does not have to be sustained for a period of 30 minutes or more, but it does need to add up to that amount.

You need to incorporate both aerobic (endurance) and anaerobic (strength) activities into your schedule. The aerobic activities include walking, running, biking, swimming, and skiing; activities that get your heart pounding and your skin sweaty. Anaerobic activities include lifting, pushing, and pulling; activities that build muscular strength.

If you plan on developing a high level of fitness, the FITT formula is used. FITT means **F**requency, **I**ntensity, **T**ime, and **T**ype of Activity. Frequency should be no less than three times a week while intensity is how hard you exercise. You should set a target heart rate to exercise at 60 to 80% of your maximum heart rate (220 – age). As a beginner you would start low (even below 60%) and gradually increase the intensity. The duration (time) of the activity should be a minimum of 20 minutes of continuous activity, however, every minute you can exercise throughout the day is beneficial. It all adds up. "Type of activity" is what you like to do. If what you are doing is not fun, you will not continue to participate!

To work physical activity into your lifestyle we recommend playing with your children, dancing to music, hiking, biking, playing, gardening, and cleaning. Remember that to continue being active you have to love what you do! This gives a brief idea about how to get started, but if you are serious you need to find a book that gives you more specifics. There are several books that will help to get you started.

Summary

This chapter focused on providing guidelines to the early childhood educator in developing learning activities on healthy lifestyles. We provided the rationale for potential lessons on: selecting meals and snacks, activity planning, disease prevention, and safety promotion. When using these ideas, the teacher of young children must not mandate the behavior but instead assist the child in making the decision to live healthy.

CHANGE AND ADVOCACY

1. Plan a community "TV-OFF" week and send fliers home with the children asking parents to plan a family activity for the week.

2. Write state legislatures demanding that they mandate that every school system receiving state money provides the children with 2½ hours of physical activity each week.

REFERENCES

Anspaugh, D., & Ezell, G. (1998). *Teaching today's health.* Boston: Allyn & Bacon.
Bruess, C., & Richardson, G. (1994). *Healthy decisions.* Madison, WI: Brown & Benchmark.
Glover B., & Shephard, J. (1989). *The family fitness handbook.* New York: Penguin Books.
Hill, J. O., & Trowbridge, F. L. (1998). Childhood obesity: Future directions and research priority. *Pediatrics, 101* (3), 570–574.

Iowa Health Book. (1997). *How to prevent foodborn illness.* Iowa Department of Public Health and Iowa Department of Inspections and Appeals.

Joint Committee on Health Education Standards. (1995). *The national health education standards: Achieving health literacy.* Kent, OH: American School Health Association.

Karpovich, P. (1937). Texbook fallacies regarding the development of the child's heart. *Research Quarterly, 8,* 33–37.

Leeds, M. (1998). *Nutrition for healthy living.* Boston, MA: McGraw-Hill.

Meeks, L., Heit, P., & Page, R. (1996). *Comprehensive school health education* (2nd ed.). Blacklick, OH: Meeks Heit Publishing Co.

Miller, D., Telljohann, S., & Symons, C. (1996). *Health education.* Madison, WI: Brown & Benchmark.

Monighan-Nourot, P. (1997). Playing with play in four dimensions. In J. Isenberg, & M. Jalongo (Eds.), *Major trends and issues in early childhood education: Challenges, controversies, and insights.* New York: Teachers' College Press

Parizkova, J. (1996). *Nutrition, physical activity, and health in early life.* New York: CRC Press.

Parten, M. (1932). Social participation among preschool children. *Journal of Abnormal and Social Psychology, 27,* 243–269.

Smilansky, S. (1968). *The effects of sociodramatic play on disadvantaged preschool children.* New York: John Wiley and Sons

Smith, J. (1999). *Understanding childhood obesity.* Jackson, MS: University Press of Mississippi.

Vollmer, M. (1999). *Class observation. Falk School.* Pittsburgh, PA.

10 Parents and Community Partnerships

CHAPTER OBJECTIVES

Knowledge

- The reader will understand the roles parents, teachers, and the community play in the education triad.

Skills

- The reader will analyze the components of positive communication.

Dispositions

- The reader will value the role early childhood educators have in instigating and maintaining the educational triad.

CHAPTER SYNOPSIS

Educational Triad
  Teachers as Partners
  Families as Partners

Communities as Partners
Expansion of the Partnership
Family and Teacher Communication

Scenario

It was parent-teacher conference time in Mrs. Peck's first-grade classroom. Nancy Hsu's parents are the next parents on the schedule. Mrs. Peck is uneasy about the meeting because she does not know Chinese, and she is aware of the fact that Nancy's parents are recent immigrants to the United States with limited use of the English language. Since the beginning of the year Nancy has been negotiating the various diverse transitions between home and school. This first conference filled

Mrs. Peck with trepidation about how she would handle the conference. At the appointed time, Mr. and Mrs. Hsu walked into the classroom accompanied by Nancy who announced, "I thought you would need me to interpret what my parents say."

Clearly, 6-year-old Nancy understood and respected the importance of her family and the role that her family played in her life and community educational setting. "Education programs and families must respect and reinforce each other as they work together to achieve the greatest benefit for all children" (NAEYC, 1996b). Children moving from the private world of their home to their educational settings, whether it is the child care environment, the Head Start environment, or the kindergarten and primary environment, must adapt to a variety of differences in rules, traditions, values, behaviors, and expectations. The adaptation to these differences can be made easier for children if parents and teachers work together to help the child bridge the gaps that may exist and provide understanding through mutual respect and appreciation. The goal for both parents and teachers is to ensure that children have the healthiest lifestyle possible and develop into adults capable of making health-enhancing decisions. In this chapter we discuss the ways that parents, teachers, and members of the community can work together to assist children in reaching the ultimate goal of a healthy lifestyle.

Education Triad

Educating children takes the efforts of all three: family, teachers, and the community. We discussed this interaction in general terms in Chapter 1 when we discussed the importance of the Bioenvironmental Reciprocity Model. It is the reciprocity of the child's genetic makeup and her environment that causes the changes in her development.

Children are competent individuals who must develop a sense of trust not only with their parents but also with the community. Parents need to build on this trust and assist the child in developing autonomy. This will permit him to become a competent member of the community. The community becomes part of this reciprocal relationship by supporting the child and the parents in the child's education, and by providing a healthy environment. When families, teachers, and the community work together, the early educational setting can be a stimulating environment filled with curiosity and joy. A cooperative, beneficial triad is formed (see Figure 10.1).

There must be mutual respect and communication between all members of the triad in order to provide a healthy lifestyle for young children. Communication and respect must be a two-way process; one part is not more important than the other.

In order for the family, community, and teacher to form a triad to promote the optimal healthy development of the child, each member must be able to communicate effectively with the other members. Therefore, in this chapter we first cover the members of the triad and the roles they play in the development of the child, followed by the role communication has in the success of the triad.

FIGURE 10.1   Interaction of Family, Teacher, and Community in the Life of the Child

Teachers as Partners

Teachers are a very important component of the triad. In 1997, 65% of women with children under age 6 were in the work force (CDF, 1998). It is increasingly evident that children are being cared for outside of the home and by someone outside of the family. This changing aspect of today's society means that teachers play a significant role in the lives of young children. They make curriculum decisions and serve as role models for children. Teacher preparation programs should reflect these aspects of the teacher's role in the development of the child.

Curriculum Decisions.   Teachers establish the curriculum that is used in educational settings. As they plan, implement, and assess curriculum issues that affect the three domains—cognitive/language, social/emotional, and motor/physical—it is important that teachers realize how salient it is that a healthy lifestyle be emphasized in all curriculum issues. Teachers can help children develop an awareness of the nutrition, safety, health, and fitness components that are needed for the children to make decisions that will lead to a healthy lifestyle. These components should be a part of the daily curriculum. If teachers emphasize nutrition issues during snack time, frequent hand washing, and provide a variety of movement activities related to music, obstacle courses, and ball play they will contribute to the development of the concept of a healthy lifestyle.

Teachers as Role Models.   Another way teachers can facilitate the development of a healthy lifestyle for young children, in addition to trust and communication within the triad, is to encourage them to practice a healthy lifestyle. The basis for this thought is the work of the American psychologists Albert Bandura and Walter Mischel, who are the designers of the cognitive social learning theory. Bandura felt that human beings learn by observing what others do. It is through observational learning, or modeling, that humans cognitively represent the behavior of others; the result may be the adoption of this behavior (Santrock, 1997).

Any observer of children is well aware of this phenomenon. We have all seen the 3-year-old boy walking down the street with his father—attempting to model his father's stride, or the 4-year-old girl carrying a purse in the same manner as her mother. This is how children learn behavior related to gender, nutrition, and physical activity—to name just a few.

Let us consider how this theory would apply to the development of a healthy lifestyle in a young child. A teacher who tells children that they should eat a healthy diet based on the food pyramid but drinks soda during lunch with the children is not serving as a good model. Additionally, educators who spend the outdoor learning period sitting rather than participating with the children in physical activity serve as negative models according to the cognitive social learning theory.

Using the cognitive social learning theory, Wilson (1990) outlined eight guidelines that educators should follow to enhance the development of children. Competent educators are physically and mentally healthy, flexible, patient, and open to learning and enjoy being caregivers. They also have a positive self-image and are positive role models.

Educators of young children should make every effort to follow the above guidelines and to be positive role models. Chapter 9 provides ways that teachers can maintain a healthy lifestyle. It is important to do this not only for the sake of the children but also for the sake of the educator and his family. Educators must be aware of their role in the triad and this role should be emphasized in all teacher preparation programs.

Teachers as Researchers.   When educators have learned to listen, to observe, and to form new hypotheses they have become researchers. Teachers become researchers by having:

- An attitude to accept change
- A disposition to be open to exploration and discovery
- A willingness to form hypotheses and to learn
- An ability for self-reflection

These characteristics lend themselves to research abilities and optimum observation skills for learning about children and communicating with parents about their child.

Teacher Preparation.   The Guidelines for Preparation of Early Childhood Professionals (NAEYC, 1996a) lists eight standards established by the National Board for

Professional Teaching Standards (NBPTS) to serve as the basis for early childhood/ generalist certificate. These standards are based on the following philosophical guidelines and clearly involve all aspects of the triad:

1. Teachers are committed to students and their learning.
2. Teachers know the subjects they teach and how to teach those subjects to students.
3. Teachers are responsible for managing and monitoring student learning.
4. Teachers think systematically about their practice and learn from experience.
5. Teachers are members of a learning community.

There is a common core of knowledge based on the above philosophical concepts that is necessary for all professionals to have when working as a member of the triad. This core of knowledge is reflected in the eight standards. Throughout this chapter we present standards that are relevant to the triad and to building strong partnerships.

In addition to the teacher as partner, the family as partner also plays a critical role in the child's development. The family as partner is covered next.

Families as Partners

Stamp and Groves (1994) suggested the involvement of the child's family should be viewed as the "third institution" with its purpose being to strengthen the links with the other two institutions: the educational setting and the community. Institutions are organizations established by customs, laws, or society. In this case, families are defined by society and refined by customs and laws. A society may have multiple customs that shape traditions and behaviors, and a society may have multiple laws, tribal and national, that will affect the structure of a family. All of these factors affect the family institution. The family institution has tentacles with far-reaching consequences in the lives of young children. Families not only nurture and protect the child by providing the child with appropriate nutrition and shelter, but they also support the child in the various developmental domains.

Definition of the Family.   While the role of the family has remained fairly consistent, the composition of the family has changed and is still in flux. Today the family may not be the two-parent family described as typical for the 1940s and 1950s in the United States. Early childhood educators must understand that the composition of the family may vary by culture and by socioeconomic grouping.

The families of today can be made up of:

- Two-parent families
- Unmarried heterosexual couples
- Skipped-generation households
- Single parent households
- Gay and lesbian couples
- Blended families

Educators working with families must be sensitive to the different family configurations and make adjustments when interacting with the child and family. The way each family provides the child with a nurturing environment, guidance, opportunity for problem solving, and modeling style will vary not only according to the family composition but also by ethnic and financial guidelines.

Role of the Family.   As suggested by Swick (1986), the role of the family is to provide:

- Nurturing environment
- Direct and indirect guidance
- Opportunities for problem solving
- Modeling

Families provide children with an environment that gives them the basic survival needs: food, clothing, and shelter. Families also assist in developing guidance opportunities for problem solving and serve as a model for the developing child. Three-year-old Ian attended Mass with his father. During Communion, Ian looked at his father and asked when he would be able to eat the "white food." Clearly, Ian had been thinking about the Communion process that he had been exposed to under the guidance and modeling of his parents. Their values and beliefs were being instilled into Ian during his early development.

Modeling and guidance are important aspects of the family role and must be considered when working within the triad. A teacher asked Brian why his math homework was difficult to read. Brian told the teacher that his mother did not permit him to work at the table. Instead, she gave him a phone book to use as a work surface. Parent expectations and teacher expectation do not always match. Parent expectations and style are factors that must be considered when communicating with families.

Family Management Styles.   Based on parental personalities and past management behaviors, parents will develop their own particular parenting style. It is important to understand the variance in parenting styles; this will lead to understanding the child's behaviors. Baumrind (1971) has defined three types of parenting styles:

- Authoritarian
- Authoritative
- Laissez-faire

The authoritarian style of parenting is punitive and restrictive. Authoritarian parents demand that the child follow the rules without discussion and/or negotiation. Children of authoritarian parents show apprehensiveness concerning social comparisons, do not take initiative, are hostile, and have poor communication skills (Berk, 1997; Santrock, 1999).

Authoritative parents set guidelines and place limits on the child but do so in negotiation with the child. The child is encouraged to be independent and in control of her own actions. Children who develop under the authoritative parenting style typically show social competence, have high self-esteem, are happy, and display less gender stereotype behavior (Berk, 1997; Santrock, 1999).

The third style, laissez-faire or permissive parenting, has two forms: neglectful or uninvolved and indulgent or permissive (Berk, 1997; Santrock, 1999). The neglectful parent is not involved in the child's life. Basic care is provided but this is the extent of the parent's involvement. The indulgent parent is very involved in the child's life but places few guidelines or restrictions on the child. The laissez-faire style leads to social incompetence and lack of self-control. These children are impulsive and lack persistence (Berk, 1997; Santrock, 1999).

These parenting styles have an effect on the personalities of the children and in turn will affect the interactions teachers have with children and parents. An understanding of the family and parenting style will help educators meet the needs of the child.

Because of its composition, each family will have its unique joys and problems based on the makeup of the family and how society perceives the family's composition. Teachers should celebrate the differences and the accomplishments of each child and his family.

Families and Children with Disabilities and Serious Illnesses.   Children may be born with disabilities or medical conditions, or accidents may occur that result in a disability. Disabilities place stress on the family, and they struggle with feelings of loss. Families proceed through the following stages of grieving:

- Denial
- Anxiety
- Guilt
- Depression
- Anger (Moses, 1983)

When parents first discover their child has a disability, they try to deny the fact. They spend time and money trying to find cures for the disability. As the parents struggle to provide the necessary medical care for the child their fears and mental anguish or anxiety provide added stress to the family unit. Part of the grieving process is the feeling of guilt. The parents blame themselves for what happened and often become depressed. As the grieving process continues the parents become angry, blaming themselves or other family members, medical personnel, or random people. At the last stage of grieving, the parents accept the disability. The parent can now focus on the positive side of the disability and see it as a positive gain instead of a loss. The parent can now focus on the positive side of the disability and be concerned with ways to enhance the quality of the child's lifestyle through interactions with intervention specialists and community programs that promote changes in the learning environment of the child. Teachers and other professionals can help a parent through this whole process.

Teachers must recognize that families are allies in their work and encourage family involvement by strengthening opportunities for observation, volunteer and assistant work, and policy and programmatic decision making. Additionally, teachers must become observers and quality communicators with children and families.

Family Involvement.   Parents can be integrated into the education setting if teachers follow the guidelines suggested by Kaiser and Rasminsky (1999) in establishing a partnership:

- Encourage the parents to communicate their goals and expectations for their child
- Inform the parents of the philosophy and the goals and objectives of the educational program
- Respect, without reservation, the cultural and socioeconomic background of the family
- Develop a familiarity with the family's routines, customs, and expectations and make programmatic adaptations whenever possible

Additionally, teachers should encourage parents to volunteer in the program. Children should be exposed early in life to a variety of cultures and backgrounds to develop an understanding and acceptance of individuals. Through casual encounters children are exposed to individuals with a variety of cultures and backgrounds. A parent can read to the children in the parent's native language, explain her culture, prepare cultural dishes, demonstrate cultural dances, or just interact with the child in her special and individual manner. Dr. Sayre took a day off from work to butter toast at her daughter's kindergarten breakfast experience. While this was a simple thing to do, and one that she was well qualified for, it provided an opportunity for her to interact with other parents, children, the classroom teacher, and her daughter, Kelly. This simple interaction provided Dr. Sayre with a deeper understanding of Kelly's school culture.

If parents work and are unable to participate during the day, asking them to do various activities at home will encourage their participation. Some suggested activities would be:

- Read to their child at home
- Make picture or writing booklets
- Write stories together
- Collect pictures for the classroom
- Walk with their child in their neighborhood
- Engage in a physical activity linked to their culture
- Make or send a recipe of a healthy ethnic food
- Plan menus

- Watch a television program together
- Visit a museum together

It is important that a healthy partnership be established early and continue as long as the child is a participant in the program. It may even continue beyond that period if it is advantageous for both parties. Family partnerships are so important the National Association for the Education of Young Children (NAEYC, 1996b) has made this concept one of the standards, Standard VII: Family Partnerships, for early childhood professionals.

The family, child, and teacher are part of a larger community. The next part of the educational triad is community as partner.

Communities as Partners

The community plays a major role in maintaining an individual's or family's health. Teachers can help parents connect with service agencies that assist in improving the quality of the child's and family's lives. Children, parents, and teachers need to know the purpose of the various health services, where they are located, and which services are of high quality. They also need to know which services are missing. Thus, teachers and parents can expand the horizon and improve the lives of children by connecting early childhood programs with services and programs at the local, state, and federal levels as well as beneficial programs and services at the colleges/universities and hospitals/clinics. The latter institutions are eager to connect with the family institution and build lasting relationships that will improve the lives of children. Families can be directed to individual-sponsored, school-sponsored, agency-sponsored, and government-sponsored programs, and public- and campus-sponsored programs that would assist them in their nurturing, guiding, and role-modeling. Additionally, teachers and families need to play a larger role in the community to improve the lives of young children. The school partnership must be expanded.

Expansion of the Partnerships

The partnership between teachers and parents can be a truly rewarding one that will profit and expand the horizons for both parties and, more important, help the child to build trust and autonomy. They must work together to provide the best services to meet the physical/motor, cognitive/language, and social/emotional needs of the child who is the focus of both their interests. Once the relationship has become productive, it is time to move to a new level and become advocates for children in general.

Advocates.   Parents and teachers must work together to provide care and education for all children in the program. Teachers and parents can become powerful advocates to the director or owners of the program or program site about a problem that may exist with policy or an environmental issue. Teachers and directors should be trained in the advocacy process and assist parents in becoming advocates.

The advocacy role can be expanded to involve issues in the immediate and expanded community. Parents and teachers can get involved in advocacy issues by:

- Voting
- Joining professionals organizations (e.g., National Association for the Education of Young Children [NAEYC] and American Alliance for Health, Physical Education, Recreation, and Dance [AAHPERD])
- Joining political campaigns
- Letter writing campaigns (e.g., legislatures: state, federal, and business)
- Community service
- Running for a political office

The above are just a few of the ways that parents and teachers can become advocates for children. A teacher wrote a letter to a major mail order catalog company bringing to their attention the fact that their full-page catalog picture of wooden outdoor play equipment did not picture absorption material under the equipment. The letter pointed out the importance of modeling safety for potential purchasers. Response to the letter came quickly from the executive assistant to the company's president. The advocate letter writer was thanked and informed that the corrections would be made in all future catalogs. This simple way to advocate resulted in far-reaching results that hopefully had a positive effect on children and their families. We can all become advocates like this. You have become an advocate by completing the Change and Advocacy sections at the end of each chapter.

Standard VIII: Professional Partnerships in **Guidelines for Preparation of Early Childhood Professionals** (NAEYC, 1996a) emphasizes this point. The standard states, "teachers work with colleagues to improve program and practices for young children and their families" (NAEYC, 1996a). One way this can be accomplished is by working with families and service agencies to assist in the development and delivery of quality programs for young children. It is important to have input from all members of the triad.

Individual Family Service Plan and Individual Education Plan. The 1990 Individuals with Disabilities Education Act (IDEA) reauthorized Public Law 94-142 and Public Law 99-457, helping to ensure a public education for all children. The Individualized Family Service Plan (IFSP) and the Individualized Education Plan (IEP) were developed to assist parents and teachers in the formation of partnerships in both the educational and community settings. The federal law and the format of the IEP and the IFSP recognize the importance of involving the family in the educational planning for a child with disabilities. We feel that IFSPs and IEPs should be standard procedures for all children—not just for children with disabilities. All parents should be involved in the development of educational plans for their children, thereby helping to ensure that family values are honored and cultivated.

The executive director of a child care program at a university had the opportunity to be involved in an IEP. It was clear from the beginning of the meeting that it was going to be a positive and productive partnership. The leader of the local educational agency quickly established a positive and cooperative tone for the meeting. All service providers matched the established tone. The result was an IEP that met the needs of the child and family without overwhelming the service providers.

To be an effective advocate and member of an IFSP or IEP team it is important for each member to possess communication skills. An awareness of these skills enhances the communication process.

Communication

Communication involves multiple aspects: speaking, listening, and reflecting. Each aspect is important and, for good communication, all must be present.

Speaking. Speaking to others is a skill. Everyone must learn to choose his words carefully. The message to the other person should not be ambiguous. Verbal communication should be positive in its message and should be accompanied with a warm tone and friendly body language. Even if the verbal message is positive, if it is stated in an aggressive or firm tone and/or body language, the speaker's intent of delivering a positive and friendly communication is lost.

Whenever possible the message should be delivered with clear articulation in the language of the listener, not the language of the educator. Nancy, in the opening scenario, knew her parents would have a problem communicating with her teacher, and on her own initiative she found a solution to the dilemma. When speaking with individuals who do not have English as their native language, every effort should be made to support the language of the home. We need to advocate for the long-term benefits that result from bilingualism (NAEYC, 1996b).

When speaking or listening, we should maintain good eye contact and a relaxed posture. By making and maintaining eye contact in a relaxed manner the receptive partner in the communication process is assured that the speaker is interested and concerned. It should be noted that in some cultures this latter statement should not be followed. In some cultures making eye contact is a sign of disrespect. This example reinforces the earlier statement that the teacher must be aware of the family's culture to be an effective teacher.

Listening. Listening is a major part of communication and is more than just hearing various sounds. Berger (1995) describes listening as "the active process of interpreting, understanding, and evaluating the spoken and nonverbal speech into a meaningful message." It is important that teachers listen rather than speak when communicating with families. To improve listening skills, Smith (1986) recommends the following steps:

- Good listeners should be receptive.
- Good listeners should make a conscious effort to concentrate on what the speaker is saying.

- Good listeners should listen in silence.
- Good listeners should ask questions to clarify issues that are not clear.
- Good listeners should be patient.
- Educators must learn to listen and hear the concerns of the family before they can work to improve the lives of the young children in their programs.

Reflection.   Reflection is another component of communication. Teachers should reflect upon what has been said or heard. Reflection in teaching and thinking involves all of our senses and the interpretation of this information into knowledge, skills, feelings, and dispositions.

John Dewey (1933) put forth the concept that reflective thinking is the "active, persistent, and careful consideration of any belief or supposed form of knowledge in light of the grounds that support it." Teachers must persevere in prudent evaluation of their beliefs surrounding educational practices, perceptions of children and their families, and current knowledge and skills. Teachers are professionals who are sincere and thoughtful in their practices and beliefs, and who constantly learn from their reflective experiences.

Pollard and Tann (1987) analyzed the work of John Dewey and identified four essential characteristics of systematic reflective teaching:

1. Reflective teaching implies an active concern with aim and consequences as well as with means and technical efficiency.
2. Reflective teaching combines inquiry and implementation skills with attitudes of open-mindedness, responsibility, and compassion.
3. Reflective teaching is applied in a cyclical or spiraling process, in which teachers continually monitor, evaluate, and revise their own practices.
4. Reflective teaching is based on teacher judgment, informed partly by self-reflection and partly by insights from educational disciplines.

To be a reflective teacher one must care and be concerned about the total child, not just the subject matter. The total child cannot be understood without understanding the family and communicating with the family. The child is a total package; he comes to a learning environment with a variety of experiences and skills that encompass a wide range of motor, cognitive, and emotional experiences and abilities.

The reflective teacher encourages children and their families to be active rather than passive participants in the learning and reflection processes. Learning for both the child and the family must be open, active, meaningful, and must incorporate inquiry and problem solving in an emotionally safe environment. Therefore, the reflective teacher should encourage the child to hypothesize, experiment, and test various methods of solving problems. Educators of young children should use problem-solving strategies to make caring and developmentally appropriate decisions about educational practices and a healthy lifestyle. Reflection when communicating and making learning environment and curriculum decisions will provide more meaningful connections for children and their families.

Reflection is so important in the communication and teaching process that the National Board for Professional Teaching Standards (NBPTS) has established reflective practices as one of the eight standards to be used as a foundation for Early Childhood/Generalist certification (NAEYC, 1996). Standard VI: Reflective Practice emphasizes the importance of the teacher evaluating results and seeking input systematically from a variety of sources. It is also essential to be open to new ideas and to continually refine practices (NAEYC, 1996).

Once the educator understands the importance of communication he can assist in developing communication within the triad. Establishing a partnership with the child and family is the primary responsibility of the teacher and should be nurtured, prior to the first physical encounter, through positive communication.

Family and Teacher Communication

Teachers have learned communication skills, but they do not always use them. Many times communication with parents is based on information gained from textbooks (what they think is occurring), rather than on astute observation skills. It is extremely important that teachers become observers to acquire the knowledge and attitudes to be quality communicators.

Children must be observed within the family environment; the child cannot be separated from the family. Teachers must listen, observe, and learn before they can link textbook knowledge with family knowledge. Teachers must also listen, observe, and learn before they can help children and the larger educational community.

Confidentiality. It is very important to remember the concept of confidentiality when communicating; it must be maintained at all times. All information on families and their children recorded on forms or obtained during formal and informal interviews or home visitations is confidential and must not be released to any unauthorized person and/or agency without parental consent. Individuals working with young children should make every effort to respect child/parental confidentiality. At times, confidentiality may be violated inadvertently by posting lists of children receiving special services and the times these services are to be delivered. Reflection on all actions is an important part of maintaining confidentially.

Communication Methods. Communication between teachers and parents and/or community members can be one-way or two-way in nature. Examples of one-way communication are:

- Notes
- Handbooks
- Newsletters

Examples of two-way communication are:

- Telephone calls
- Home visits

- Classroom interaction visitations
- E-mail
- Conferences

The best method of communication to involve all individuals and groups is two-way communication. Communication is the transference of information, and it should be two-way for optimum results. Teachers need to listen, observe, and learn from family members. This can only be accomplished through two-way communication.

Summary

Teachers and families are dependent on each other to provide the positive experiences that will assist young children in their total development. Teachers and schools must view the family as an institution with whom they must establish a partnership. While the role of the family has not really changed, the composition of the family has changed. This fact should be considered by teachers when interacting with families. Communication must take place freely on the level of the family, and educators must reflect on all aspects of the communication. Finally, the family-teacher partnership should advocate for all children in the community, and the community must also provide a safe and nurturing environment for the child.

CHANGE AND ADVOCACY

1. Research and make a list of legislators and community businesses that are advocates for children.

2. Design social programs to involve parents in the child care early education program.

REFERENCES

Baumrind, D. (1971). Current patterns of parental authority. *Developmental Psychology Monographs, 4* (1, Pt. 2).

Berger, E. H. (1995). *Parents as partners in education.* Upper Saddle River, NJ: Prentice-Hall, Inc.

Berk, L. (1997). *Child development.* Boston: Allyn & Bacon.

Children's Defense Fund. (1998). *The state of America's children 1998 yearbook.* Washington DC: CDF.

Dewey, J. (1933). *How we think: A restatement of the relation of reflective thinking to the educational process.* New York: Houghton Mifflin.

Kaiser, B., & Rasminsky, J. (1999). *Meeting the challenge.* Ottawa, Ontario: Canadian Child Care Federation.

Moran, R. (1999). Evaluation and treatment of childhood obesity. *American Family Physician, 31,* 861.

Moses, K. (1983). The impact of initial diagnosis: Mobilizing family resources. In J. Mulick, & S. Pueschel (Eds.). *Parent-professional partnerships in developmental disabilities services* (pp. 11–34). Cambridge, MA: Academic Guild.

NAEYC. (1996a). *Guidelines for preparation of early childhood professionals.* Washington, DC: NAEYC.

NAEYC. (1996b). NAEYC position statement: Responding to linguistic and cultural diversity—Recommendations for effective early childhood education. *Young Children, 51,* 4–12.

Pollard, A., & Tann, S. (1987). *Reflective teaching in the primary school.* London, Great Britain: Cassell.

Santrock, J. W. (1997). *Life-span development.* Boston, MA: McGraw-Hill.

Smith, V. (1986). Listening. In O. Hargie (Ed.), *A handbook of communication skills* (pp. 246–265). New York: New York University Press.

Stamp, L. N., & Groves, M. N. (1994). Strengthening the ethic of care: Planning and supporting family involvement. *Dimensions of Early Childhood, 22,* 5–9.

Swick, J. J. (1986). Parents as models in children's cultural development. *The Clearinghouse, 60* (2), 72–75.

Wilson, L. (1990). *Infants and toddlers: Curriculum and teaching.* Albany, NY: Delmar.

Food and Nutrition Board, National Academy of Sciences

1989 National Research Council Recommended Dietary Allowances

Dietary Allowance	Infants		Children		
	0.0–0.5	*0.5–1.0*	*1–3*	*4–6*	*7–10*
Protein	13	14	16	24	28
Vitamin A	375	375	400	500	700
Vitamin D	7.5	10	10	10	10
Vitamin E	3	4	6	7	7
Vitamin K	5	10	15	20	30
Vitamin C	30	35	40	45	45
Thiamin	0.3	0.4	0.7	0.9	1.0
Riboflavin	0.4	0.5	0.8	1.1	1.2
Niacin	5	6	9	12	13
Vitamin B-6	0.3	0.6	1.0	1.1	1.4
Folate	25	35	50	75	100
Vitamin B-12	0.3	0.5	0.7	1.0	1.4
Calcium	400	600	800	800	800
Phosphorus	300	500	800	800	800
Magnesium	40	60	80	120	170
Iron	6	10	10	10	10
Zinc	5	5	10	10	10
Iodine	40	50	70	90	120

Infant (0.0–0.5) Recommended Dietary Allowances based upon weight of 13 pounds and 24 inches long.

Infant (0.5–1.0) Recommended Dietary Allowances based upon weight of 20 pounds and 28 inches long.

Children (1–3) Recommended Dietary Allowances based upon weight of 29 pounds and 35 inches long.

Children (4–6)   Recommended Dietary Allowances based upon weight of 44 pounds and 44 inches long.

Children (7–10)   Recommended Dietary Allowances based upon weight of 62 pounds and 52 inches long.

The allowances are average daily intakes. Diets should be based on a variety of foods.

APPENDIX B

Clorox—409 Glass & Surface Cleaner I

CLOROX—409 GLASS & SURFACE CLEANER
MATERIAL SAFETY DATA SHEET
NSN: 793000F048884
Manufacturer's CAGE: 93098
Part No. Indicator: A
Part Number/Trade Name: 409 GLASS & SURFACE CLEANER

General Information
Company's Name: CLOROX CO (HEADQUARTERS)

Company's Street: 1221 BROADWAY

Company's P.O. Box: 24305

Company's City: OAKLAND

Company's State: CA

Company's Country: U.S.

Company's Zip Code: 94612

Company's Emerg Ph #: 510-847-6100

Company's Info Ph #: 510-847-6796

Distributor/Vendor # 1: THE CLOROX CO

Distributor/Vendor # 1 Cage: CLORO

Record No. For Safety Entry: 001

Tot Safety Entries This Stk#: 001

Status: SE

Date MSDS Prepared: 01SEP94

Safety Data Review Date: 18JUL96

Preparer's Company: CLOROX CO (HEADQUARTERS)

Preparer's St Or P.O. Box: 1221 BROADWAY

Preparer's City: OAKLAND

Preparer's State: CA

Preparer's Zip Code: 94612

MSDS Serial Number: BZTZY

Ingredients/Identity Information
Proprietary: NO

Ingredient: ISOPROPANOL (ISOPROPYL ALCOHOL), 2-PROPANOL, DIMETHYL CARBINOL

(IARC CANCER REVIEW GROUP 3) *96~2*

Ingredient Sequence Number: 01

Percent: 2–9

NIOSH (RTECS) Number: NT8050000

CAS Number: 67-63-0

OSHA PEL: 400 PPM

ACGIH TLV: 400 PPM

Other Recommended Limit: 400 PPM

Physical/Chemical Characteristics
Appearance And Odor: CLEAR PURPLE LIQUID

Specific Gravity: 0.981

Solubility In Water: COMPLETE

pH: 9.5

Fire and Explosion Hazard Data
Flash Point: 10SF

Flash Point Method: CC

Unusual Fire And Expl Hazrds: PRODUCT DOESN'T IGNITE WHEN EXPOSED TO OPEN FLAME.

Reactivity Data
Stability: YES

Hazardous Poly Occur: NO

Health Hazard Data
Route Of Entry—Inhalation: NO

Route Of Entry—Skin: NO

Route Of Entry—Ingestion: NO

Health Haz Acute And Chronic: EYES: IRRITATION. TEMPORARY CONJUNCTIVAL REDNESS.

Carcinogenicity NTP: NO

Carcinogenicity—IARC: NO

Carcinogenicity—OSHA: NO

Explanation Carcinogenicity: NONE

Signs/Symptoms Of Overexp: EYES: IRRITATION. TEMPORARY CONJUNCTIVAL REDNESS.

Emergency/First Aid Proc: EYES: FLUSH THOROUGHLY W/WATER. SKIN: WASH W/WATER. INGESTION: DRINK A GLASSFUL OF WATER. INHALATION: REMOVE TO FRESH AIR. OBTAIN MEDICAL ATTENTION IN ALL CASES.

Precautions for Safe Handling and Use

Steps If Matl Released/Spill: ABSORB & CONTAINERIZE. WASH RESIDUAL DOWN TO SANITARY SEWER. CONTACT THE SANITARY TREATMENT FACILITY IN ADVANCE TO ASSURE ABILITY TO PROCESS WASHED DOWN MATERIAL.

Waste Disposal Method: DISPOSE OF IN ACCORDANCE WITH FEDERAL, STATE & LOCAL REGULATIONS.

Precautions-Handling/Storing: DON'T USE ON ALUMINUM. ON PAINTED SURFACES & WALL COVERINGS, TEST A SMALL INCONSPICUOUS AREA BEFORE USING.

Other Precautions: MINIMIZE SKIN CONTACT & INHALATION OF VAPOR/MIST.

Control Measures

Ventilation: GENERAL VENTILATION

Protective Gloves: RECOMMENDED

Eye Protection: SAFETY GLASSES

Transportation Data

Disposal Data

Label Data

Label Required: YES

Label Status: G

Common Name: 409 GLASS & SURFACE CLEANER

Special Hazard Precautions: EYES: IRRITATION. TEMPORARY CONJUNCTIVAL REDNESS. EYES: IRRITATION, TEMPORARY CONJUNCTIVAL REDNESS.

Label Name: CLOROX CO (HEADQUARTERS)

Label Street: 1221 BROADWAY

Label P.O. Box: 24305

Label City: OAKLAND

Label State: CA

Label Zip Code: 94612

Label Country: U.S.

Label Emergency Number: 510-847-6100

Listed at website address: http:llmsds.pdc.cornell.edu/msds/siri/q3I91q202.html (Retrieved from World Wide Web August, 1999)

APPENDIX C

Emergency Procedures

Staff member closest to injured party and/or volatile situation should:

1. assess the situation
2. wearing gloves, initiate first aid, CPR, etc. if necessary
3. alert the coordinator or other staff member if necessary
4. accompany injured party to hospital if necessary
5. transportation should be in an emergency vehicle and/or with age-appropriate safety restraints
6. remain with the child until the parent assumes responsibility for child's care

Coordinator or other staff member not involved directly in the emergency care should:

1. call 911 and Public Safety if necessary
2. give directions: map is on file at EMS. Additional directions are: Follow Wood Street toward University to Wilson Avenue. Turn right onto Wilson Avenue. Turn right at the first driveway. Follow driveway until the "Y." Take the left branch at the "Y." Park in the unloading zone.
3. call parent. (Detailed records should be kept of all attempts to reach parent.)
4. clear the area, if necessary
5. stay with evacuated children
6. assume the following duties only if two staff members are present

Staff member not involved directly in emergency care should:

1. wait outside of Center for emergency help if necessary
2. call the Director and/or other members on the authority list
3. make arrangements for a substitute staff person to take the place of the staff member who accompanies the child to a source of emergency care if necessary.

AUTHORITY LIST

Name/Address	Position	Office Phone	Home Phone
Dr. Mary Jones 369 Hope Rd. Bingo, PA 16020	Executive Director	2209/2020	378-637-2333

Name/Address	Position	Office Phone	Home Phone
Ron Brown 10 Line St. Mark, PA 16242	Director	2020	378-102-4399
Public Safety	Campus Security	2111	

No staff member is to make any comments or statements to reporters, witnesses, or bystanders. Reports may be made to anyone on the Authority List, *NO ONE ELSE.*

Accident Reports should be filed. Follow up within 24 hours.

Call Department of Welfare if one or more of the following occurs: 1–inpatient hospitalization; 2–emergency room treatment of a child receiving care at the facility; 3–death of a child receiving care at the facility; 4–a facility fire that requires the service of a fire department. Administrator will file a written report to the regional office of the Department of Health & Welfare within 72 hours after the occurrence of the above events.

Children's Learning Complex Injury Report Form

Program Name: _____ Phone:_____

Program Address: _____

Injured Child's Name: _____ Sex: M F   Birthdate: __/__/__

Injury Date:__/__/__   Time of Injury: ___:___ a.m./p.m.

Witnesses: _____

Parent(s) notified by: _____ Time: notified: ___:___ a.m./p.m.

CIRCLE ALL DESCRIPTORS AS APPLICABLE

Location where injury occurred: playground; classroom; bathroom, hall, doorway; gross motor room; office; unknown; other (specify): _____

Equipment involved: climber; slide; sandbox; trike/wagon; toy (specify): _____

_____

Other equipment (specify):_____

Describe Cause of Injury: _____

_____

Parts of Body Injured: _____

_____

Type of Injury: cut; bruise; puncture; scrape; broken bone; sprain; burn; loss of consciousness; unknown, other (specify): _____

First aid given to the injured child at the program: _____

_____

Action taken by doctor or dentist: _____

Child Hospitalized: yes no

Follow-up Care of the Child: _____

Corrective action taken to prevent reoccurrence: _____

Signature of staff member _____ Date: __/__/__

Signature of Parent _____ Date: __/__/__

Form adapted from PA-ECELS

APPENDIX E

Children's Learning Complex Evacuation Procedures

If it is necessary to evacuate the Children's Learning Complex during operating hours the following procedures should be followed:

- The children will be prepared for evacuation by the staff and will be removed from the building by the staff with 2½ minutes.
- The staff will evacuate the building with the children and stay with the children at all times.
- At the time of evacuation the staff will take with them the following items:
  Emergency Child Information Folders
  First Aid Kit
  Children's Activity Kit
- The staff will evacuate the children to the Student Center until permission is given by Public Safety to return to the Children's Learning Complex.
- After one hour, if permission has not been given to return to the Children's Learning Complex, parents will be called and requested to pick up their child(ren).
- The following will be informed of the evacuation in a timely manner:
  Public Safety
  Executive Director, Children's Learning Complex
  Director, Children's Learning Complex
- The charge person will file an **Evacuation Report** within 24 hours following the evacuation.

Developmental Sequence for What the Body Can Do

General Concepts
Self-Space
General Space

Spatial Orientation
under
in front
on top
between

Directions
forward
backward
sideways
right
left

Balance

Line
walk forward
walk backward
walk heel-toe
walk over object

Beam
Wide Beam
walk forward
walk backward
walk heel-toe
walk over an object

Narrow Beam
walk forward
walk backward

walk heel-toe
walk over an object

Bilateral Coordination
bilateral—arms
bilateral—legs
unilateral—right
unilateral—left
arms and legs together
right arm/left leg
left arm/right leg

Fundamental Motor Patterns
run straight
run and change directions
jumping
step down from height/support
step down from height
jump down with support
jump down
2-foot jump up/support
2-foot jump (use object)
2-foot jump
2-foot jump for distance
jump over barrier
1-foot take-off
2-foot landing
hop with 2 feet
hop with 1 foot

Gallop
dominant side leads
non-dominant side leads

Hop
supported
not supported

Skip
step—hop

Throwing
rolling—2 hands—large ball (LB)
rolling—1 hand—small ball (SB)
underhand—distance—2 hand LB

underhand—distance—1 hand SB
underhand—accuracy—2 hand LB
underhand—accuracy—2 hand SB
underhand—A/D—2 hand
underhand—A/D—1 hand
overhand—distance—2 hands—LB
overhand—distance—1 hand—SB
overhand—accuracy—2 hand—LB
overhand—accuracy—1 hand—SB
underhand—to moving target—LB
underhand—to moving target—SB
overhand—to moving target—LB
overhand—to moving target—SB

Catching

large rolling ball
drop—catch
large ball chest height
large ball below waist
large ball above shoulders
move to catch large ball
small ball chest height
small ball below waist
small ball above shoulders
move to catch ball

Kicking

large stationary ball
toe—dominant
inside of foot—dominant
toe—non-dominant
inside of foot—non-dominant

performer moving
toe—dominant
inside of foot—dominant
toe—non-dominant
inside of foot—non-dominant

large moving ball
toe—dominant
inside of foot—dominant
toe—non-dominant
inside of foot—non-dominant

performer/ball moving
> toe—dominant
> inside of foot—dominant
> toe—non-dominant
> inside of foot—non-dominant

Striking

> stationary ball/2-hand underhand
> stationary ball/1-hand underhand
> large rebounding ball/2-hand underhand
> large light stationary
> ball/short paddle
> underhanded
> large rolling ball
> short paddle underhand
> large ball on tee
> short paddle side arm
> small ball suspended
> waist high/short paddle
> small ball suspended
> shoulder high/short paddle
> small ball suspended
> overhead/short paddle
> large ball on tee
> plastic bat
> large ball in one hand
> 1 hand underhand
> large rebounding ball
> 1 hand underhand
> large rebounding ball

Rope Jumping

> turn in dominant hand
> turn in non-dominant hand
> both hands turning
> jump-bounce
> jump-bounce/long rope
> jump-bounce/2 ropes
> jump-bounce 1 rope

INDEX

Note: Citations to figures and tables are indicated by an italicized *f* or *t* immediately following the page number on which the item appears.